RIGHT TO WORK?

Titles in the Equity and Development Series

The Equity and Development Series addresses the distributional consequences of macroeconomic policies and showcases techniques for systematically analyzing the distributional consequences of policy reform. Titles in this series undergo internal and external review under the management of the Research Group in the World Bank's Development Economics Vice Presidency.

Free access to titles in the Equity and Development Series is available at https://openknowledge.worldbank.org/handle/10986/2160

RIGHT TO WORK?

Assessing India's Employment Guarantee Scheme in Bihar

Puja Dutta

Rinku Murgai

Martin Ravallion

Dominique van de Walle

ISBN (paper): 978-1-4648-0130-3
ISBN (electronic): 978-1-4648-0131-0
DOI: 10.1596/978-1-4648-0130-3

Cover design: Debra Naylor, Naylor Design, Inc.

Library of Congress Cataloging-in-Publication Data
Dutta, Puja.
   Right-to-work? : assessing India's employment guarantee scheme in Bihar / Puja Dutta, Rinku Murgai, Martin Ravallion, and Dominique van de Walle.
      pages cm. — (Equity and development)
   Includes bibliographical references and index.
   ISBN 978-1-4648-0130-3 (alk. paper) — ISBN 978-1-4648-0131-0 (electronic)
   1. Manpower policy, Rural—India—Bihar. 2. Right to labor—India—Bihar. 3. Guaranteed annual income—India—Bihar. 4. Unemployment—India—Bihar. I. World Bank. II. Title.
   HD5710.85.I42B5435 2014
   331.01'10954123—dc23   2014001155

Contents

Boxes

Figures

Tables

Foreword

India's Mahatma Gandhi National Rural Employment Guarantee Scheme (MGNREGS) is one of the world's largest experiments in running a public employment generation scheme. The Act to initiate this program was passed by the Indian parliament in 2005, making a certain minimal amount of paid employment a justiciable right of rural Indian households. Soon thereafter, MGNREGS was rolled out in India's most backward districts, spanning the length and breadth of the nation. During this process MGNREGS was, by turns, praised, criticized, hailed, and castigated, but what was unquestionable and recognized by all was the ambitious scale of the experiment.

Not surprisingly, many studies of MGNREGS have been undertaken, from anthropological sketches to village-level statistical, econometric analyses. However, a scientifically controlled, evidence-based, large-scale study of this important program was still needed, especially in regions in which administrative and organizational capacity is not high. This book, by Puja Dutta, Rinku Murgai, Martin Ravallion, and Dominique van de Walle, focuses on Bihar, India's third largest state, and one of its poorest. The book fills that analytical need and will no doubt be viewed as one of the most comprehensive and dispassionate research monographs on the subject. I expect this book to be of value not just to the government and researchers in India but also to economists the world over and to policy makers in other emerging market economies who want to learn from India's experience on job creation to inform their fight against extreme poverty. They will learn from MGNREGS's successes (the study finds, for instance, that the rationing process is pro-poor and the scheme is reaching poor families) and from its failures (for instance, large leakages, and large unmet demand for work—unmet demand that is not revealed by the administrative data).

The study draws on a wide variety of methods, including subjective assessments by respondents, observational (econometric) and experimental methods, and qualitative field work. A specially designed panel survey of 3,000 households, representative of all of rural Bihar, was implemented. A distinctive feature of the methodology was the use of individual-specific counterfactual questions to assess the micro-impacts of the program. This technique allowed the authors to provide a very detailed picture of the impacts of the scheme.

What makes this study especially important and topical is that employment is, today, a major concern across the world. Evidence indicates that, worldwide, the aggregate wage-bill-to-GDP ratio is declining. This outcome seems to go hand in hand with a propensity to have fewer jobs and lower wages, which is, of course, a matter of some concern since such a large fraction of the world population lives by wages alone. If this trend persists it will weaken our ability to fight poverty and deprivation, and can become a source of social unrest and political turbulence.

It is not surprising that "jobs" is a matter of concern across the world, from the United States and Europe to South Asia and Sub-Saharan Africa. The problem is exacerbated by the march of technology, which brings more and more workers from far corners of the world into a common labor market. Our focus on labor market policies and the challenges therein is bound to increase. The problem will have to be tackled by many different methods, and one contender in emerging economies is public employment programs. The final word is not out on the role and efficacy of such government-run employment programs. Important questions remain about their fiscal viability, inflationary impact, and effect on the incidence of poverty. The present book does not try to answer all these questions, but focuses on some important ones, especially those pertaining to chronic poverty. The questions it takes on, it answers more fully and comprehensively than any other book or paper that I have read. The book clearly sketches out areas where the program has succeeded and those where it has failed. It also sheds light on the challenges of running such a program in poorer regions where the need for jobs is great but the available organizational capital is low.

I hope this book will not just answer important questions, as it does, but will also provide a foundation for asking other questions, especially those relating to the macroeconomic consequences of large-scale public employment programs. I expect the book to enable policy makers, even when they design and operate temporary employment programs to battle famine and other short-term calamities, as they have done for centuries, to glean ideas to increase their effectiveness in creating meaningful employment.

India's MGNREGS is the largest state-run employment-generation scheme in the world. This book is the most comprehensive study of this scheme. It is natural to expect it to find a large readership with or without my urging, but let me, nevertheless, use this Foreword to put my urging on record.

Kaushik Basu
Chief Economist and Senior Vice President
The World Bank
Washington, DC
January 2014

Acknowledgments

The study has benefited greatly from the support and insights of Santhosh Mathew (former principal secretary, Rural Development Department, government of Bihar) throughout the project. Anup Mukerji (former chief secretary, government of Bihar) gave the initial impetus for the study. At the World Bank, Philip O'Keefe, Mansoora Rashid, Pablo Gottret, and N. Roberto Zagha have shown constant interest and support for this work.

We were fortunate to receive excellent research assistance from Arthur Alik-Lagrange, Maria Mini Jos, and Manasa Patnam. The field work for both rounds of the survey was carried out by GfK Mode. Sunai Consultancy Private Ltd., under the able leadership of Khurshid Akhtar, provided critical support on all aspects of the field work related to this study, including piloting of questionnaires, supervision of field work, data entry, qualitative process assessments, and rollout of the information intervention using a movie. Juan Muñoz provided guidance on sample design and household tracking for the panel survey. The movie used a trial information campaign that was produced by Praxis with assistance from Soumya Kapoor. The qualitative research for this study was undertaken by action research teams from Development Alternatives, Indian Grameen Services, MART, and Sunai Consultancy Pvt. Ltd. We are grateful to the Rural Development Department, government of Bihar, for making available administrative data for this analysis and for providing insights into the challenges and ongoing initiatives in Bihar. Pranav Chaudhury, Anindita Adhikari, and Devesh Sharma provided the data required for the analysis for funds flow and for further information on administrative processes.

Funding for this study was received from several sources, including the Trust Fund for Environmentally and Socially Sustainable Development (TFESSD), the Spanish Impact Evaluation Fund (SIEF), and the Gender Action Plan Trust Fund. Funding from the government of the United Kingdom's Department for International Development is also gratefully acknowledged; however, the views do not necessarily reflect the U.K. government's official policies.

The authors are grateful to Jean Drèze, Emanuela Galasso, Markus Goldstein, Pablo Gottret, Ghazala Mansuri, Santhosh Mathew, Giovanna Prennushi, Abhijit Sen, and Theresa Jones for comments on this manuscript or presentations based on it. While the study has benefited from discussions with the Rural Development Department (government of Bihar), the Ministry of Rural Development (government of India), and the Department of Economic Affairs, Ministry of Finance (government of India), the study is neither sponsored by the government of India, nor will the findings be binding on the government. Valuable feedback was also received from seminars at the U.K. Department for International Development, the World Bank, and at various conferences and universities.

These are the views of the authors and do not necessarily represent those of the World Bank or its member countries.

About the Authors

Puja Vasudeva Dutta is a senior economist in the World Bank's East Asia Human Development Unit. She holds a DPhil in economics from the University of Sussex. Dutta has worked primarily on the issues of social protection design, delivery and evaluation, poverty and inequality, and labor markets in India, Maldives, Vietnam, Cambodia, and Republic of the Union of Myanmar.

Rinku Murgai is a lead economist in the World Bank's South Asia Poverty Reduction and Economic Management Unit. She holds a PhD in agricultural and resource economics from the University of California at Berkeley. Murgai has worked on a range of issues in the areas of poverty measurement, impact evaluation of public programs, social protection, and functioning of rural land and water markets.

Martin Ravallion holds the inaugural Edmond D. Villani Chair of Economics at Georgetown University. Before taking up this position in December 2012, he had been director of the World Bank's Research Department. Ravallion's main research interests have long concerned poverty and policies for fighting it. He has advised numerous governments and international agencies on this topic, and he has written extensively on this and other subjects in economics, including three books and 200 papers in scholarly journals and edited volumes. He currently serves on the editorial boards of 10 economics journals, is a senior fellow of the Bureau for Research in Economic Analysis of Development, a founding council member and president (elect) of the Society for the Study of Economic Inequality, a research associate of the National Bureau of Economic Research (U.S.), and nonresident fellow of the Center for Global Development, Washington, DC. Among various prizes and awards, in 2012 he was awarded the John Kenneth Galbraith Prize from the American Agricultural and Applied Economics Association.

Dominique van de Walle is a lead economist in the World Bank's Development Research Group. She holds a master's degree in economics from the London School of Economics and a PhD in economics from the Australian National University, and began her career at the Bank as a member of the core team that produced the 1990 *World Development Report* on poverty. Van de Walle has spent many years in the Bank's Research Department, as well as six years in the Gender and Development Group and in Social Protection and Labor. Her research interests are in the general area of poverty, vulnerability, gender and public policy, encompassing social protection, safety nets, and impact evaluation; rural development, land distribution, rural infrastructure, and poverty; infrastructure (water and electricity); and women's labor force participation. Much of her recent past research has been on Vietnam, South Asia, and Sub-Saharan Africa.

Abbreviations

BDO	block development officer
BPL	Below Poverty Line
BREGS	Bihar Rural Employment Guarantee Scheme
CBO	community-based organization
CSO	civil society organization
CSS	centrally sponsored scheme
GIS	geographic information system
GP	Gram Panchayat
ICT	information and communications technology
IT	information technology
km	kilometer(s)
MGNREGS	Mahatma Gandhi National Rural Employment Guarantee Scheme
MIS	(MGNREGS) Management Information System
MoRD	Ministry of Rural Development
NGO	nongovernmental organization
NREGA	National Rural Employment Guarantee Act
NSS	National Sample Survey
NSSO	National Sample Survey Organization
OBC	Other Backward Class
PO	program officer
PRI	Panchayati Raj Institution
PRS	panchayat rozgar sewak
PW	public works
R1	round 1
R2	round 2
Rs	rupees

SC	Scheduled Caste
SHG	self-help group
SoR	Schedule of Rates
ST	Scheduled Tribe

Introduction

In 2006, India embarked on an ambitious attempt to fight poverty by attempting to introduce a wage floor in a setting in which many unskilled workers earn less than the minimum wage. The 2005 National Rural Employment Guarantee Act creates a justiciable "right to work" by promising 100 days of wage employment in every financial year to all rural households whose adult members volunteer to do unskilled manual work. Work is provided in public works projects at the statutory minimum wage notified for the program by state governments that are responsible for implementing the Act under the Mahatma Gandhi National Rural Employment Guarantee Scheme (MGNREGS). Work must be made available within 15 days of receiving an application to work, failing which, the state government is liable for paying an unemployment allowance.

MGNREGS is the largest antipoverty public employment program anywhere. Yet until recently, it has been subject to very little rigorous evaluative research. If the scheme worked in practice the way it is designed, there would be little or no unmet demand for work among unskilled workers. Anyone who wanted work at the stipulated wage rates would get it. Under ideal conditions, such a scheme could almost certainly have a large impact on poverty in India. The work requirement will create a "self-targeting" mechanism, in that nonpoor people are unlikely to demand such work. The scheme could also help reduce future poverty through its second-round effects, including providing insurance in risk-prone environments, empowering workers and villagers generally, and creating useful assets.

This study asks: Are these ideal conditions met in practice? How much impact on poverty do the earnings from the scheme have? Why might that impact fall short of its potential? How can the scheme bridge that gap?

The impacts can be expected to vary across the states of India, as well as within them. The extent of poverty (or its correlates) can be expected to condition the impact. We confirm expectations that the demand for this work tends to be higher in the poorer states.

However, actual participation rates in MGNREGS are not (as a rule) any higher in poorer states. A likely reason for the lower participation is that poorer states face extra constraints on their ability to implement the scheme effectively. Among the important factors, they face shortages in the types of skilled manpower needed for effective administration of such a complex scheme. A common characteristic of poor states and countries is that skilled manpower is scarce, which constrains their ability to absorb funds and implement such schemes. Without reasonably rigorous and professional supervision and monitoring at the local level, with firm reporting links up the chain of command, and strong overall leadership, one might find that the scheme works less well in poor areas—ironically, the places where it is probably needed most. That is indeed what we find across the states of India: the incidence of unmet demand for work tends to be higher in poorer states, even though demand for the scheme is higher there. On balance, the scheme is no more effective in the states where it is needed the most.

Thus, the bulk of this volume tries to provide a better understanding of this finding by undertaking a closer study of the performance of MGNREGS in what is by most measures one of India's poorest states, Bihar. To address the questions about the scheme, we implemented a panel survey of 3,000 households in the rural areas of Bihar during the months of May and June in 2009 and 2010. In using the results of the survey and administrative data to address the key questions about performance of the scheme in Bihar, we draw on a variety of methods, including subjective assessments by respondents, observational (econometric) and experimental methods, and qualitative field work. A distinctive feature of this methodology is the use of individual-specific counterfactual questions in assessing the microimpacts of the program. This methodology allows us to provide a very detailed picture of the impacts of the scheme.

The results confirm the potential for the labor earnings from this scheme to reduce poverty in Bihar, but also point to a number of specific performance issues that impede realization of that potential in practice. We find that there is large unmet demand for work on the scheme—unmet demand that is not revealed by the administrative data. However, we also find that the rationing process is pro-poor and the scheme is reaching poor families, though richer households also share in the gains.

Among those who do participate, we also find a sizable gap between the wages actually reported by workers and those they are supposed to receive under the scheme. A similar gap is revealed by administrative records on wage disbursements. The gap is nowhere near as large as some casual observers have claimed; grossing up our representative sample estimates to the state as a whole, we find that one-fifth of the claimed wage payments are unaccounted for. Leakage is the likely explanation for the discrepancy between the survey results and the administrative data.

So workers are not getting all the work they want, and they are not getting the full wages to which they are due. Unsurprisingly, we find that their participation in the scheme is far from costless to them. Many participants report that they had to give up another income-earning activity when they took up work on the scheme.

These factors have greatly reduced the scheme's impact on poverty. Whereas we estimate that under ideal conditions the extra labor earnings from the scheme would bring down the poverty rate in Bihar 14 percentage points or more, in actuality the impact is closer to 1 percentage point. We find that more than two-thirds—about 10 percentage points—of "lost impact" is attributable to the ways in which the scheme is not fulfilling the provisions of the Act. In particular, if there were no rationing (so that anyone who wanted work got work), the impact of the scheme on poverty would be 8 percentage points. The gap between actual wages received and stipulated wages accounts for 2 percent of the gap. The rest is due to forgone income, which is hard to avoid. Thus, unmet demand for work is the single most important policy-relevant factor in accounting for this gap between actual performance and the scheme's potential.

In probing the factors underlying this performance gap, we find very low public awareness of what needs to be done to obtain work and low participation by poor people in decisions about the scheme. Knowledge is lower for women than for men, and higher for those who are better educated. The sharing of information between men and women within the household appears to be weak. There are also strong village effects on knowledge about the scheme. Holding constant individual and household characteristics, levels of awareness of the scheme are lower in villages with higher inequality and where there are more signs of tension between different social groups. The characteristics of the village leader (such as whether he or she lives in the village) also matter.

We use a randomized control trial of an awareness intervention—a specially designed fictional movie—to show how knowledge of rights and processes can be enhanced as a key step toward better performance. The main story line centered on a temporary migrant worker returning to his village to see his wife and young daughter. He learns that there is work available in the village, even though it is the lean season, so he can stay there. The movie was effective in raising awareness, but had little discernible effect on actions such as seeking employment when needed.

A number of specific supply-side constraints to work provision are also identified, including poor implementation capacity and weak financial management and monitoring systems. The resultant bottlenecks in the funds flow and planning and work sanctioning processes indicate that the implementation of the scheme differs significantly from the intent. We find evidence of unpredictability of work provision, delays in wage payments, and deviations from the scheme guidelines in the management of worksites and provision of facilities to workers. These factors both discourage participation and lead to the creation of poor-quality assets, thereby reducing the overall impact on poverty.

We argue that if the potential impact of MGNREGS is to be realized, eliminating the extensive unmet demand for work under the scheme is crucial—to make it a genuine "employment guarantee." The extent of unmet demand we demonstrate in poor states, including Bihar, is undermining the ability of the scheme to reach those in need, and also greatly reducing the insurance and empowerment benefits of the scheme, making it less likely that women will be reached by the scheme, creating opportunities for leakage, and vastly decreasing the overall impact on poverty.

Addressing this problem will require coordinated action on two fronts. First, enhanced central and local administrative capacities for implementation and monitoring are needed. Second, far greater public awareness of the obligations, rights, and rules of the scheme, more active public mobilization, and better mechanisms for addressing grievances are required. These two sets of reforms are complements; doing one without the other may have little impact.

Overview

Fighting poverty in poorer places may be hard for many reasons. Credit market failures may be more severe, leaving many more unexploited investment opportunities than in better-off economies, leading to lower long-term growth rates and less poverty reduction. Poor nutrition and health (especially in the early years of life) can have the same consequences. The various dimensions of inequality that often accompany high poverty may limit the scope for cooperative action to fight poverty. Thus, poverty can self-perpetuate.

Poverty can persist for another potentially important reason: poorer places tend to have weaker public administrations. Employees with the skills to implement and monitor public programs, including programs for fighting poverty, are relatively scarce in poorer economies. Even when governments care about reducing poverty today, they can face trade-offs with other demands on their budgets and staff resources that also have a bearing on future poverty. No doubt other factors come into play to influence the terms of this trade-off, such as strong political will to fight poverty, but a trade-off can still be expected.

In attempting to fight poverty in poor places with weak administrative capabilities, the idea of "rights" has often been invoked. Although rights-based ideas about distributive justice have a long history (back to the 18th century), they have not had great traction in development policy discussions until recently. We have seen calls for the "right to health care," "right to schooling," "right to food," and "right to work." Because poor people tend to have few rights, it is hoped that creating new rights will empower them to take actions that will help them escape poverty. Whether this tactic will work is another matter. The same factors that made people poor in the first place may operate to undermine attempts to expand their effective rights.

This book aims to contribute to the understanding of the efficacy of poor states in fighting poverty using an ambitious rights-based program—the largest antipoverty public employment program in India, and possibly anywhere in the world. We study how that program works in one of India's poorest states—where one would hope that such a scheme would work well. Some comparisons are also made with other, less poor Indian states.

The program we study is India's Mahatma Gandhi National Rural Employment Guarantee Scheme (MGNREGS), which was launched to implement the National Rural Employment Guarantee Act (here the Act for short; the abbreviation NREGA is common in India). The Act was passed by the Indian Parliament in September 2005. It created a justiciable right to work for all households in rural India by promising 100 days of work per financial year to all rural households whose adults are willing to do unskilled manual labor at the statutory wage established for the program. Work is to be made available to anyone who demands it within 15 days of receipt of an application, failing which the applicant is entitled to an unemployment allowance. The work is supposed to be undertaken with a view to creating sustainable assets in rural villages to promote future livelihoods. In addition, the scheme's delivery processes, particularly the stress placed on community participation, transparency, and accountability, are designed to strengthen village-level governance.

MGNREGS is a prominent example of a class of direct interventions against poverty, also called workfare or public works programs, that impose work requirements on participants. Such programs have desirable incentive effects as second-best policies for situations in which the set of feasible redistributive policy instruments is limited.[1] It is also known that, under certain conditions, these programs can yield efficiency gains, given the existence of factor-market distortions (see, for example, Ravallion 1990; and Basu, Chau, and Kanbur 2009).

The program became operational in February 2006. In the first phase, MGNREGS operated in the country's 200 most backward districts and was expanded to an additional 130 districts in 2007.[2] The remaining districts in the country were eligible under the Act beginning April 1, 2008. Since 2008, the program has reached the entire country with the exception of districts with entirely urban populations. A description of the key features of MGNREGS is provided in box O.1.

India has long experience with using rural public works to implement antipoverty and famine-relief policies.[3] However, several aspects of MGNREGS distinguish it from earlier public works programs:

• MGNREGS recognizes the right to work as a legal right. The state government is legally bound to provide employment to a household within 15 days of its demanding work or to pay the

Box O.1 Key Features of MGNREGS

Each rural household guaranteed 100 days of work per year upon demand. Each rural household is entitled to a free job card with photographs of all adult members living in the household. Adult members of these registered households with job cards may then apply for employment, and the government is obligated to provide the work within 15 days, failing which the applicant is entitled to an unemployment allowance. Furthermore, work must be provided within 5 kilometers of the applicant's residence or there is a 10 percent premium on the scheme's wage. How the household distributes the 100 days among its members is entirely the household's decision.

All-India uniform wage of 100 rupees (Rs) per day established in the scheme, but adjusted for state-specific inflation. In 2009, the central government uncoupled MGNREGS wages from state-level statutory minimum wage rates.[a] Payment is made according to a Schedule of Rates that is based on the amount of work done by a person. The Act requires the Schedule of Rates to be set such that an able-bodied worker working for nine hours, with one hour of rest, is able to earn the established program minimum wage.

Wages paid directly into post office or bank accounts. Beginning April 1, 2008, all MGNREGS wages began to be paid directly into workers' bank or post office accounts (opened free of charge). Exceptions are made if a state government acquires an exemption from the central government. Wages should be paid no later than a fortnight after work completion.

Provision of basic facilities at the worksite. Basic facilities include shade, drinking water, child care for children under age six, first aid facilities to attend to the injured in case of an accident, and a notice board with all relevant information about the worksite.

Several provisions of the Act encourage the participation of women. First, the Act mandates that one-third of the workers be women. Second, it ensures equal wages for men and women, with gender-specific productivity norms in the Schedule of Rates. Finally, the scheme mandates provision of work locally (within 5 kilometers of one's residence) and child care facilities (if more than five children younger than age six are present at a worksite).

Focus on labor-intensive rural development works, with a heavy focus on water and irrigation activities as well as connectivity. In addition to the list of specific types of works allowed under the Act, additional types of works may be acceptable based on consultations between the state and the central governments. Overall, the scheme maintains a 60:40 labor-to-capital ratio. Use of contractors or machinery in the execution of works is banned.

(Continued on the following page)

Box O.1 (Continued)

Local village governments (referred to as Panchayati Raj Institutions [PRI]) and communities play a central role. PRI leaders and communities are meant to identify the list of works through discussions in village meetings (Gram Sabha). PRIs also participate in the execution (at least 50 percent of works by value are to be implemented through the Gram Panchayat), supervision, and monitoring of works (including through social audits).

A dedicated administrative structure for MGNREGS implementation. The Act makes specific provision for administrative costs to be borne by the center and supplemented by states. There is provision for a dedicated cadre of MGNREGS officials and functionaries at the district, block, and Gram Panchayat levels that are responsible for implementing the program.

Emphasis on accountability through the use of information and communication technology tools and by relying on communities and third-party monitoring. Management information systems have been developed based on administrative reporting of employment generated and assets created. Field-based monitoring is carried out through the Ministry of Rural Development's national field-level monitors and local Village Vigilance and Monitoring Committees. Community-based monitoring through social audits is also occurring in some states.

Center and state financing. The central government share amounts to 90 percent of total expenditure on the program. This share includes 100 percent of wage costs and 75 percent of the nonwage component (including materials and wage payments to skilled and semiskilled workers, and most administrative tasks, subject to a maximum limit), working under an assumed 60:40 labor-to-capital ratio. States are responsible for paying 100 percent of unemployment allowance costs.

Source: World Bank 2011, based on MGNREGS operational guidelines (www.nrega.nic.in) and various government orders.

a. Wage determination rules may change further because setting MGNREGS wages below the state-mandated minimum wage rates under the Minimum Wages Act has been challenged in court as a violation of the law and tantamount to "forced labor." This stand was upheld in September 2011 by a Karnataka High Court verdict that affirms that the central government is obligated to pay wages in line with the state minimum wage rate. In January 2012, the Supreme Court refused to stay the Karnataka High Court verdict.

unemployment allowance. The scheme is universal in that all rural households can apply for work. In this, the MGNREGS follows a demand-driven, rights-based approach that differs from the supply-based approaches adopted by most earlier public works schemes. It is closest in spirit to the Maharashtra Employment Guarantee Scheme (MEGS) initiated in the 1970s.[4]

• Wage payments under MGNREGS are entirely in cash, unlike previous programs that also had food components.

• MGNREGS is the first social protection scheme to devolve significant resources to Gram Panchayats (GPs) and under which Panchayati Raj Institutions (PRIs) are given a central role in planning, execution, and oversight.[5] In practice, the leader of the GP—called the Mukhiya in Bihar—plays an important role in how the Act is implemented.

• The design of MGNREGS emphasizes transparency and accountability to a greater degree than previous schemes.

Advocates of this scheme have claimed that it could largely eliminate poverty in rural India. For example, Drèze (2004) claims that the scheme "would enable most poor households in rural India to cross the poverty line." That might appear to be a tall order, but there can be no denying that this is an ambitious and well-intentioned effort to fight poverty in India and that, in principle, it has tremendous promise.

Such a workfare scheme tries to reduce poverty in a number of distinct ways. The most direct and obvious way is by providing extra employment and income to the poorest in rural areas. The long-standing incentive argument is that the work requirements in such a scheme mean that it will be self-targeting, that is, the nonpoor will not want to do such work, and poor people will readily turn away from the scheme when better opportunities arise.

Furthermore, by linking the wage rate to the statutory minimum wage rate, and guaranteeing work at that wage rate, the scheme becomes a means of enforcing that minimum wage rate on *all* casual work, including work not covered by the scheme. Indeed, the existence of such a program can radically alter the bargaining power of poor men and women in the labor market, and also of poor people living in not-so-poor families, by increasing the reservation wage (the fallback position if a bargain is not struck). They may then benefit even if they do not participate (Dasgupta 1993).

Such second-round effects may be huge. Murgai and Ravallion (2005b) show that before the program started (based on the 2004/05 National Sample Survey [NSS] round), three-quarters of India's casual laborers were paid less than the country's state-level statutory minimum wage rates. The 2009/10 NSS round indicates that two-thirds of agricultural labor days were paid less than the minimum wage for agricultural unskilled labor. Probably the only way to enforce a living wage in a developing rural economy is for the government to act as the employer of last resort. The spillover effect on nonparticipants could account for a large share of the poverty impact of such a scheme, as shown by Murgai and Ravallion (2005a, 2005b).

The scheme also tries to address some of the underlying causes of poverty in rural India. It can help reduce future poverty by creating useful assets. For example, it can help regenerate the natural resource base and expand rural connectivity through road rehabilitation. The guarantee of work can provide valuable insurance against the many risks faced by India's rural poor in their daily lives and help underpin otherwise risky investments. Even those who do not normally need such work can benefit from knowing it is available. The gains to the poor can also be accompanied by efficiency gains given existing labor market distortions.[6] Also, by its bottom-up, demand-driven nature, the scheme aims to empower marginalized communities. It would be naive to think that self-efficacy in demanding work will emerge overnight among poor people. However, creating the legal right is certainly a first, positive step.

The idea of an employment guarantee is important to the realization of these benefits. The gains depend heavily on the scheme's ability to originate a supply of work to match the demand. Doing so is not going to be easy, given that it requires an open-ended public spending commitment; similarly to an insurance company, the government must pay up when shocks hit. This kind of uncertainty about disbursements in risky environments would be a challenge for any government at any level of economic development. Even if flexibility in spending is not an issue, accommodating supply to demand will require state and local government administrative capabilities that could be a challenge, particularly in poor areas. If creating a right to work is not in the interests of those in power locally, and public capabilities for enforcement are weak, rationing can emerge at the local level even when the central government is committed to providing funds.

Along with financial resources and government capacity to implement, public awareness is also essential for success. Interest in the use of information-based interventions to improve service delivery and governance has increased recently. The premise is that lack of information is a decisive demand-side factor inhibiting successful participatory action by poor people to get the services to which they are entitled. Past studies lend support to this premise.[7] However, incomplete information is only one of the reasons that poor people do not access the services due to them.[8] Imparting information about the available services does not necessarily make that information relevant and meaningful in their daily lives. People might not know their legal rights because there is no point to knowing them when the reality of their lives will never admit those rights. Greater knowledge will not then be sufficient for people to be willing and able to take action to get what they are due. The same factors that make poverty and underdevelopment persist may also make information about one's legal rights largely irrelevant to one's agency in accessing services.

The word "public" in "public awareness" is key. Specific individuals may know that they were denied work, but may not be aware that this is true of others as well. Local officials can exploit a degree of "plausible deniability" of large-scale rationing of work, as long as it is not too obvious. Supporters of MGNREGS have argued for active monitoring through social audits and local public disclosure of payments (see, for example, Drèze 2004). The little quantitative evidence available on the performance of Gram Sabhas (GS) suggests that when the GS is held it does improve the performance of public programs in reaching the poor in southern states (Besley, Pande, and Rao 2005).[9] However, generalizing from this evidence to the rest of India would clearly be hazardous; some states, including Bihar, have weak PRIs, which have a critical role in MGNREGS implementation.[10] At the same time, the experience of civil-society-led social audits across the country (particularly in Rajasthan) shows that mobilization of village communities is possible. However, making social audits a regular public scrutiny process in the absence of strong local community organizations is a challenge. Andhra Pradesh is one example in which the state government has developed an institutional mechanism for undertaking audits of all MGNREGS works across the state (Aiyar, Kapoor Mehta, and Samji 2011; Aiyar and Samji 2009; Aakella and Kidambi 2007).

The Bihar Rural Employment Guarantee Scheme

Bihar is the third largest, poorest, and most densely populated state in India. With a population of 104 million, which is 8.6 percent of India's total, it is the largest state after Uttar Pradesh and Maharashtra. Population density is very high and nearly four times the national average. One in six poor Indians lives in Bihar. In 2009/10, more than half (55 percent) of the rural population lived below the poverty line.[11] Because of population growth, between 2004/05 and 2009/10, the number of rural poor people increased to 50 million from 45.4 million. Poverty rates have remained persistently high.[12] The state has had one of the lowest long-run trend rates of poverty reduction in India; indeed, there is virtually no long-run trend reduction for the period 1960–2000 (Datt and Ravallion 2002).

Bihar is predominantly a rural state. The average level of urban-ization in India is low, but at 11.3 percent it is even lower in Bihar (about one-third of India's average). Changes in the structure of the economy are proceeding rapidly. During the past decade, agricul-ture's share in total output has fallen from 30.6 percent (in 2001–03) to 18.2 percent (in 2009–11). However, the drop in output has come at a time when the agricultural workforce has declined very slowly, leading to stagnant household incomes from farming. The state has one of the highest levels of rural landlessness and fragmented land holdings in the country. Because of its topographic and climatic con-ditions, Bihar is also vulnerable to natural disasters (for example, droughts in the region south of the Ganges). About 73 percent of the state's geographical area is flood prone, particularly in the north. Bihar accounts for 17 percent of the flood-prone area and 22 percent of the flood-affected population in India.[13]

For these reasons, MGNREGS should have great significance to Bihar. The government of Bihar launched the program in 22 districts in February 2006 with central government funding.[14] Simultaneously, it launched the Bihar Rural Employment Guarantee Scheme (BREGS) in the remaining 16 districts with state government funding. The two schemes followed a common set of guidelines and processes, so in effect the scheme started in all districts in 2006 albeit with different sources of funding. In the second phase, beginning April 1, 2007, central government financing was extended to all districts. This study refers to the whole scheme in Bihar as BREGS.

The formal processes followed by BREGS closely follow the Act, as figure O.1 illustrates. The starting point is when the household obtains a job card, which forms the basis of identification for demanding employment. Job card holders can make an applica-tion seeking work to the GP or block office, stating the time and duration for which work is sought. Applicants are issued a dated receipt against which the guarantee of providing employment within 15 days operates. On the supply side, open assemblies of the GS are intended to identify suitable projects. The expressed demand for work is then to be accommodated on those projects emerging from the GS that obtain administrative and technical clearances.[15] Failing this, the worker is entitled under the Act to an unemploy-ment allowance.

The scale of the program is unprecedented for Bihar. Expenditure on public works increased nearly four times from Rs 7,183 million in 2006/07 to Rs 26,320 million in 2010/11 (table O.1). By 2010/11, about 13 million households—more than three-quarters of rural households—were registered for the program, that is, they had been issued job cards (table O.1). Administrative data

Figure O.1 Bihar Rural Employment Guarantee Scheme
Flowchart

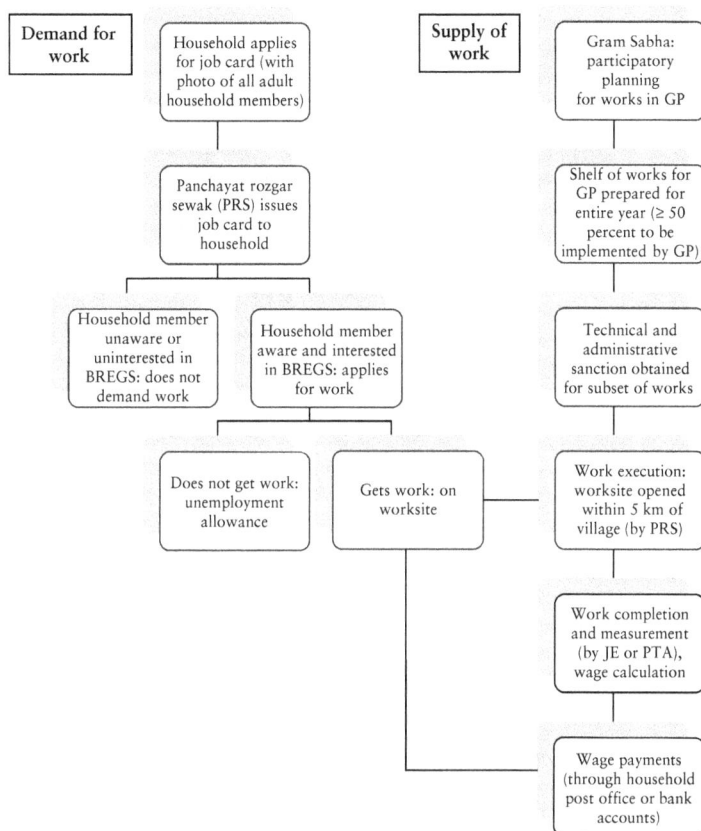

Source: Based on government of Bihar guidelines available at http://rdd.bih.nic.in/.
Note: GP = Gram Panchayat; JE = junior engineer; km = kilometers; PTA = panchayat technical assistant; PRS = panchayat rozgar sewak.

indicate that 4.7 million households—nearly 30 percent of rural households—were provided employment, amounting to approximately 160 million person days. Of this, nearly half was performed by Scheduled Caste and Scheduled Tribe (SC/ST) workers and nearly 30 percent by women.[16] These figures suggest significant expansion relative to previous public works programs in Bihar. For instance, previous programs generated only about 62 million person days in 2005/06, just before the introduction of BREGS. Although about half of this employment was provided to SC/ST households, only about 21 percent was provided to women.

Table O.1 Summary Statistics on the Bihar Rural Employment Guarantee Scheme from Administrative Data

	2006/07	2007/08	2008/09	2009/10	2010/11
Allocation and expenditure					
Total available funds (Rs, millions)	12,289	14,729	21,433	23,967	31,938
Total expenditure (Rs, millions)	7,183	10,534	13,058	18,177	26,320
Total wage expenditures (Rs, millions)	4,222	6,806	8,396	11,087	15,961
Expenditures per household (Rs)	442	638	779	1,069	1,526
Utilization of funds (percent)	58	72	61	76	82
Registration					
Households issued job cards (millions)	3.6	8.1	10.3	12.4	13.0
Rural households with job cards (percent)	23	52	65	77	80
SC/ST households issued job cards (millions)	1.6	3.8	4.8	5.5	5.7
Households provided employment					
Households provided employment (millions)	1.7	3.9	3.8	4.1	4.7
Households provided 100 or more days of employment (millions)	0.0	0.1	0.1	0.3	0.3

Rural households provided employment (percent)	11	25	24	26	29
Rural households provided 100 or more days of employment (percent)	0.2	0.3	0.6	1.8	1.6
Employment provided					
Person days generated (millions)	60	84	99	114	160
Person days generated for SC/ST (millions)	30	41	52	54	76
Person days generated for women (millions)	—	—	30	34	45
Person days per household provided employment	35	22	26	28	34
Person days per rural household	4	5	6	7	10
Person days among SC/ST (percent)	50	49	53	47	47
Person days among women (percent)	—	—	30	30	28

Sources: Program expenditure (all years) and program outcomes (2006/07, 2007/08): Monthly Progress Report, Rural Development Department, government of Bihar. Data on annual projected population from government of India (2006).

Note: The number of rural households was computed by dividing the population projections by the mean rural household size computed from the 2009/10 National Sample Survey (NSS 66th round, Schedule 1.0). Rs = rupees; SC/ST = Scheduled Caste and Scheduled Tribe; — = not available.

This Study

This study shows that BREGS has the potential to substantially reduce poverty in Bihar. If every rural household that indicates they want this work were to get the full 100 days at the stipulated wage rate, and did not have to give up any other source of income to take up this work, the poverty rate in rural Bihar would have been 37.6 percent in 2009—12 percentage points lower than the 50 percent rate obtained by using median household consumption per capita as the poverty line, or a 14 percentage point impact compared with the estimated poverty rate in the absence of the program. Therefore, an idealized version of BREGS has the potential to achieve a sizable reduction in poverty in one of India's poorest states.

But that potential is a long way from being met in practice. The estimates suggest that BREGS reduced poverty in 2009 by 1 percentage point.

To inform policy discussions about how to ensure greater future impact, we need to understand why the scheme is falling so far short of its potential. There are a number of ways that an ambitious anti-poverty intervention such as this might not realize its potential in practice:

• The work requirements may deter some of the poorest, who may not be fit for such work as the result of undernourishment or disability, or poor health generally.

• The process of actually applying for work may also discourage some poor people, notably those who have faced a history of social exclusion and marginalization that has led to limited self-efficacy in expressing their demand for any form of public entitlement.

• There may be unmet demand for work, in that not everyone who wants work can get it, or some get fewer days of work than they want. Inadequate funds, restrictions on the flow of funds, or limited administrative capacity for implementation at the local level can result in less work being available on the scheme than is demanded, leading to rationing of the work.

• The full wage rate stipulated under the scheme might not be received by workers because of leakage.

• There is also likely to be forgone income, that is, some opportunity cost to the worker from some forgone economic activity; these costs are largely unavoidable "deadweight losses."

• The selection process for projects may be captured by local elites, and not reflect the needs of poor people.

To try to shed light on the overall impact and the importance of these various factors, we rely on a wide range of sources:

administrative data, household surveys, a randomized intervention, and qualitative observations from field work. Administrative data sources are known to be questionable in some respects, notably in assessing demand for work on the scheme (Drèze and Oldiges 2011). For that purpose, household surveys are clearly better instruments. In fact, very little systematic information about demand for work is currently available.

This book presents survey-based estimates for India as a whole as well as results for Bihar. Results for India are based on the 2009/10 National Sample Survey (Schedule 10.0). The bulk of the analysis on Bihar draws on a panel survey of rural households commissioned by the authors for the purpose of this study (referred to as the BREGS survey). Two surveys were carried out in 2009 and 2010 and spanned 150 villages spread across all 38 districts in Bihar. These data are supplemented by qualitative research in six districts to better understand supply-side challenges.

This study is not a standard "impact evaluation" in which average outcomes for those who participate in a program (sometimes randomly assigned to it, sometimes not) are compared with outcomes for those who do not participate. We cannot observe any areas of Bihar in which the program was not in effect because Bihar fully scaled up almost immediately, rather than phasing the program into operation as occurred elsewhere in India.[17]

We need a different approach that still respects the principle of evaluation, namely, that impact is assessed relative to explicit counterfactuals. A distinctive feature of our methodology is that we identify the key counterfactual outcomes of interest—that is, what BREGS participants would have done in the absence of the program—by directly asking individual BREGS participants.[18] The advantage of this approach is that it produces an individual-specific estimate of impact—exploiting the information available for each participant—rather than delivering only a mean impact. Thus, it is well suited to distributional analysis. Its disadvantage is that it requires that a counterfactual question be asked, which is never easy (although not fundamentally different from the common method of asking about expectations of the future).

A potential shortcoming of this methodology is that counterfactual outcomes reported by households do not provide a valid estimate of mean impact on the treated for an employment guarantee scheme such as MGNREGS *if* the guarantee is being implemented. As Ravallion (1990) argues, the gains from such a program are very likely to spill over into the private labor market. If the employment guarantee is effective, the scheme will establish a firm lower bound to the entire wage distribution—assuming that no able-bodied worker would accept any work, including in the private sector, at a wage rate below the public works wage. In such a case, one will incorrectly conclude that the scheme has no impact, because even the counterfactual wages will be the same for participants and non-participants. That would entirely miss the impact, which could be large for both groups.[19] However, as we show later in this book, although we cannot rule out the possibility that the scheme is causing a tightening of the agricultural labor market, the extent of the unmet demand for BREGS work does make one skeptical.

Another potential shortcoming of the analysis is that we follow the standard practice in India of using household consumption per person as the welfare indicator when measuring poverty and assessing performance in targeting the poor. However, this practice does not allow for the likely disutility of doing casual manual wage labor. This type of work (including working on MGNREGS) is physically taxing, of uncertain duration, and provides no employment benefits. Yet the consumption-based measures of welfare used for measuring poverty and assessing targeting performance in India attach no disutility to doing such work. Two people with the same real consumption expenditure are deemed to be equally poor regardless of how each derives that consumption.

We first examine participation in MGNREGS across states using the 2009/10 National Sample Survey (Schedule 10.0). Chapter 1 uses these data to document a substantial degree of unmet demand ("rationing") in the scheme across states. The chapter identifies likely reasons for rationing, including that state governments also care about the cost of providing employment under MGNREGS. These costs comprise identifying, hiring, training, and supervising the skilled manpower needed for organizing and supervising projects as well as establishing adequate systems for ensuring smooth flow of funds to local implementing agencies and for monitoring scheme performance. A state government may value the objectives of the Act, but it still faces a trade-off between guaranteeing employment to all who want it (as stipulated by the Act) and the costs of doing so.[20]

Alarmingly, we find that the degree of rationing is greatest in the poorer states that arguably need the scheme more. By and large, MGNREGS is working best where it is needed least. As chapter 1 also shows, Bihar stands out as having not only the highest extent of rationing, but also above-average rationing given its level of poverty. The rest of the volume analyzes why the scheme seems to be working worst in one of the very poorest states.

In chapter 2 we use the BREGS survey to look at the demand for work and how much of that demand is actually being met. We demonstrate that the unmet demand for work on the scheme in

Bihar is large. We also show considerable churning in the form of exits and entries into the scheme, and argue that this churning was largely involuntary in that many more households than did so would have liked to enter as well as remain employed in the scheme over time. We turn in chapter 3 to the task of providing a profile of people attracted to the program, and of these, who gets work. Chapter 4 examines the wages received, and we demonstrate that there is a sizable gap between the wages reported by workers in the survey and the stipulated wages for the scheme as well as wages for other casual work. There is a similar gap with the wages recorded in the administrative data. We also explore the differences in wages between men and women and how wages are determined in the scheme versus in the casual labor market. Chapter 5 uses the survey responses to assess likely forgone incomes from BREGS participation.

By combining the main elements in these chapters, we are able in chapter 6 to assess how closely BREGS is able to approximate the potential impact on poverty. Instead of a 14 percentage point reduction in poverty as would be expected under ideal conditions—though (we would contend) not unlike the conditions envisaged by the scheme's designers—we estimate that BREGS has reduced poverty by about 1 percentage point.

We then turn to the task of trying to explain why the actual performance of BREGS in reducing poverty falls so far short of potential, and suggest specific actionable areas for reform. Both demand- and supply-side factors constrain participation. Chapter 7 describes the impact on awareness of a randomized awareness intervention using a specially designed fictional movie about BREGS rights and entitlements. Finally, chapter 8 provides insights into supply-side constraints to work provision.

Main Lessons from the Study

India cannot claim success for its MGNREGS unless the scheme is working adequately where it is needed most, that is, in the country's poorest areas. This study investigates the scheme's performance in what is by some measures the country's poorest state, Bihar, and provides comparisons with other states.

Under the idealized conditions that the scheme's founders appear to have had in mind, everyone who wants work at the stipulated minimum wage rates should get it, up to 100 days per household per year, without having to give up any other income source to take up the work. We show that BREGS should then have a large impact on rural poverty in Bihar, bringing the poverty rate down by some

14 percentage points. If anything, this is likely to be an underesti-mate given that it ignores likely spillover effects to casual wage rates for other unskilled work; it also ignores consumption gains from the extra assets created. However, the reality falls far short of this ideal. We estimate that the actual impact is about 1 percentage point.

When we use the survey data to understand this clearly disap-pointing performance we learn a lot about how the scheme might work better. Even though public awareness of the existence of the scheme is growing, we find that there is little understanding of even its most basic features. Few people understand that after getting a job card, they need to apply for work to get employment. In that sense, the fundamental principle of employment on demand has yet to sink in. Similarly, knowledge of other entitlements, such as the statutory wage, employment within 15 days, weekly wage pay-ments, unemployment allowances, and facilities to be provided at the worksite, is minimal.

We find compelling evidence that the scheme is reaching relatively poor families. Certain types of households are rationed, in that they want this work but do not get it. The rationing exhibits a clear gender dimension—households with large shares of adult women and female-headed households will not get the work they want. In general, the rationing process tends to favor those with characteristics associated with poor households: among richer households, those who have Below-Poverty-Line cards are less likely to be rationed. Those who lack the typical profile of the poor appear to be more likely to be excluded from access to the scheme when they want it. This is evident in the effects of education and landholding on participation in the scheme, given other controls (including wealth).

Among those who do participate, we also find a sizable gap between the wages actually reported by workers and the wages they are supposed to receive under the scheme. So workers are not getting all the work they want, and they are not getting the full wages to which they are due. In addition, leakage to unintended beneficiaries (estimated as the gap between survey-based estimates and adminis-trative records on wage disbursements) is substantial even though it is nowhere near as large as some casual observers have claimed or in comparison with that in other antipoverty programs.

If the potential gains to India's poor are to be realized by MGNREGS, policy makers will need to focus on the substan-tial unmet demand for work. Given the scheme's current level of complexity, meeting this unmet demand will probably not be pos-sible unless administrative capacity for implementing the scheme is strengthened. Better performance will require better state- and local-level administration, monitoring, and reporting. The shortage of the skilled manpower needed for these tasks clearly constrains the state's ability to absorb funds and implement the scheme. Developing local administrative capabilities through training and providing incentives to staff and setting up strong financial management and monitoring systems are high priorities. In particular, initiatives such as creating a state-level corpus fund and putting in place a centralized fund management system can smooth fund flows, thereby limiting one potential source of work rationing.

These enhanced administrative capabilities can also be used to ensure local public knowledge of households' rights and of the scheme's rules and local monitoring and grievance redress, and to facilitate better administrative response to demands for work. The essential aim is to radically change the entire calculus of costs and benefits facing local leaders and officials. If workers know and are confident that they can demand work at the stipulated wage, they will resist any attempts by officials to deny them or to take a cut from their wages. We have demonstrated that a public information campaign using a movie can significantly enhance workers' knowledge. However, it has little discernible average impact on actions such as seeking employment when needed or on the key scheme outcomes of wages and employment. Among selected subgroups, the only exception to the latter finding is that the movie helped illiterate people secure extra work on existing BREGS projects. If such a campaign can be combined with more effective implementation of the scheme's supply-side provisions and a more rapid flow of funds, it should be possible to realize a greater share of the potential impact on poverty of this ambitious scheme.

It is important that reform efforts for MGNREGS work on *both* of these aspects—a stronger, more capable, local administration, *plus* more effective participation by civil society. One without the other will not ensure a true "right to work."

Notes

1. For further discussion, see Ravallion (1991) and Besley and Coate (1992).

2. During the first two phases, districts that were not covered by MGNREGS continued to be covered by previous public works programs (that is, the Sampoorna Grameen Rozgar Yojana and the National Food for Work Program).

3. See the discussions in Drèze (1990) and World Bank (2011).

4. On this scheme see the discussions in Echeverri-Gent (1988), Drèze and Sen (1989), and Ravallion, Datt, and Chaudhuri (1993).

5. The GP is a cluster of villages and is the primary unit of the three-tier structure of local self-governance in rural India. The next higher level of administration is the block, followed by the district. Locally elected bodies at the GP, block, and district levels are referred to as the PRIs. The 73rd Amendment (1992) to the Indian Constitution mandated the devolution of powers and responsibilities to PRIs.

6. The distortions could be caused by monopsony power in rural labor markets (Basu, Chau, and Kanbur 2009) or labor-tying (Basu 2013). Nor does the distortion need to be felt only in the rural labor market; it could instead be manifested in the urban labor market by generating excess migration to urban areas (Ravallion 1990).

7. Strömberg (2004) reports evidence that U.S. antipoverty programs have worked better in places with greater access to radios. For India, Besley and Burgess (2003) find that the governments of states in which newspaper circulation is greater are more responsive in their relief efforts for negative agricultural shocks. In Uganda, Reinikka and Svensson (2005) find significant impacts on schooling of a newspaper campaign. Access to a televised soap opera in Brazil is found by La Ferrara, Chong, and Duryea (2012) to lower fertility, especially among poor women. Jensen and Oster (2009) find that access to television led to less domestic violence and lower fertility rates in India. Not all studies have been supportive. Results of Banerjee and others (2010) are less encouraging on the scope for using information interventions to improve the monitoring of education service providers in India. Using a different community-based information campaign, Pandey, Goyal, and Sundararaman (2009) report more supportive results in the same setting.

8. What follows is not a complete list of the reasons. Useful overviews of the arguments and evidence on other social and behavioral factors relevant to the success of information campaigns can be found in Keefer and Khemani (2005) and, in the context of immunization campaigns, Cappelen, Mæstad, and Tungodden (2010).

9. A GS is a body of all persons in the electoral roll for a Gram Panchayat. The Gram Panchayat convenes meetings of the GS to disseminate information as well as to enable all households to participate in decisions relating to development of the village.

10. Bihar was one of the first states to introduce PRIs, and GP elections were held every three to six years from 1952 until 1978. However, subsequently, no GP-level elections were held in the state until as late as 2001. For evidence on the differing performance of the panchayats across India, see Mathew and Buch (2000).

11. Estimates are based on official Planning Commission poverty lines for 2009/10.

12. In a marked departure from past trends, official estimates for 2011–12 indicate a steep reduction in rural poverty to 34 percent in the two-year period since 2009–10.

13. Flood Management Information System, Water Resources Department, government of Bihar, available at http://fmis.bih.nic.in/history.htm.

14. These districts were Araria, Aurangabad, Bhabhua, Bhojpur, Darbhanga, Gaya, Jamui, Jehanabad, Katihar, Kishanganj, Lakhisarai, Madhubani, Munger, Muzaffarpur, Nalanda, Nawada, Patna, Rohtas, Samastipur, Sheohar, Supaul, and Vaishali.

15. Works can also be introduced by the block- and district-level bodies, but have to be approved by the GS, which may accept, amend, or reject them.

16. SC/STs comprise population groupings that are explicitly recognized by the Indian Constitution. SC/STs are earmarked for special treatment such as reservations in public sector employment and government-run educational institutions.

17. A number of studies use the phasing in of the scheme across districts to evaluate the impacts of MGNREGS using a double-difference approach (see Azam 2011; Liu and Deininger 2013; Ravi and Engler 2013; Imbert and Papp 2012; and Berg and others 2012).

18. Jha, Gaiha, and Pandey (2012) also ask survey respondents working on MGNREGS whether they thought any other work was available. They do not, however, ask for forgone incomes, but instead use prevailing wage rates for the imputation.

19. See Ravallion (2008). Note that this would be true even if one could observe a group of participants randomly assigned to the program and compare them with those "randomized out" of the program, or if a counterfactual outcome were estimated by propensity score matching procedures.

20. Very few states actually exhaust the central funds for administrative expenditure so do not, in general, have to invest from their own budgets. However, there are opportunity costs of time with regard to state capabilities being mobilized to develop systems and recruit and manage the skilled manpower, such as the panchayat rozgar sewak, and so forth.

References

Aakella, K. V., and Sowmya Kidambi. 2007. "Social Audits in Andhra Pradesh: A Process in Evolution." *Economic and Political Weekly* 42 (47): 18–19.

Aiyar, Yamini, Soumya Kapoor Mehta, and Salimah Samji. 2011. "Strengthening Public Accountability: Lessons from Implementing Social Audits in Andhra Pradesh." Accountability Initiative Working Paper, Center for Policy Research, New Delhi.

Aiyar, Yamini, and Salimah Samji. 2009. "Transparency and Accountability in NREGA: A Case Study of Andhra Pradesh." Accountability Initiative Working Paper No. 1, Center for Policy Research, New Delhi.

Azam, Mehtabul. 2011. "The Impact of Indian Job Guarantee Scheme on Labor Market Outcomes: Evidence from a Natural Experiment." IZA Discussion Paper No. 6548, Institute for the Study of Labor, Bonn.

Banerjee, Abhijit, Rukmini Banerji, Esther Duflo, Rachel Glennerster, and Stuti Khemani. 2010. "Pitfalls of Participatory Programs: Evidence from a Randomized Evaluation in Education in India." *American Economic Journal: Economic Policy* 2 (1): 1–30.

Basu, Arnab K. 2013. "Impact of Rural Employment Guarantee Schemes on Seasonal Labor Markets: Optimum Compensation and Workers' Welfare." *Journal of Economic Inequality* 11 (1): 1–34.

———, Nancy H. Chau, and Ravi Kanbur. 2009. "A Theory of Employment Guarantees: Contestability, Credibility and Distributional Concerns." *Journal of Public Economics* 93: 482–97.

Berg, Erlend, Sambit Bhattacharyya, Rajasekhar Durgam, and Manjula Ramachandra. 2012. "Can Rural Public Works Affect Agricultural Wages? Evidence from India." Working Paper WPS/2012-05, University of Oxford, Center for the Study of African Economies, Oxford, U.K.

Besley, Timothy, and Robin Burgess. 2003. "The Political Economy of Government Responsiveness: Theory and Evidence from India." *Quarterly Journal of Economics* 117 (4): 1415–51.

Besley, Timothy, and Stephen Coate. 1992. "Workfare vs. Welfare: Incentive Arguments for Work Requirements in Poverty Alleviation Programs." *American Economic Review* 82 (1): 249–61.

Besley, Timothy, Rohini Pande, and Vijayendra Rao. 2005. "Participatory Democracy in Action: Survey Evidence from South India." *Journal of the European Economic Association* 3 (2–3): 648–57.

Cappelen, Alexander, Ottar Mæstad, and Bertil Tungodden. 2010. "Demand for Childhood Vaccination—Insights from Behavioral Economics." *Forum for Development Studies* 37 (3): 349–64.

Dasgupta, Partha. 1993. *An Inquiry into Well-Being and Destitution.* Oxford: Oxford University Press.

Datt, Gaurav, and Martin Ravallion. 2002. "Has India's Post-Reform Economic Growth Left the Poor Behind?" *Journal of Economic Perspectives* 16 (3): 89–108.

Drèze, Jean. 1990. "Famine Prevention in India." In *The Political Economy of Hunger*, Volume 2, edited by Jean Drèze and Amartya Sen, 13–122. Oxford: Oxford University Press.

———. 2004. "Employment as a Social Responsibility." *The Hindu*, November 22. http://www.hindu.com/2004/11/22/stories/2004112205071000 .htm.

————, and Christian Oldiges. 2011. "NREGA: The Official Picture." In _The Battle for Employment Guarantee_, edited by Reetika Khera. New Delhi: Oxford University Press.

Drèze, Jean, and Amartya Sen. 1989. _Hunger and Public Action._ Oxford: Oxford University Press.

Echeverri-Gent, John. 1988. "Guaranteed Employment in an Indian State: The Maharashtran Experience." _Asian Survey_ 28: 1294–310.

Government of India. 2006. "Report of the Technical Group on Population Projections Constituted by the National Commission on Population." Office of the Registrar General and Census Commissioner, New Delhi.

Imbert, Clément, and John Papp. 2012. "Equilibrium Distributional Impacts of Government Employment Programs: Evidence from India's Employment Guarantee." Paris School of Economics Working Paper No. 2012 - 14. Paris School of Economics, Paris.

Jensen, Robert, and Emily Oster. 2009. "The Power of TV: Cable Television and Women's Status in India." _Quarterly Journal of Economics_ 124 (3): 1057–94.

Jha, Raghbendra, Raghav Gaiha, and Manoj K. Pandey. 2012. "Net Transfer Benefits under India's Rural Employment Guarantee Scheme." _Journal of Policy Modeling_ 34 (2): 296–311.

Keefer, Philip, and Stuti Khemani. 2005. "Democracy, Public Expenditures, and the Poor: Understanding Political Incentives for Providing Public Services." _World Bank Research Observer_ 20 (1): 1–28.

La Ferrara, Eliana, Alberto Chong, and Suzanne Duryea. 2012. "Soap Operas and Fertility: Evidence from Brazil." _American Economic Journal: Applied Economics_ 4 (4): 1–31.

Liu, Yanyan, and Klaus Deininger. 2013. "Welfare and Poverty Impacts of India's National Rural Employment Guarantee Scheme: Evidence from Andhra Pradesh." Policy Research Working Paper No. 6543, World Bank, Washington, DC.

Mathew, George, and Nirmala Buch. 2000. _Status of Panchayati Raj in the States and Union Territories of India 2000._ New Delhi: Institute of Social Studies.

Murgai, Rinku, and Martin Ravallion. 2005a. "Employment Guarantee in Rural India: What Would It Cost and How Much Would It Reduce Poverty?" _Economic and Political Weekly_, July 30, 3450–55.

————. 2005b. "Is a Guaranteed Living Wage a Good Anti-Poverty Policy?" Policy Research Working Paper No. 3460, World Bank, Washington, DC.

National Sample Survey Organization (NSSO). 2009/10. "Socio-Economic Survey Sixty-Sixth Round Schedule 10: Employment and Unemployment." Government of India, New Delhi.

Pandey, Priyanka, Sangeeta Goyal, and Venkatesh Sundararaman. 2009. "Community Participation in Public Schools: Impacts of Information

Campaigns in Three Indian States." *Education Economics* 13 (3): 355–75.

Ravallion, Martin. 1990. "Market Responses to Anti-Hunger Policies: Wages, Prices, and Employment." In *The Political Economy of Hunger,* Volume 2, edited by Jean Drèze and Amartya Sen, 241–78. Oxford: Oxford University Press.

———. 1991. "Reaching the Rural Poor through Public Employment: Arguments, Evidence, and Lessons from South Asia." *World Bank Research Observer* 6 (2): 153–75.

———. 2008, "Evaluating Anti-Poverty Programs." In *Handbook of Development Economics,* Volume 4, edited by Paul Schultz and John Strauss. Amsterdam: North-Holland.

———, Gaurav Datt, and Shubham Chaudhuri. 1993. "Does Maharashtra's 'Employment Guarantee Scheme' Guarantee Employment? Effects of the 1988 Wage Increase." *Economic Development and Cultural Change* 41: 251–75.

Ravi, Shamika, and Monika Engler. 2013. "Workfare as an Effective Way to Fight Poverty: The Case of India's NREGS." http://ssrn.com/abstract=1336837.

Reinikka, Ritva, and Jakob Svensson. 2005. "Improving Schooling by Combating Corruption: Evidence from a Newspaper Campaign in Uganda." *Journal of the European Economic Association* 3(2–3): 259–67.

Strömberg, David. 2004. "Radio's Impact on Public Spending." *Quarterly Journal of Economics* 119 (1): 189–221.

World Bank. 2011. *Social Protection for a Changing India.* Human Development Unit, South Asia Department. Washington, DC: World Bank.

1

Does India's Employment Guarantee Scheme Guarantee Employment?

The idea of an "employment guarantee" is clearly important for the full benefits of the Mahatma Gandhi National Rural Employment Guarantee Scheme (MGNREGS) to be realized. The gains depend heavily on the scheme's ability to accommodate the supply of work to the demand for it. If MGNREGS in practice worked the way it was designed, there would be no unmet demand for work on the scheme. Anyone who wanted that work would get it. This is, of course, an exacting standard. In reality there may be frictions in implementation leading to some unmet demand for work, such that those wanting work do not get it in a timely manner. The extent to which the employment guarantee is honored will depend, in part, on how effectively and quickly the scheme responds to demand.

We begin this chapter with some theoretical arguments about why we might observe rationing of MGNREGS work even when there are no such frictions in responding quickly to demand. In other words, the employment guarantee required by the National Rural Employment Guarantee Act (the Act, or NREGA) is not necessarily attainable for more fundamental reasons. We then turn to the evidence for India as a whole before, in subsequent chapters, taking a much closer look at the scheme's performance in Bihar.

Why an Employment Guarantee Need Not Be Attainable

The simplest way that unmet demand can emerge is when an employment guarantee scheme faces a hard budget constraint and the wage rate is set too high, given the demand for work on the scheme. A condition must be satisfied—expenditure on the program must not exceed the budget available—and rationing may be the only way to keep expenditure in check given the wage rate and the budget. For example, compelling evidence indicates that rationing emerged in the antecedent scheme to MGNREGS, Maharashtra's Employment Guarantee Scheme, when the wage rate on the scheme was increased substantially in line with revised statutory minimum wage rates (Ravallion, Datt, and Chaudhuri 1993).[1] The rationing occurred mainly because of sluggishness in the opening of new work sites in response to demand.

Unmet demand can also emerge as an equilibrium outcome even when the central government makes an open-ended commitment for funding. We consider three ways this can happen. First is the scheme's role in local electoral politics. MGNREGS provides important resources for locally elected leaders to use to attract voters (see, for example, the interesting discussion in Witsoe 2012). For this purpose, local officials up for reelection must be able to control access to the scheme—to be seen as the benefactor, not simply the conduit for the central government. Thus, the very idea of an "employment guarantee" can be antithetical to local political processes. Those in power locally have little or no incentive to give up their ability to control who benefits from public spending, for that is in large part the way they maintain their power.

Second, local administrative costs, not all of which are evident in official data, must be considered. The provisions of the Act do not imply that there will be zero cost to local (state or lower level) budgets when employing workers under MGNREGS. As described in box O.1, the center covers a large share of the cost, but relatively skilled manpower at the local level is still required for organizing projects and workers. This cost will tend to be higher for governments with generally weak administrative capabilities or weak Panchayati Raj Institutions, which have a key role to play in MGNREGS implementation. This need not be true of all governments in poor areas. However, as a rule, just as unskilled manpower tends to be abundant in poor areas, skilled manpower is scarce. And relatively skilled manpower is needed to manage a scheme such as MGNREGS, including for registering demand, vetting project proposals, drawing up the technical estimates and engineering plans, ensuring the required monitoring and reporting take place, and managing scheme funds, including reporting back to the center to access funds. The scarcity of skilled manpower or strong Panchayati Raj Institutions tends to make it harder, and more costly, for poor areas to implement such a complex scheme. The limited available skilled manpower will have a high opportunity cost if diverted to MGNREGS projects.

Arguably no less important to the functioning of the scheme at the local level will be the availability of "brokers" (variously called *vichawlia* or *dalal*) who can be trusted by local leaders to mediate between them and the various stakeholders, including workers but also local officials and landowners. Based on close observation from field work, Witsoe (2012, 50) explains the role of NREGA brokers in Bihar as follows:

> NREGA brokers had to be trusted allies of the mukhia [Mukhiya] (or else the mukhia would be unwilling to delegate so much power to them), had to have experience working with the block staff and bank manager, had to be able to recruit and manage laborers, while also "managing" landowners, and had to have the liquidity and drive to "invest" in a potentially rewarding but also somewhat risky enterprise. People with such a specialized skill set were in short supply. Given the complexities of implementing NREGA, and the realities of weak state capacity at the local level, without brokers, the project would likely not have functioned at all.

Thus, the local administrative cost of such a scheme may be quite high, especially when one takes into account these typically hidden and scarce brokerage functions. To see what the scarcity of capacity implies for the scheme, we assume that the local government faces a trade-off between the administrative cost incurred per worker employed on MGNREGS and the benefits of extra local employment. ("Local government" can mean any level below the center; similar trade-offs will presumably apply for both the state government and the local village-level government.) Of course, the local government cares about the cost, given by the unit cost times the number of workers employed under the scheme. At the same time, we assume that it also cares about the amount of unmet demand for work on MGNREGS. The local government has the option of not hiring everyone who wants work, but it does not want to drive employment on the scheme down to zero. We can imagine that the central government imposes some explicit penalty (in this case, an unemployment allowance), or that the local government is sympathetic with the objectives of the scheme, or that it perceives a likely political penalty of unmet demand for work. For example, unemployment might generate protests from those whose demands for work are unsatisfied or from civil society groups sympathetic with the interests of potential MGNREGS workers. Future prospects for reelection might also be jeopardized. These penalties can be assumed to fall to zero when there is no unmet demand for work on the scheme but to rise with higher unmet demand. It seems plausible that the penalties will rise more steeply as the excess demand rises; at very high levels of unmet demand the protests may be vastly greater than at low levels.

So in implementing the scheme, the local government faces a trade-off between the cost of employing workers under MGNREGS and its desire to meet the demand for work as required by the Act. In the states with high administrative capability, there may be little trade-off. Indeed, if the unit administrative cost is sufficiently low (in the precise sense defined in box 1.1), the local government will choose to honor the employment guarantee. But that cost may be quite high in very poor states with weak capability for organizing, supervising, and administering the work. Scarce skilled manpower within the local administration will need to be diverted to the scheme, at a potentially high opportunity cost, which cannot be covered by the center.

In fact, with a sufficiently high administrative unit cost facing the local government, its desired level of employment has a particularly simple form, as described in box 1.1. There will be a critical minimum level of demand before any work will be provided on the scheme. The higher the unit cost of providing work, the higher will be this critical minimum. As long as demand rises above this point, work will be provided, given by the difference between the level of demand actually observed in the state and its own critical minimum. At sufficiently low administrative costs, the local government will choose to comply with the employment guarantee and employ all those who want work.

The third way that the guarantee might not be attainable locally is through what is often called "local corruption" (see box 1.2). Much discussion of corruption on MGNREGS has occurred, particularly in the Indian media. Some have also tried to explain, model, or assess leakage (Niehaus and Sukhtankar forthcoming; Imbert and Papp 2011). Of course, corruption is hardly unique to this scheme, and is also found in schemes that favor the nonpoor. However, the fact that MGNREGS is intended to fight poverty adds extra indignation about corruption.

"Corruption" is not easily identified, though we note a number of suggestive instances from both the field observations and the survey data; for example, corruption is one possible interpretation of

Box 1.1 Effect of Local-Level Costs on Meeting Demand under MGNREGS

The central government dictates that the local government should provide work for all those who want it at the stipulated wage rate. The central government pays the unskilled labor cost. The local government chooses the level of employment E to minimize a generalized cost function:

$$cE + p(D - E) \quad \text{subject to} \quad E \leq D, \qquad (1.1.1)$$

in which c is the unit administrative cost of the skilled labor that the local government must finance and $p(\cdot)$ penalizes the unmet demand for work, given an exogenous demand for work, D. It is assumed that the penalty function p is strictly increasing and convex with $p(0) = 0$. Let E^* denote the level of employment that equates the marginal penalty with the unit cost of skilled labor: $p'(D - E^*) = c$. Inverting this function we have

$$E^* = D - f(c), \qquad (1.1.2)$$

in which $f(\cdot)$ is the inverse function of $p'(\cdot)$. The value of $f(c)$ can be interpreted as the minimum level of demand for work before the local government will begin to hire any MGNREGS workers. It is readily verified that $f(c) > 0$ and $f'(c) > 0$. If there is rationing in equilibrium, it will be in the amount $f(c)$. Above this, E^* rises one for one with D.

We can distinguish two regimes: In Regime 1, the level of c is "sufficiently high," in that $c > c^*$ where $c^* = p[f(c)]/f(c)$, which is the

Figure B1.1.1 Theoretical Relationship between Work Provided and Demand for Work

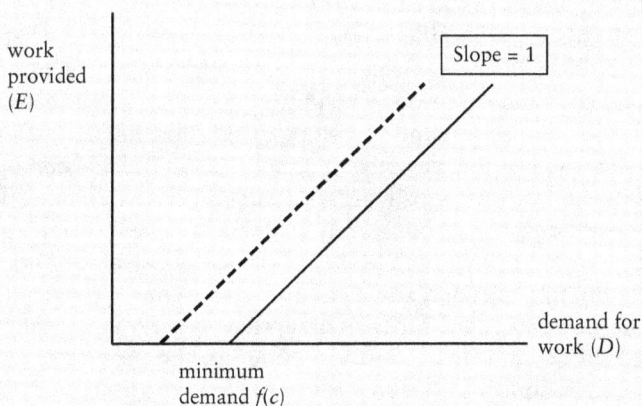

minimum
demand $f(c)$

(Continued on the following page)

Box 1.1 (Continued)

penalty at the minimum level of demand per unit of demand. If c exceeds this critical level, the cost of employing E^* workers is less than the cost of employing all those who want work. Then E^* is the optimal level of employment provided and there will be unmet demand in equilibrium, in that $E^* < D$ with $f(c)$ workers rationed out of jobs. A reduction in the unit administrative cost will increase employment and reduce rationing. In Regime 2 we have $c \leq c^*$, so the local government will choose to comply with the dictate to employ all those who want work.

the discrepancies between the survey-based estimates of wages paid and the administrative data for Bihar, although measurement errors may also be playing a role. However, we do not pay a great deal of explicit attention to corruption in this book. Instead, we focus on the public administrative processes that can either foster or help reduce corruption.

Nonetheless, one issue pertaining to corruption merits attention here, namely, the possibility that it might undermine the guarantee. At first this claim seems surprising. One might expect corruption at the local level on such a scheme to eliminate any unmet demand for MGNREGS work. By this view, corrupt local officials will gain by hiring more workers and taking their "slice" of wage outlays. Thus, corruption would eliminate any rationing.

However, this argument ignores the complexity of MGNREGS and how it works in the context of village politics. There are many checks in force, as is evident from the description of the scheme in box O.1. These checks mean that local officials can face a steep marginal cost of corruption. Corruption may then be perfectly consistent with unmet demand for work in equilibrium. To make this point sharply, box 1.2 describes a simple model of local corruption that will yield rationing of work as an equilibrium outcome. There is a demand constraint, but it only requires that the officials cannot employ more workers than want work; the constraint is not necessarily binding. Beyond some level of employment, local officials will risk being exposed for the corruption. For example, they may need to go beyond their "comfort zone" in the people (especially the aforementioned "NREGA brokers") they trust to collude in the corruption. The "bribes bill" will start to rise sharply. The steep marginal cost faced by local leaders will then limit the scope for expansion in the scheme, leaving unmet demand in equilibrium.

Box 1.2 Corruption and the Unmet Demand for Work

Suppose that local officials choose the level of employment E given an exogenous demand for work on the scheme D to maximize profit:

$$R(E) - C(E) \quad \text{subject to} \quad E \leq D. \tag{1.2.1}$$

Here $R(E)$ is the official's own revenue from corruption at employment level E and $C(E)$ is the cost of corruption. The marginal benefit (MB) is $R'(E)$ and the marginal cost (MC) is $C'(E)$. It is assumed that $R''(E) < C''(E)$. Then there will be unmet demand in equilibrium if $E^* < D$, where $R'(E^*) = C'(E^*)$, as illustrated in figure B1.2.1. (The MB function need not be decreasing, though we draw it as such.)

To make these functions more concrete we can suppose that for each person employed, the local official gets a share of their wage on the scheme, but is constrained by the local market wage rate for unskilled labor, denoted w. The official's share will then be $1 - w/w^{EGS}$ and $R(E) = (w^{EGS} - w)E$. One can generalize this further by allowing for the possibility that higher E puts upward pressure on the market wage rate, implying that MB is not constant. The cost of corruption $C(E)$ can be interpreted as the side payments that the local official must make to cooperating agents. The total cost rises with the number of workers employed because more workers will require that more worksites be opened and that "ghost workers" be paid more, with further side payments required to cooperating officials. It can also be expected that the marginal cost will rise as employment rises; the local official may have to expand the set of people he bribes beyond his own "comfort zone" of those he trusts, and even those he trusts will face larger risks of exposure at large scale, and so require higher compensation.

Figure B1.2.1 Theoretical Model of the Optimal Employment Provided by a Corrupt Local Official

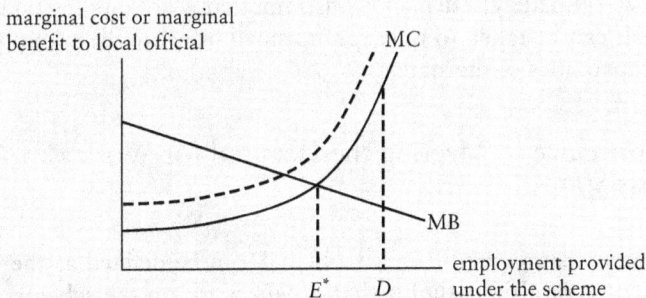

(Continued on the following page)

Box 1.2 (Continued)

Two remarks can be made about the implications of this model. First, notice that an increase in the marginal cost of corruption facing the local official will decrease employment and increase rationing (as can be seen in the figure B1.2.1). Second, notice that an increase in the wage rate on the scheme (where $R(E) = (w^{EGS} - w)$) will increase employment on the scheme, even though there is rationing. However, the gain in wages will go entirely to the local officials, not to the workers on the scheme.

This model suggests that efforts to reduce local corruption by increasing its marginal cost will increase the extent of rationing (box 1.2). To the extent that efforts to "tighten up" the scheme focus on poor states and aim to increase the marginal cost of local corruption—such as by introducing more checks or imposing stricter reporting requirements or higher penalties that vary with the scale of the corruption uncovered—this model can explain why we might find more rationing in poor states, especially if they already have weaker monitoring mechanisms.

The solution to corruption in this situation is to make the model outlined in box 1.2 irrelevant to the behavior of local officials. That requires that local officials have no power to enforce rationing in the first place, so that the demand constraint becomes binding on their behavior. For the demand constraint to be binding those who want work under the scheme must be aware that the law entitles them to that work (or to an unemployment allowance if the work cannot be provided) and must be able to act on that awareness. Thus, adequate administrative and legal processes must be in place for addressing grievances and for punishing local officials who do not comply with the law. Ultimately, a demand constraint that is not binding on local officials can be taken to reflect in no small measure the administrative capabilities of the state.

Performance in Meeting the Demand for Work across States

The participation rate P in MGNREGS can be defined as the proportion of rural households that obtain work on the scheme. The participation rate can be thought of as the product of the demand rate D, defined as the proportion of rural households that want work on the scheme, and one minus the rationing rate R, defined as the proportion of those who wanted work but did not get it. Thus, for state i we have the following identity:

$$P_i = (1 - R_i)D_i, (i = 1, ..., n). \tag{1.1}$$

Notice that the share of households that are rationed is the product of the rationing rate and the demand rate. We shall call this the unmet demand, denoted $U_i \equiv R_i D_i = D_i - P_i$.

How can the true demand for work, and hence the rationing rate, be measured? The administrative data indicate virtually no unmet demand for work on MGNREGS. According to the administrative data, 52.865 million households in India demanded work in 2009/10, and 99.4 percent of them (52.530 million) were provided work.[2]

However, these numbers are deceptive. What is called "demand for work" in the administrative data is the official registration of demand, recorded by local officials. For instance, in Bihar, as in several other states, the administrative data claim that exactly 100 percent of those who demanded work got it. Yet we know from several studies that the work application process and the system for recording demand for work accurately are not yet in place (Khera 2011). Furthermore, state and local governments have an incentive not to report unmet demand given that they should then be paying unemployment allowances (box O.1). Also, some people will undoubtedly be deterred from formally demanding work from the officials, or do not even know that they have the right to make such demands.

A better measure of demand for work can be obtained by asking people directly in their homes and independently of the scheme. That is what the surveys used in this study provide. In this section we will rely on the 66th Round of the National Sample Survey (NSS), conducted between July 2009 and June 2010, in all states. The Employment-Unemployment module (Schedule 10.0) of the survey included questions on participation and demand for work in MGNREGS, which allows us to estimate the demand and rationing rates across states. Three questions on the program were included: (1) whether the household has a job card; (2) whether it got work on the scheme during the last 365 days, for which responses were coded under three options—got work, sought but did not get work, and did not seek work on MGNREGS; and (3) if the household got work, number of days of work and mode of payment. In addition, the "daily status" block collected information on activities for all household members during the week preceding the survey, including number of days worked and wages received, if they worked on MGNREGS public works.

In this chapter we limit the definition of participation and rationing to whether households got work or did not get work. Unmet demand can also take the form of getting fewer days of work than desired. Many households that participated were no doubt rationed in that they would have liked more days of work and still had fewer than the 100 days stipulated by the Act. We have no choice but to ignore this aspect of the scheme's performance because the NSS did not ask how many more days of work the household wanted; all we know is whether the household wanted more work on the scheme. (We were able to relax this constraint in the Bihar survey, as is discussed in later chapters.)

Table 1.1 gives the results by state for the participation rate, the demand rate, and the rationing rate. (The table also gives the female share of employment, to which we return later.) "Demand" is defined as either getting work on the scheme or seeking work but not getting it. For India as a whole, 45 percent of rural households wanted work on the scheme. Of these, 56 percent got work—a national rationing rate of 44 percent. The rationing rate varied from 15 percent in Rajasthan to 84 percent in Maharashtra. Only three states have rationing rates of less than 20 percent. Bihar has the third-highest rationing rate. There is clearly large excess demand for work.

The data in table 1.1 display a puzzling feature: participation rates are only weakly correlated with rural poverty rates across states as further illustrated in figure 1.1. If MGNREGS worked the way the Act intended, this weak correlation would be surprising because one would expect the scheme to be more attractive to poor people, and hence to have higher take-up in poorer states. The same point holds for public spending on MGNREGS. Table 1.2 provides summary statistics on spending per capita for 2009/10 and 2010/11. The correlation between MGNREGS spending per capita and the poverty rate is −0.02 using spending in 2009/10 and 0.04 for 2010/11.

Bihar stands out in these data as having one of the highest rural poverty rates and one of the lowest MGNREGS participation rates. Bihar's participation rate is 0.22 below the regression line in figure 1.1, making it an outlier (t-statistic = −3.16, using a White standard error).[3] This is in stark contrast to states like Chhattisgarh, Rajasthan, Madhya Pradesh, and West Bengal, which perform better in providing employment under the scheme. As noted above, at the all-India level, 56 percent of those households that wanted work on MGNREGS actually got it. In Bihar, rationing was 78 percent; fewer than one-quarter of those rural households that reported in the NSS that they wanted work on the scheme actually got it.

However, when we look at variation in the demand rate, we see the expected positive correlation with the poverty rate (with a correlation coefficient r = 0.50) (figure 1.2). Poorer states tend to have

Table 1.1 Summary MGNREGS Statistics, 2009/10

State	Headcount index of poverty (% of population below poverty line)	Participation rate (share of rural households working on MGNREGS)	Demand rate (share of rural households that want work on MGNREGS)	Rationing rate (share of rural households that wanted work but did not get it)	Female share of employment on MGNREGS (% of total person days)
Andhra Pradesh	20.6	0.354	0.472	0.249	58.1
Assam	42.3	0.182	0.413	0.559	27.7
Bihar	56.5	0.099	0.461	0.785	30.0
Chhattisgarh	56.4	0.479	0.690	0.306	49.2
Gujarat	32.5	0.215	0.382	0.438	47.5
Haryana	24.2	0.051	0.195	0.738	35.6
Himachal Pradesh	11.9	0.334	0.418	0.202	46.0
Jammu and Kashmir	—	0.097	0.334	0.709	7.0
Jharkhand	43.5	0.192	0.517	0.628	34.3
Karnataka	31.3	0.080	0.228	0.648	36.8
Kerala	11.7	0.112	0.232	0.517	88.2
Madhya Pradesh	45.9	0.406	0.646	0.371	44.3
Maharashtra	33.9	0.044	0.277	0.840	39.8

(Continued on the following page)

Table 1.1 (Continued)

State	Headcount index of poverty (% of population below poverty line)	Participation rate (share of rural households working on MGNREGS)	Demand rate (share of rural households that want work on MGNREGS)	Rationing rate (share of rural households that wanted work but did not get it)	Female share of employment on MGNREGS (% of total person days)
Orissa	49.9	0.220	0.507	0.567	36.3
Punjab	19.4	0.052	0.312	0.833	26.0
Rajasthan	31.2	0.618	0.732	0.155	66.9
Tamil Nadu	22.8	0.335	0.414	0.190	82.9
Uttar Pradesh	40.8	0.162	0.350	0.536	21.7
Uttarakhand	—	0.292	0.406	0.280	40.1
West Bengal	35.1	0.432	0.658	0.344	33.4
All India	36.4	0.249	0.447	0.444	48.1

Sources: Poverty rates are based on 2004/05 Tendulkar poverty lines updated to 2009/10 using state-specific consumer price indices for agricultural laborers (CPIAL) and per capita consumption expenditures in Schedule 1.0 of the National Sample Survey. Poverty rates for Jammu and Kashmir and Uttarakhand are not reported because data are not available on state-level CPIAL. The female share of person days is from MGNREGS administrative data (http://nrega.nic.in). The remaining columns are from the authors' calculations from unit record data of 2009/10 National Sample Survey Schedule 1.0 (for headcount index) and Schedule 10.0.

Note: Households with missing values (that did not respond to the question on whether they got, sought, or did not want work on MGNREGS) are excluded from the sample when participation, demand, and rationing rates are estimated. MGNREGS = Mahatma Gandhi National Rural Employment Guarantee Scheme; — = not available.

Figure 1.1 There Is No Correlation between Participation
Rates in MGNREGS and the Incidence of Poverty across
Indian States

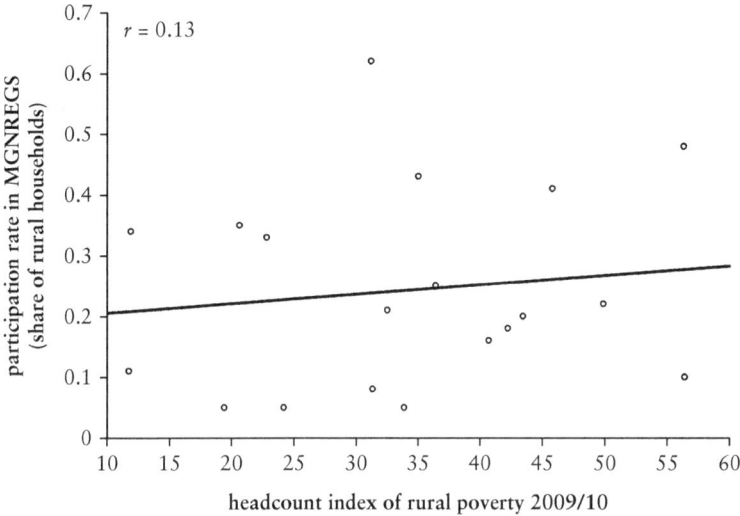

Source: Table 1.1.
Note: MGNREGS = Mahatma Gandhi National Rural Employment Guarantee
Scheme.

a higher percentage of households that want work on MGNREGS,
as one would expect. The reason this is not evident in figure 1.1 is
that the rationing rate also varies and is no lower in poorer states;
indeed, it is positively correlated with the poverty rate, though only
weakly so ($r = 0.183$). It is this interstate variation in the rationing
rate that explains why the participation rate is uncorrelated with the
poverty rate across states.

The demand for MGNREGS work is also lower in Bihar than
would be expected, even given the state's high poverty rate. Bihar
is an outlier in figure 1.2, with a demand rate for MGNREGS 0.14
below the regression line ($t = -2.58$). At a similar poverty rate,
Chhattisgarh has a participation rate almost five times higher than
that in Bihar. Public spending in Bihar is also lower than one would
expect, and roughly one-third the level in Chhattisgarh.

Poorer states have greater excess demand for MGNREGS, as
can be seen in figure 1.3. Figure 1.3 plots the share of the rural
population that is rationed—that is, the rationing rate times
the demand rate—against the poverty rate. The extent of this
unmet demand is not only greatest in Bihar but high given its
poverty rate, with a value 0.05 above the regression line, making

Table 1.2 Program Expenditure per Capita across States

	Expenditure per capita (rupees)	
State	*2009/10*	*2010/11*
Andhra Pradesh	749	896
Assam	406	358
Bihar	214	309
Chhattisgarh	723	884
Gujarat	214	226
Haryana	87	128
Himachal Pradesh	936	837
Jammu and Kashmir	221	445
Jharkhand	586	539
Karnataka	742	683
Kerala	186	276
Madhya Pradesh	734	707
Maharashtra	54	60
Orissa	281	455
Punjab	89	98
Rajasthan	1,133	647
Tamil Nadu	555	744
Uttar Pradesh	389	365
Uttarakhand	406	539
West Bengal	335	399
All India	464	477

Sources: Cumulative expenditures (including wage and nonwage spending) in current prices during the 2009/10 and 2010/11 fiscal years were obtained from the Ministry of Rural Development website (http://nrega.nic.in).

Note: To calculate expenditure per capita, the population projections for 2009 and 2010 from the Registrar General of India were used.

it a statistical outlier ($t = 2.93$). Therefore, the extent of unmet demand is greater in Bihar for reasons in addition to its high poverty rate. Something else is going wrong. We will learn more about this in later chapters.

The rationing rate is highly negatively correlated with the participation rate ($r = -0.882$). This outcome is not surprising given how the rationing rate is defined, though the strength of the correlation will also depend on the way the participation rate varies with the demand rate, to which we now turn.

Although rationing is common, there is much less evidence of rationing at the margin than on average. As the model in box 1.1 indicates, the average participation rate could be lower than the marginal participation rate among those who wanted work on MGNREGS, given that a certain minimum level of demand in a

Figure 1.2 Demand for MGNREGS Work Is Greater in Poorer States

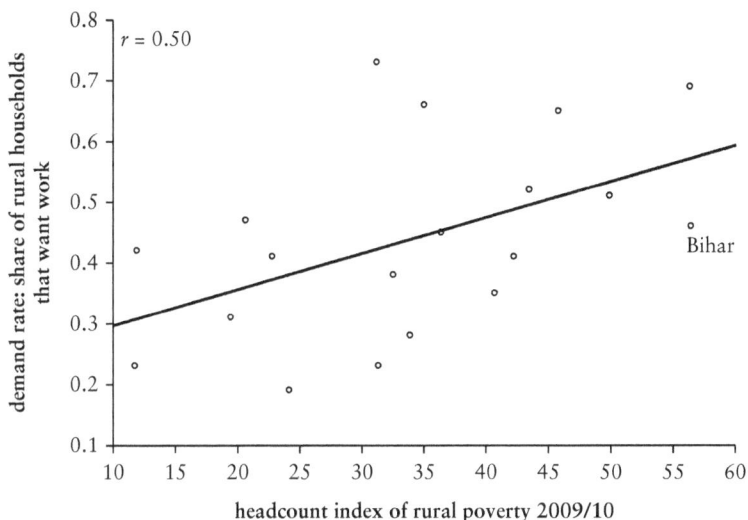

Source: Table 1.1.
Note: MGNREGS = Mahatma Gandhi National Rural Employment Guarantee Scheme.

Figure 1.3 Poorer States Have Greater Unmet Demand for Work on MGNREGS

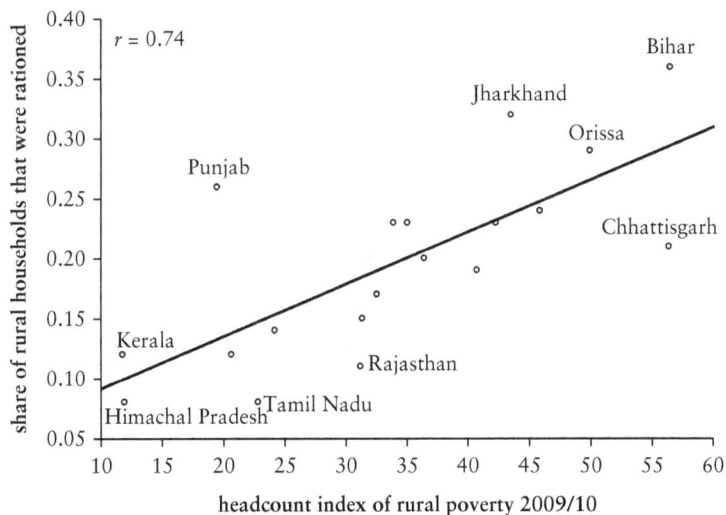

Source: Table 1.1.
Note: MGNREGS = Mahatma Gandhi National Rural Employment Guarantee Scheme.

given state is probably necessary before work is provided. Indeed, the marginal rate could also exceed unity. For example, it is possible that when an extra household expresses demand for work, not only does that household get work, but there is a spillover effect on others who wanted work but had not yet gotten it.

The data across the states provide striking confirmation of the model in box 1.1. Figure 1.4 shows the relationship between the MGNREGS participation rate and demand for MGNREGS work. Whereas the average participation rate among those who want work is 0.56, the marginal rate (as indicated by the regression coefficient of employment on demand for work) is 0.91 (with a robust standard error of 0.09); the intercept on the horizontal axis is 0.17 (standard error = 0.03), implying that the scheme would not have come into action if demand for work was less than 17 percent of the population of rural households.

Thus, once the minimum level of demand for work is reached, extra demand is being met, on average. The low average participation rate reflects the existence of the positive lower bound on demand, below which work is not provided. Following the logic of box 1.1, this lower bound can be interpreted as the effect of the costs incurred by state and local governments.

Figure 1.4 There Is Less Rationing at the Margin Than on Average across States

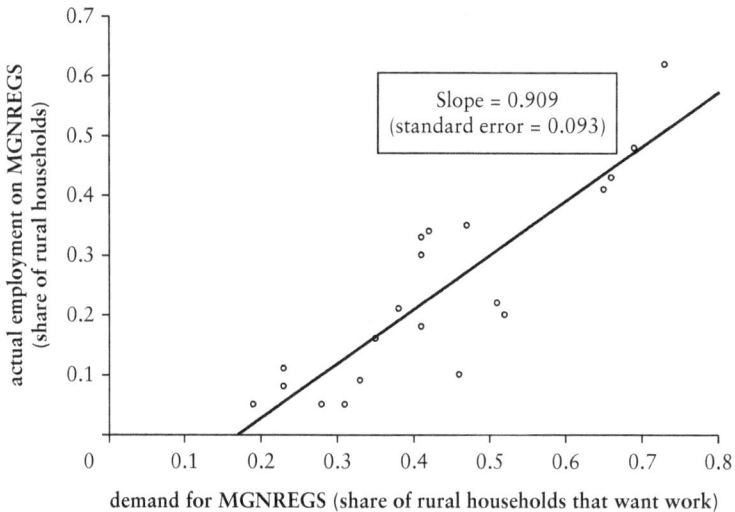

Slope = 0.909
(standard error = 0.093)

actual employment on MGNREGS (share of rural households)

demand for MGNREGS (share of rural households that want work)

Source: Table 1.1.
Note: MGNREGS = Mahatma Gandhi National Rural Employment Guarantee Scheme.

Again, Bihar is performing poorly relative to other states. Bihar has roughly the national average demand for work on MGNREGS, with 46 percent of rural households saying they want this work, as compared with 45 percent in India as a whole. However, as we have already seen, the extent of rationing is particularly high in Bihar; the actual level of employment on MGNREGS is 10 percent of Bihar's rural households, while the relationship for all of India implied by the regression line in figure 1.4 indicates that 26 percent of rural households in Bihar would have gotten work.[4]

Why is MGNREGS not more active in poorer states? We postulate that being a poor state has two opposing effects on participation. First, greater poverty has an effect via a higher demand for MGNREGS work. Call this the "demand effect" of poverty. We see confirmation of this in figure 1.2, which illustrates the expected positive correlation between demand for work and the poverty rate. The second effect is that poorer states tend to have greater unmet demand for work on the scheme. Call this the "rationing effect."

We suggest three reasons for the rationing effect on participation to work in a direction opposite that of the demand effect. First, poorer states will be less able to afford that share of the costs that are borne by state and local governments. Second, poorer states will tend to have weaker capacity for administering such a scheme, or may have weak Panchayati Raj Institutions, which have a key role in implementation. Third, the poor may be less empowered in poorer states. As shown in the next section, both poor and nonpoor people have a demand for work on the scheme, though the demand is greater among the poor. If poor people tend to have less power to influence local decision making (reflected in lower awareness of their rights under the Act), a higher poverty rate will lead the state government to put less weight on the need to accommodate their demand for work.[5]

These data tell us nothing about the relative importance of these three factors on the overall rationing effect. But we can certainly confirm evidence of a rationing effect. Poorer states have greater unmet demand for MGNREGS, as can be seen in figure 1.3. However, the variation among poorer states should be noted. Some of the poorest states (Bihar, Jharkhand, and Orissa) have low participation rates and high levels of unmet demand. In contrast, other poor states such as Chhattisgarh, Madhya Pradesh, Rajasthan, and West Bengal perform better in providing employment under the scheme. For example, even with a similar poverty rate, Chhattisgarh has a participation rate almost five times that of Bihar (table 1.1). Public spending is also lower in Bihar, at roughly one-third of the level in Chhattisgarh.

Using the identity in equation (1.1), a simple regression decomposition can be used to identify these two effects in the data:[6]

$$D_i = \alpha^D + \beta^D H_i + \varepsilon_i^D, \tag{1.2}$$

$$U_i = \alpha^U + \beta^U H_i + \varepsilon_i^U. \tag{1.3}$$

(Here ε_i^k for $k = D, U$ are zero-mean regression error terms, and α^k, β^k are parameters.) Thus, equation (1.2) minus equation (1.3) gives how the overall participation rate varies with the state headcount index of rural poverty H. The regression coefficient of demand for MGNREGS (based on the NSS responses) on the state poverty rate is 0.583 (standard error = 0.189), meaning that a 10 percentage point increase in the poverty rate comes with about a 6 percentage point increase in the share of rural households demanding MGNREGS work, on average. The regression coefficient of U on H is 0.434 (standard error = 0.097). The net effect (the estimate of $\beta^D - \beta^U$) is 0.149, but it is not significantly different from zero (standard error = 0.293). Statistically, the two opposing effects can be said to cancel each other out, giving the relationship in figure 1.1, whereby poorer states have no higher participation in MGNREGS, despite the greater demand for work on the scheme.

Note that Bihar is, again, an outlier, with a participation rate that is about 7 percentage points lower than one would expect given both its demand for work and its poverty rate. Something else is going on in Bihar. We have seen that demand for work is lower than expected given Bihar's poverty rate (figure 1.2). The chapters that follow examine the role of both of the factors identified above—weak capacity to implement and lower awareness of entitlements and processes among poor people. Furthermore, we argue that changing one alone will not ensure that the scheme will achieve its potential in Bihar. Effective action on both fronts will be necessary.

Targeting

By insisting that participants do physically demanding manual work at a low wage rate, workfare schemes such as MGNREGS aim to be self-targeted, in that nonpoor people will not want to participate. The substantial unmet demand demonstrated above raises the question of how well this self-targeting mechanism works in practice. The rationing of the available work does not mean that targeting will not be pro-poor. For one thing, the manual work requirement at a low wage rate will still discourage many nonpoor people from wanting to participate. For another, the local authorities doing the rationing may favor the poor. The local officials who are deciding who gets work could either enhance or diminish the scheme's targeting performance. A number of quantitative studies have explored the targeting performance of MGNREGS based on selected samples. The tests used have often been problematic.[7] Dutta and others (2012) use India's 2009/10 NSS to provide the first comprehensive national assessment of targeting performance. Liu and Barrett (2013) expand on that analysis to provide more state-specific detail. What, then, does the evidence from the NSS survey for 2009/10 suggest?

Table 1.3 gives the participation rate, demand rate, and rationing rate by rural household quintiles defined using household consumption per person from the NSS.[8] Results for both India as a whole and Bihar are provided.

As expected, demand for work on MGNREGS declines with consumption per person. Richer households are less likely to want to do this work, although there is demand even from the richest quintile in rural areas. Consistent with the incidence of expressed demand, the proportion of households that have obtained job cards declines with consumption per person. But notice that the demand rate is higher than the proportion with job cards; there are many households that expressed demand for work but have not obtained job cards.

Strikingly, however, across India as a whole, and for Bihar in particular, the rationing rate also tends to rise with consumption per person. The local-level processes of deciding who gets work from among those who want it mean that poorer households are less likely to be rationed, although the difference is modest.

The quintile averages in table 1.3 hide much detail. Figure 1.5 provides a finer representation of the data from the NSS. The top panel illustrates the nonparametric regression function of the household participation rate against consumption per person, with the latter converted into ranks and normalized to be between 0 and 100. Thus, the horizontal axis gives the percentile of the consumption distribution.[9] The lower panel illustrates the rationing rate. (The demand rate exhibits a similar pattern to the top panel, so is not shown separately.) Both panels show the regression functions adding state dummy variables to control for state effects.[10]

The participation rate declines rather slowly until about the 50th percentile of the rural distribution. In fact, no decline in participation between the 30th and 40th percentile, in the neighborhood of the national poverty rate, can be discerned; households just below the poverty line are no more likely to participate in MGNREGS than those just above the line. The marked decline in participation

Table 1.3 Coverage of MGNREGS across Consumption Quintiles, 2009/10

Quintiles	Participation rate	Demand rate	Rationing rate	Share of households with job cards	Mean person days among participating households	Mean person days among all rural households
All India						
Q1 (Poorest)	0.344	0.599	0.426	0.465	33.7	11.3
Q2	0.305	0.528	0.423	0.414	36.2	10.7
Q3	0.280	0.493	0.432	0.385	38.3	10.4
Q4	0.233	0.417	0.441	0.329	40.0	9.0
Q5 (Richest)	0.142	0.289	0.509	0.218	39.7	5.5
All	0.249	0.447	0.444	0.347	37.4	9.0
Bihar						
Q1 (Poorest)	0.142	0.524	0.728	0.256	21.5	2.9
Q2	0.131	0.526	0.751	0.216	29.4	3.7
Q3	0.125	0.511	0.754	0.206	19.5	2.4
Q4	0.086	0.488	0.824	0.162	25.4	2.1
Q5 (Richest)	0.049	0.331	0.853	0.020	28.9	1.3
All	0.099	0.461	0.785	0.172	24.5	2.3

Source: Estimates from the National Sample Survey (2009/10).

Note: The participation rate is the share of rural households working on MGNREGS. The demand rate is the share of rural households that want work on the program. The rationing rate is the share of households who wanted work but did not get it. Households with missing values (that did not respond to the question on whether they got, sought, or did not want work on MGNREGS) are excluded from the sample when participation, demand, and rationing rates are estimated. MGNREGS = Mahatma Gandhi National Rural Employment Guarantee Scheme.

Figure 1.5 Participation and Rationing by Consumption per Person, Rural India

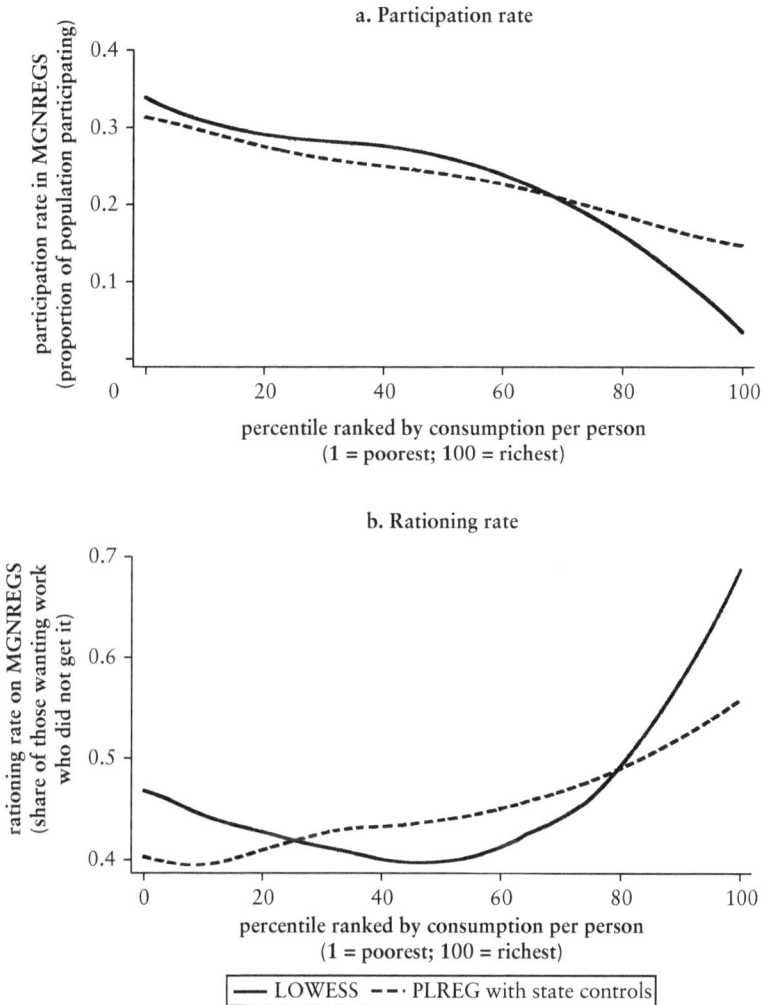

a. Participation rate

percentile ranked by consumption per person
(1 = poorest; 100 = richest)

b. Rationing rate

percentile ranked by consumption per person
(1 = poorest; 100 = richest)

—— LOWESS – – · PLREG with state controls

Source: Estimates from Schedule 10.0 of the National Sample Survey (2009/10).
Note: LOWESS = locally weighted smoothed scatter plot; MGNREGS = Mahatma Gandhi National Rural Employment Guarantee Scheme; PLREG = partial linear regression.

rates does not emerge until the upper half of the rural consumption distribution. By the 90th percentile, the participation rate reaches about 10 percent. Although far fewer "rich" rural households participate, some do. This phenomenon could reflect recent shocks, or poor individuals within generally well-off households.

The rationing rate follows a U-shape, declining initially as consumption increases until about the median, but then rising. However, this path clearly stems from the high rationing rates in most poor states demonstrated above. Thus, when we add state fixed effects, a steady increase in the rationing rate emerges as consumption increases across the whole distribution (the lower panel of figure 1.5). The greater unmet demand observed in poorer states is clearly not because the rationing process within states is biased against the poor. As emphasized, the more plausible interpretation is that implementation capacity is weaker in poorer states.

The lower rationing rate for the poor does not, however, imply that more rationing would improve targeting. What the numbers in table 1.3 and the lower panel of figure 1.5 reflect is the rationing process at a given level of participation. When the participation rate rises as a result of a reduction in rationing, the self-targeting mechanism will start to play a bigger role. We will see evidence of this when we compare targeting performance across states with very different participation rates.

Also notice that, among participants, the days of work received shows a slightly positive gradient with consumption per person. The pro-poor targeting is achieved through both demand for work and the rationing of work, not by the amount of work actually received.

It is of interest to compare targeting performance across states. Many measures of targeting performance in the literature might be used for this purpose. Ravallion (2009) surveys the various measures and tests their performance in predicting the impacts on poverty of a large antipoverty program in China, called the Di Bao program. (This program provides cash transfers targeted to those with income below the locally determined Di Bao poverty lines.) Among all standard targeting measures, the one that performed the best (and by a wide margin) in predicting the program's impact on poverty was the "targeting differential" (TD). The TD better reflects differences in coverage, that is, the proportion of the poor receiving the program, than do other standard measures, which focus more on how well the scheme avoids leakage—the proportion of the nonpoor receiving the program.

In the present context, the TD can be defined as the difference between the MGNREGS participation rate for the poor and that for the nonpoor. To interpret the TD, note that when only the poor get help from the program and all of them are covered, TD = 1, which is the measure's upper bound; when only the nonpoor get the program and all of them do, TD = -1, its lower bound. This measure is easy to interpret, and it automatically reflects both leakage to the nonpoor and coverage of the poor.

Table 1.4 gives the TD and participation rates for the poor and nonpoor. Participation rates among the poor vary enormously across states, from a low of 0.10 in Maharashtra to a high of 0.73 in Rajasthan. They also vary among the nonpoor. Although participation rates are always higher for the poor, the gap with that for the nonpoor is not large. The targeting differential for India as a whole is 0.12. (The TD for China's Di Bao program was 0.27.) Madhya Pradesh has the highest TD, at 0.22, while Kerala has the lowest, at 0.01.

Table 1.4 also gives the rationing rates for the poor and nonpoor. Consistent with the all-India results in table 1.3, the nonpoor are rationed more than the poor in almost all states (the only exceptions are Kerala and Rajasthan).

The *TD* in equation (1.4) is determined by how the demand rates and the rationing rates vary between the poor and nonpoor. A simple decomposition method can be used to show how much of the targeting differential for state *i* is due to each factor:

$$TD_i = P_i^{poor} - P_i^{nonpoor} = (1 - \overline{R})(D_i^{poor} - D_i^{nonpoor}) -$$

$$\overline{D}(R_i^{poor} - R_i^{nonpoor}) + residual.$$

$$(1.4)$$

The bars above the variables in equation (1.4) denote fixed reference values, while P^k, D^k, and R^k are the participation rates, demand rates, and rationing rates, respectively, for k = poor, nonpoor. TD can thus be interpreted as the "self-targeting effect" (greater demand for work among the poor—the first term on the right-hand side of equation 1.4) net of the rationing effect (the extent to which the poor might be rationed more—the second term). (Because the decomposition is not exact—given the nonlinearity in equation (1.1)—there is also a residual.)

Applying this decomposition, and using the all-India values for the reference, we find that 85.6 percent of the national TD is attributable to the difference in demand between the poor and nonpoor while 13.7 percent is due to the difference in rationing rates. (The residual is negligible.) There are differences across states, though the demand effect dominates in 17 of the 20 states. So, despite rationing, the bulk of the pro-poor targeting is coming through the self-targeting mechanism.

Targeting performance is better in states with higher overall participation rates. Figure 1.6 plots the two participation rates from table 1.4 against the overall participation rate (table 1.1).

Table 1.4 Targeting Performance of MGNREGS across States

State	Participation rate for the poor	Participation rate for the nonpoor	Targeting differential	Rationing rate for the poor	Rationing rate for the nonpoor
Andhra Pradesh	0.513	0.322	0.191	0.215	0.259
Assam	0.233	0.149	0.085	0.523	0.590
Bihar	0.127	0.075	0.052	0.756	0.816
Chhattisgarh	0.571	0.386	0.186	0.260	0.366
Gujarat	0.298	0.185	0.114	0.319	0.490
Haryana	0.106	0.037	0.069	0.701	0.760
Himachal Pradesh	0.510	0.318	0.192	0.173	0.206
Jharkhand	0.237	0.163	0.075	0.613	0.641
Karnataka	0.126	0.065	0.061	0.503	0.703
Kerala	0.116	0.112	0.005	0.535	0.516
Madhya Pradesh	0.534	0.319	0.215	0.297	0.438
Maharashtra	0.096	0.025	0.071	0.738	0.898
Orissa	0.317	0.135	0.182	0.509	0.650
Punjab	0.145	0.035	0.110	0.729	0.872
Rajasthan	0.728	0.579	0.149	0.166	0.150
Tamil Nadu	0.484	0.302	0.182	0.093	0.219
Uttar Pradesh	0.242	0.120	0.122	0.483	0.582
West Bengal	0.559	0.379	0.179	0.282	0.376
All India	0.325	0.210	0.115	0.428	0.463

Source: Calculations from the National Sample Survey (2009/10).

Note: Households are classified as poor or nonpoor based on poverty lines for the National Sample Survey Schedule 10.0 that would yield the same state-specific poverty rates as estimated from the National Sample Survey Schedule 1.0, and reported in table 1.1. All-India figures reported in this table include only the states shown. MGNREGS = Mahatma Gandhi National Rural Employment Guarantee Scheme.

The TD—the gap between the two lines—rises with the overall participation rate, and the two are strongly correlated ($r = 0.748$).

Targeting performance also tends to be worse in the states with higher levels of rationing (the correlation between TD and rationing rate is -0.71). However, this arises because (as already seen) overall participation rates are low in states with higher degrees of rationing. Once the participation rate is controlled for, there is no significant partial correlation between the TD and the rationing rate (the *t*-statistic is -0.611).[11]

So we find that targeting performance tends to improve with higher overall participation rates, which also tend to come with lower rationing rates. The fact that targeting performance improves as the program expands makes this an example of what Lanjouw and Ravallion (1999) call "early capture" by the nonpoor, which they show to be a common feature of access to safety nets and schooling in India (using data for the 1990s).[12] Lanjouw and Ravallion (1999) also show in a theoretical model of the political economy of targeted programs that for programs with relatively large start-up costs, early capture by the nonpoor may be the only politically feasible option (especially when the start-up costs must be financed domestically). So this feature of MGNREGS is possibly not surprising.

Targeting by social groups (castes and tribes) is another dimension of interest in India. Qualitative studies have suggested that Scheduled Castes (SCs), Scheduled Tribes (STs), and women—groups that have traditionally been excluded—have benefited disproportionately from the scheme (Drèze and Khera 2011). We shall return to discuss participation by women. The focus here is on the scheme's performance in reaching ST, SC, and Other Backward Class (OBC) households.

Figure 1.6 Targeting Performance Rises with the Overall Participation Rate across States

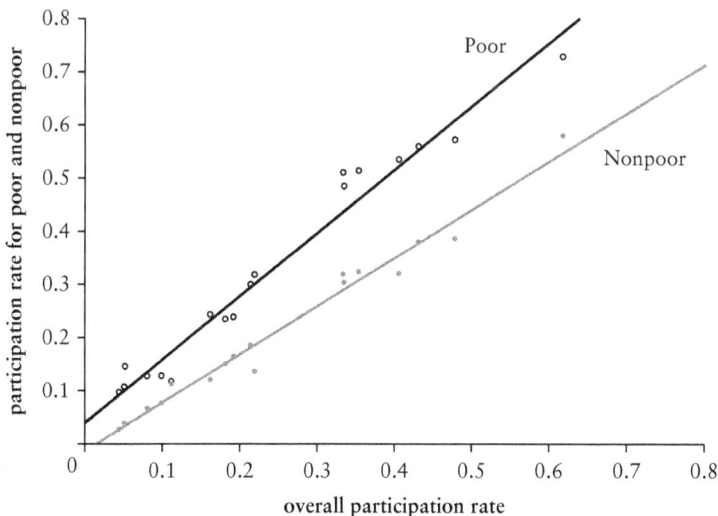

Source: Estimates from Schedule 10.0 of the National Sample Survey (2009/10).

Table 1.5 gives the participation rates by these groupings. Nationally, 42 percent and 34 percent of rural ST and SC households, respectively, participated. Participation was lower for OBCs at 21 percent, and lowest for all others at 16 percent. But there is a wide range across states. For STs, the range is from 6 percent of households in Maharashtra to 82 percent in Rajasthan, whereas for SC households it is from 2 percent to 65 percent, and for the same states. Table 1.5 also reports the targeting differential for STs, SCs, and OBCs together, defined as their weighted average participation rate less the participation rate for "others." This "caste TD" varies from –0.02 in Assam to 0.29 in Chhattisgarh, with a national mean of 0.12, almost identical to the national "poverty TD" in table 1.4.

As with the poverty TD, the caste TD is positively correlated with overall participation rates ($r = 0.723$). This correlation is also evident in figure 1.7, which plots participation rates against the overall participation rates across states. The participation rates for STs, SCs, and OBCs rise faster than that for "others" as the overall participation rate rises, suggesting that the targeting of disadvantaged castes improves with program expansion.

Wages and Rationing on MGNREGS

A number of concerns about the stipulated wage rates for the program have arisen. On the one hand, it has been argued that setting scheme wages below the state-mandated rates under the Minimum Wages Act is a violation of the law and tantamount to "forced labor," a stand that was upheld by the Supreme Court in January 2012.[13] On the other hand, concerns have been raised that the wage rate on MGNREGS is being set too high relative to actual casual labor market wages. The concern is that the scheme will divert workers from market work and so bid up the market wage rate.[14] (Supporters of the scheme usually count this as a benefit.)

What does the evidence suggest? Table 1.6 reports average wage rates from the administrative data. These are calculated as total MGNREGS spending on unskilled labor divided by total person days of employment provided.[15] The table also reports estimates for average wages in private casual labor from the NSS for the same year.[16]

The MGNREGS wage rate is not well above the market wage rate everywhere. Indeed, for India as a whole the two wages are quite close. If rural India were a single labor market, it could be conjectured that the scheme has brought the two wage rates into parity. However, rural India is not one labor market because mobility is

Table 1.5 Participation Rates and Targeting by Social Group

			Participation rates			
State	Scheduled Tribes (STs)	Scheduled Castes (SCs)	Other Backward Classes (OBCs)	Weighted mean for STs, SCs, and OBCs	Others	Targeting differential[a]
Andhra Pradesh	0.567	0.434	0.382	0.412	0.150	0.262
Assam	0.192	0.179	0.163	0.174	0.191	-0.017
Bihar	0.087[b]	0.185	0.089	0.116	0.016	0.100
Chhattisgarh	0.519	0.435	0.504	0.500	0.214	0.286
Gujarat	0.340	0.289	0.180	0.252	0.070	0.181
Haryana	0.000[b]	0.105	0.044	0.071	0.018	0.054
Himachal Pradesh	0.392	0.413	0.294	0.376	0.298	0.077
Jammu and Kashmir	0.054[b]	0.134	0.109	0.114	0.090	0.024
Jharkhand	0.204	0.268	0.155	0.197	0.149	0.048
Karnataka	0.186	0.160	0.042	0.089	0.054	0.035
Kerala	0.168[b]	0.238	0.098	0.123	0.088	0.035

(Continued on the following page)

49

Table 1.5 (Continued)

| State | Participation rates | | | | | Targeting differential[a] |
	Scheduled Tribes (STs)	Scheduled Castes (SCs)	Other Backward Classes (OBCs)	Weighted mean for STs, SCs, and OBCs	Others	
Madhya Pradesh	0.567	0.442	0.334	0.433	0.211	0.222
Maharashtra	0.442	0.017	0.074	0.058	0.015	0.044
Orissa	0.334	0.220	0.224	0.253	0.100	0.153
Punjab	0.433	0.104	0.016	0.082	0.009	0.074
Rajasthan	0.211	0.654	0.581	0.644	0.444	0.200
Tamil Nadu	0.222	0.523	0.279	0.338	0.069	0.269
Uttar Pradesh	0.140[b]	0.325	0.118	0.191	0.044	0.146
Uttarakhand	0.388	0.513	0.082	0.321	0.278	0.043
West Bengal	0.656	0.507	0.449	0.521	0.362	0.159
All India	0.415	0.336	0.214	0.279	0.155	0.124

Source: Calculations from the National Sample Survey (2009/10).
Note: All-India figures include states not shown.
a. Targeting differential is the difference between the weighted mean participation rate of STs, SCs, and OBCs and that for others.
b. ST figures were from fewer than 100 sampled households and may be unreliable.

Figure 1.7 Participation Rates for Scheduled Tribes, Scheduled Castes, and Other Backward Classes Rise Faster Than That for "Other" Castes as the Overall Participation Rate Increases across States

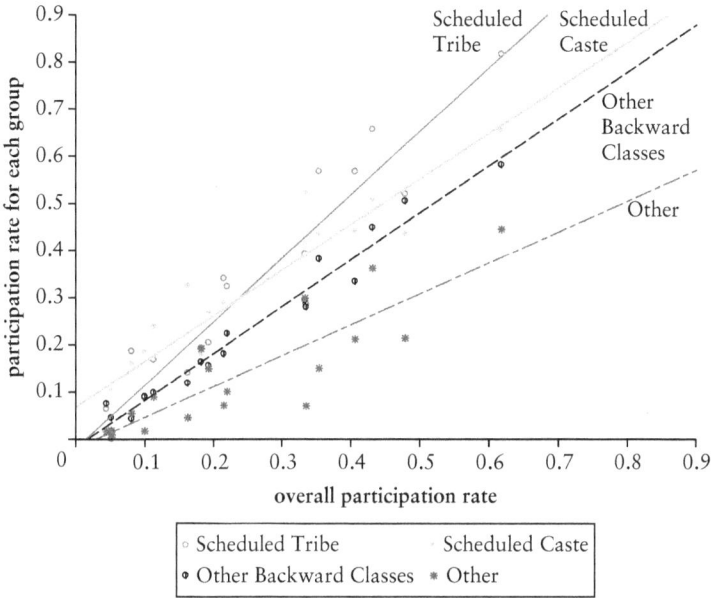

Source: Estimates from Schedule 10.0 of the National Sample Survey (2009/10).

imperfect. In half of the states, the MGNREGS wage rate in 2009/10 was actually lower than the average wage rate for casual labor.

Given the extent of rationing in a number of states (including most of the poorest half), it seems implausible that the scheme would be having a large impact on wages for other casual work in those states, let alone resulting in a higher casual wage than for MGNREGS. For example, with only 17 percent of those who wanted work on the scheme in Punjab getting that work, the casual (non-public-works [non-PW]) wage rate being greater than the MGNREGS wage rate is not likely to be due to competition for workers.

The relative wage—the mean wage rate for casual non-PW labor divided by the MGNREGS wage—does tend to be lower in states with higher levels of unmet demand. Let W_i/W_i^{EGS} be the relative wage in state i, where W_i is the wage rate in the non-PW casual labor market and W_i^{EGS} is the MGNREGS wage rate. The correlation coefficient between $\ln(W_i/W_i^{EGS})$ and unmet demand (U_i) is −0.558, which is significant at the 1 percent level.[17] However, there

Table 1.6 Average Wages on MGNREGS and in Casual
Labor, 2009/10

State	Average wage rate on MGNREGS (rupees/day)	Average casual wage rate (rupees/day)		
		Overall	Male	Female
Andhra Pradesh	91.9	98.5	115.4	75.7
Assam	87.0	90.1	94.4	74.9
Bihar	97.5	79.4	81.0	65.8
Chhattisgarh	82.3	68.8	70.8	65.5
Gujarat	89.3	83.3	87.3	71.0
Haryana	150.9	139.6	146.1	99.1
Himachal Pradesh	109.5	139.6	141.4	110.2
Jammu and Kashmir	93.3	158.3	157.5	—
Jharkhand	97.7	101.2	103.6	82.2
Karnataka	86.0	84.5	96.9	62.8
Kerala	120.6	206.5	226.6	119.3
Madhya Pradesh	83.7	69.0	74.5	58.1
Maharashtra	94.3	75.2	86.0	58.2
Orissa	105.9	75.6	81.0	59.1
Punjab	123.5	130.4	133.5	91.8
Rajasthan	87.4	125.7	132.3	94.3
Tamil Nadu	71.6	110.8	132.1	72.6
Uttar Pradesh	99.5	94.3	97.0	69.2
Uttarakhand	99.0	118.7	122.1	96.7
West Bengal	90.4	85.3	87.8	65.9
All India	90.2	93.1	101.5	68.9

Sources: Casual wages from *Key Indicators of Employment and Unemployment in India, 2009/10,* National Sample Survey Organization, government of India (June 2011). MGNREGS expenditure and employment data are from the state-wise Monthly Progress Reports available at www.nrega.nic.in.

Note: MGNREGS wage rates estimated as total expenditure on wages for unskilled labor divided by total number of person days of employment for fiscal year 2009/10 (April 2009 to March 2010). Casual wages for June 2009 to July 2010 period are based on the National Sample Survey 66th round. "All India" includes smaller states not reported. Female wage rate for Jammu and Kashmir not reported on account of small sample (seven observations). MGNREGS = Mahatma Gandhi National Rural Employment Guarantee Scheme; — = not available.

are reasons to question whether this really reflects greater tightening of the casual labor market in states where there is less unmet
demand for work on the scheme. The implied relative wage rate at
zero rationing seems too high to be believed. To see why, postulate
that the relative wage depends on the excess demand as follows:[18]

$$\ln(W_i/W_i^{EGS}) = \alpha + \beta(D_i - P_i) + \varepsilon_i. \tag{1.5}$$

The expected value of the log relative wage rate when all demand for work on MGNREGS has been satisfied is then given by α. Using the data in tables 1.1 and 1.6, the estimated (least squares) value of α is 0.398 (standard error = 0.105) and the estimate of β is –1.777 (standard error = 0.519; R^2 = 0.311). These results imply that, when all demand for work is satisfied, the market wage rate would be 50 percent higher than the MGNREGS wage rate.[19] Yet the work is very similar, and there is no obvious reason why such a differential would exist in equilibrium. The incidence of rationing across states could be picking up some other factor correlated with it. Following the earlier discussion, poverty is a plausible candidate. Adding the poverty rate to equation (1.5), the effect of unmet demand becomes insignificant (probability = 0.19) whereas the poverty rate is significant (a coefficient of 0.828, with standard error of 0.333). A higher poverty rate may be associated with greater landlessness and hence a larger supply of casual labor, bringing down the wage rate.

So the argument that these data suggest a causal effect on relative wages of greater competition between the scheme and the casual labor market in India's poorer states is not persuasive. We return to this issue for Bihar in chapter 4.

Participation by Women

Nationally, almost half (48 percent) of the employment registered in the administrative data for 2009/10 was for women.[20] This share is very high for a country in which a minority of women participate in the paid labor force; for example, it is about twice their share of other (non-PW) casual wage work.[21] The variation across states is striking; between the two extremes, only 7 percent of the work goes to women in Jammu and Kashmir as compared with 88 percent in Kerala (table 1.1). The female share on MGNREGS work is greater than their share of the work in the casual wage labor market in all states, but the gap tends to be larger in states in which women participate less in the casual labor market (figure 1.8).

In this respect also, poorer states are different. Women are less likely to participate (relative to men) in MGNREGS in poorer states. Figure 1.9 plots the share of person days of employment going to women against the poverty rate. We see a negative correlation (r = –0.47). By contrast, women's share of casual (non-PW) wage work tends to be slightly higher, on average, in poorer states, although the difference is not statistically significant (r = 0.09).

Why is less of the available work going to women in poorer states? The NSS does not allow rationing at the individual level to be identified

Figure 1.8 Women Get a Larger Share of MGNREGS Work
Than of Casual Wage Labor across States

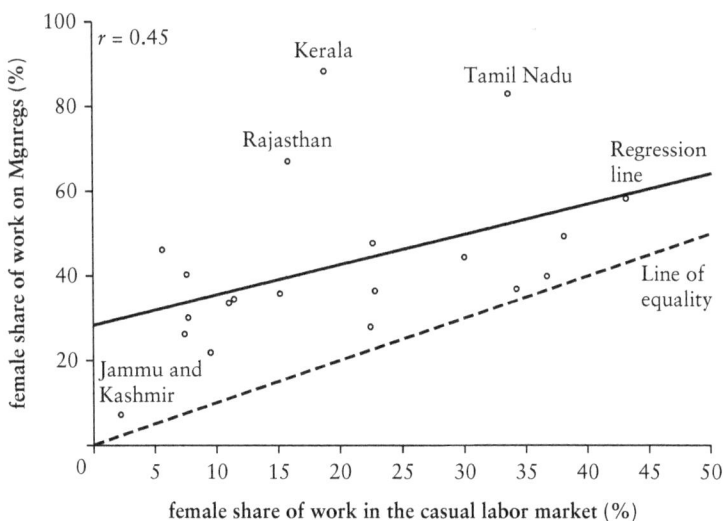

Source: Estimates from MGNREGS administrative data and Schedule 10.0 of the
National Sample Survey (2009/10).

Note: MGNREGS = Mahatma Gandhi National Rural Employment Guarantee
Scheme.

(it is a household variable). However, some clues to how rationing has
affected women can be gained from the interstate comparisons. It
would seem unlikely that the effect of household poverty on demand
for work among women is any different than among men.[22] Assuming that the effect of being a poorer state on demand for work is the
same for men and women, the pattern in figure 1.10 suggests that the
rationing process is worse for women in poorer states.

Do women have equal access to the scheme when they need it?
Again, the NSS data do not provide a direct answer. However, the
patterns in the interstate data are suggestive. We observe a negative
correlation between the female share of work and the overall rationing rate (figure 1.10). It might be conjectured that this negative
correlation reflects differences in the extent of poverty. Women may
be less aware of their rights and less empowered to demand work in
poorer states. For example, when other work is scarce, women may
get crowded out by men. However, the negative correlation between
the female share of work and the rationing rate persists when we
control for the poverty rate, as can be seen in table 1.7, which gives
regressions for the female share of employment on MGNREGS

Figure 1.9 The Share of Work Going to Women Tends to Be Lower in Poorer States

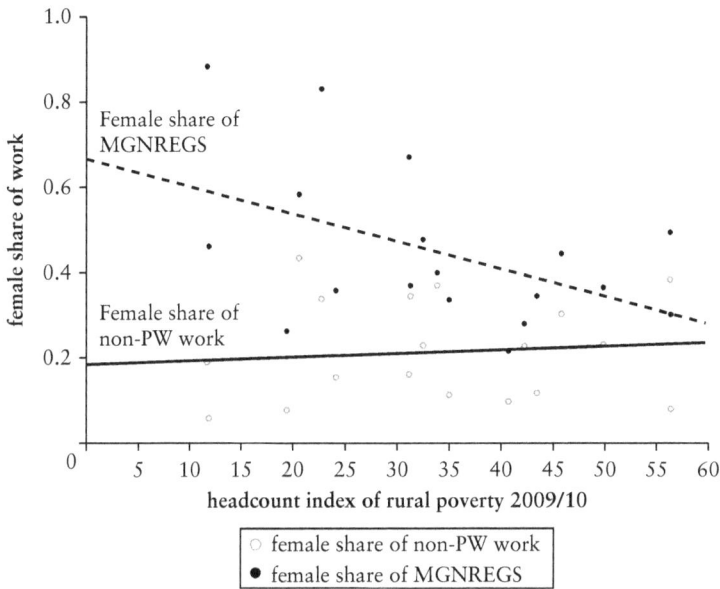

Source: Estimates from MGNREGS administrative data and Schedule 10.0 of the National Sample Survey (2009/10).

Note: MGNREGS = Mahatma Gandhi National Rural Employment Guarantee Scheme; PW = public works.

against both the rationing rate and the poverty rate. This negative correlation between the overall rationing rate and the share of work going to women implies that women are more likely to be rationed out of work than are men.

Chapter 2 directly measures rationing at the individual level in Bihar, using the specially designed survey. That chapter provides direct evidence that the rationing rate is higher for women than for men in Bihar.

Gender differences in the opportunities available in the casual labor market can also be expected to influence demand for work. We find that the female market wage rate has a significant negative effect on women's share of the work provided, whereas the male wage rate has the opposite effect (table 1.7).[23] This outcome suggests that there is an intrahousehold substitution effect; for example, when casual labor market opportunities are good for men but bad for women, women find it easier to get the (limited) number of jobs available

Figure 1.10 The Share of Work Going to Women Tends to Be Lower in States with Higher Rationing

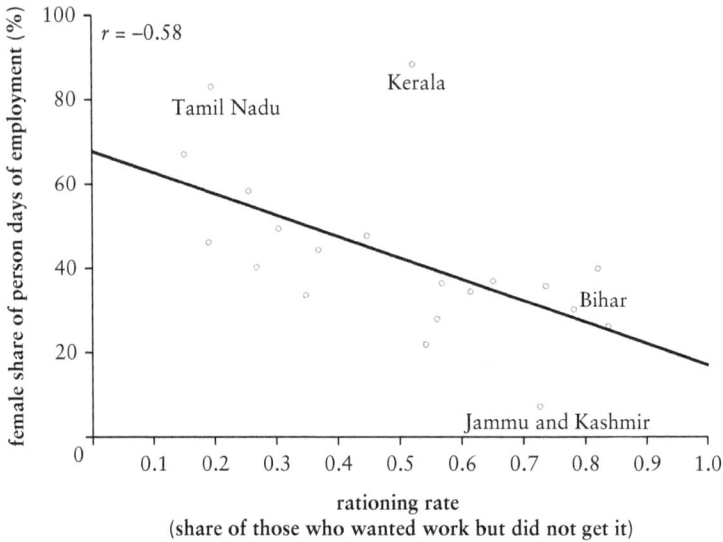

Source: Estimates from Mahatma Gandhi National Rural Employment Guarantee Scheme (MGNREGS) administrative data and Schedule 10.0 of the National Sample Survey (2009/10).

on the scheme.[24] The wage effect is strong statistically, and greatly increases the explanatory power.[25]

The negative effect of rationing on women's access to the scheme also persists when we control for differences in the wages received for private (non-PW) casual work. The final column gives the preferred regression in which the share of MGNREGS work going to women depends on the overall rationing rate—implying that women are more rationed than men—and the female market wage relative to the male wage.

Conclusion

Demand for work on MGNREGS tends to be higher in poorer states. This higher demand appears to reflect the scheme's built-in "self-targeting" mechanism, whereby nonpoor people find work on the scheme less attractive than do poor people. However, actual participation rates in the scheme are not, as a rule, any higher in poorer states, where it is needed the most. The reason for this paradox lies in the differences in the extent to which the employment guarantee is honored. The answer

Table 1.7 Regression Results for Female Share of
Employment in MGNREGS

	Full sample	Sample with headcount index available		Sample with male and female wages available	
Constant	0.676	0.829	0.193	0.131	0.697
	(8.671)	(5.341)	(0.887)	(0.246)	(3.922)
Rationing rate	−0.505	−0.419	−0.307	−0.456	−0.469
	(−3.758)	(−2.898)	(−2.904)	(−5.108)	(−5.972)
Headcount index of rural poverty		−0.515 (−1.538)	0.241 (1.518)		
Female casual non-PW wage (log)			−0.549 (−2.056)	−0.744 (−3.475)	
Male casual non-PW wage (log)			0.675 (5.156)	0.806 (3.556)	
Female wage relative to male wage (log)					−0.836 (−3.301)
R^2	0.336	0.467	0.811	0.692	0.687
Standard error of estimate	0.164	0.145	0.093	0.111	0.108
Number of observations	20	18	18	19	19

Source: Estimates from National Sample Survey 2009/10 data.

Note: The dependent variable is the share of total person days of employment on MGNREGS going to women. The rationing rate is the share of households who wanted work but did not get it. The headcount index is the percentage of population below the poverty line. The *t*-ratios in parentheses are based on White standard errors. MGNREGS = Mahatma Gandhi National Rural Employment Guarantee Scheme; PW = public works.

to the question posed in the title of this chapter is clearly "no." Rationing is common, but far more so in some of the poorest states.

We do not find that the local-level processes determining who gets work among those who want it are generally skewed against the poor. There are sure to be places where this is happening (and qualitative field reports have provided examples), but it does not appear to stand up as a generalization. We do find evidence that the poor fare somewhat less well when it comes to the total number of days of work they manage to get on the scheme. However, despite the pervasive rationing, it is plain that the scheme is still reaching poor people and also reaching the Scheduled Tribes, Scheduled Castes, and Other Backward Classes.

Participation rates on the scheme are higher for poor people than for others. This finding holds at the official poverty line, but the scheme is also reaching many families just above the official line. It is only at relatively high consumption levels that participation drops off sharply. This participation of people above the poverty line should not be interpreted as indicating that well-off families in rural India are turning to MGNREGS. There may be shocks that are not evident in the household consumption aggregates, and there may be individual needs for help that are not evident in those aggregates.

Targeting performance varies across states. The overall participation rate seems to be an important factor in accounting for these interstate differences, with the scheme being more pro-poor and reaching Scheduled Tribes, Scheduled Castes, and Other Backward Classes more effectively in states with higher overall participation rates.

Although the allocation of work through the local-level rationing process is not working against the poor, there are clearly many poor people who are not getting help because the employment guarantee is not in operation almost anywhere (Himachal Pradesh, Rajasthan, and Tamil Nadu could be the exceptions, where 80 percent or more of those who want work got it). And other potential benefits of the scheme, notably the empowerment gains and the insurance benefits, are almost certainly undermined by the extensive rationing. The first-order problem for MGNREGS is the level of unmet demand.

The scheme is popular with women—their participation rate is double their participation rate in the casual labor market—but the rationing process does not appear to be favoring them. We also find evidence of a strong effect of relative male-to-female market wages on women's participation. As one would expect, poor families appear to choose whether it is the man or the woman who goes to the scheme according to relative wages.

It has been claimed by some observers that the scheme is driving up wages for other work, such as in agriculture; some observers see this as a good thing, others not. For India as a whole, we find that the scheme's average wage rate was roughly in line with the casual labor market in 2009/10. This equivalence might look like a competitive labor market equilibrium, but that view is hard to reconcile with the extensive rationing we find. It is interesting that we do find a significant negative correlation between the extent of rationing and the wage rate in the casual labor market relative to the wage rate on the scheme. Although this is suggestive, on closer inspection we are more inclined to think that other economic factors are at work. Indeed, the correlation largely vanishes when we control for the level of poverty. Poorer states tend to see both more rationing of work on the scheme and lower casual wages—possibly as the result of a greater supply of labor given the extent of rural landlessness.

Notes

1. There is also evidence that the scheme's targeting performance deteriorated when the wage rate rose substantially (Gaiha 1997).

2. See government of India website for MGNREGS (http://nrega.nic.in).

3. Note that Bihar's participation rate of 10 percent in table 1.1 is well below the 26 percent implied by the administrative data reported in table O.1. We turn to the issue of discrepancy between survey aggregates and administrative data in chapter 4.

4. The standard error of the predicted value for Bihar is 1.9 percent, so the 95 percent confidence interval is from 23 percent to 30 percent.

5. Note that this third reason for the direct effect of poverty is not consistent with a model of public decision making based on standard utilitarian calculus, for then one would expect the policy weight on accommodating the demand for work to be higher in states with a higher share of poor people who need that work more than do the nonpoor.

6. Dutta and others (2012) provide a "structural model" of participation rates as a function of demand rates and poverty incidence, also suggesting that states with higher poverty incidence tend to have greater unmet demand for work on the scheme.

7. Jha and others (2009) report evidence that households with larger landholdings were *more* likely to participate in the scheme in Andhra Pradesh (AP), though they find evidence of better targeting in Rajasthan. They conclude that the scheme is being "captured" by the nonpoor in AP. Note, however, that their regressions control for other variables that may capture poverty, including occupation and whether the household has a Below-Poverty-Line (BPL) card. The full regressions are not presented in their paper, but it may be that, for example, having a BPL card is already capturing the pro-poor targeting of MGNREGS, but that the BPL card puts too high a weight on landlessness from the point of view of explaining participation. Then the amount of land may appear to have the wrong sign, even though the scheme is targeting the poor. By contrast, the results of Liu and Deininger (2013) suggest quite pro-poor targeting of MGNREGS in AP. Shariff (2009) reports participation regressions for MGNREGS in selected backward districts of northern states (including some districts in Bihar). Some of the regression coefficients also suggest perverse targeting. Shariff is careful in interpreting the results though the same inferential concerns hold as for the study by Jha and others (2009).

8. Household quintiles were drawn after correcting per capita consumption for cost-of-living differences across states using the price deflators implicit in the Tendulkar poverty lines.

9. Alternatively, one can just use, for example, log consumption per person. However, given the uneven spread of the data across levels of

consumption, this can be deceptive at the tails. Using percentiles instead ensures a uniform distribution of the data.

10. The curve without controls is based on a locally weighted smoothed scatter plot (LOWESS). The curve with state controls is fitted using a partial linear regression model procedure described in Lokshin (2006).

11. The TD is also positively correlated with the demand rate ($r = 0.671$), but this too vanishes when one controls for the participation rate (the t-statistic for the partial correlation coefficient is 0.151).

12. Lanjouw and Ravallion (1999) study public works programs, the Integrated Rural Development Program, the Public Distribution System, and school enrollment.

13. The Supreme Court has refused to stay a September 2011 Karnataka High Court verdict that affirms that the central government is liable for paying wages in tandem with the states' minimum wage rates.

14. Evidence for the impact of the scheme on raising market wages is reported by Imbert and Papp (2012) who compare districts that started early on the scheme with those that started later. However, they do not examine the extent of rationing.

15. The scheme stipulates both piece rates and daily rates. Under the piece rate, whether a given worker can earn the mandated wage rate depends on her work effort. If the scheme attracts workers with lower-than-average physical ability, the realized average wage rate by our calculations can fall short of the mandated wage.

16. Note that the reference periods for MGNREGS and casual market wages reported in the table are slightly different.

17. The fit is slightly better using the log relative wage; using W_i/W_i^{EGS} instead, the correlation coefficient is −0.520.

18. Using W_i/W_i^{EGS} as the dependent variable, the estimated intercept is 1.466 (standard error = 0.132). Given the uncertainty about the true functional form, we also tried a quadratic function of excess demand but it did not improve the fit.

19. Note that exp (0.398) = 1.489 is the implied ratio of the levels of wages.

20. Although the administrative data are inadequate for measuring aggregate demand for work, there is no obvious reason to question their veracity for measuring the gender composition of the work provided.

21. We estimate that the share of women in the total person days of casual labor in 2009/10 was 23.3 percent, based on the 2009/10 NSS.

22. Alternatively, the point could be made that men may be more likely to be unemployed in poorer households and that the effect of household poverty on demand for MGNREGS work may be different for men and women.

23. We tested an encompassing specification in which the log of the male wage rate, log of the female wage rate, and log of the MGNREGS wage rates entered separately. The homogeneity restriction that the sum of the

coefficients equals zero could not be rejected ($F(1,14) = 0.41$; probability = 0.53), but nor could we reject the null that it was the log of the female wage relative to the male wage that mattered, with the MGNREGS wage having no effect ($F = 1.49$; probability = 0.26). Also, the MGNREGS wage rate on its own was not significant. So we opted for a specification in which the log of the relative wage is the regressor as in table 1.7. Table 1.7 also gives a specification with male and female wages entering separately.

24. A similar result was found by Datt and Ravallion (1994) in studying time allocation within households in response to the availability of work under Maharashtra's Employment Guarantee Scheme.

25. We also tested for an effect of the female share of other (non-PW) casual labor. This is endogenous but it allows us to control for local social norms that influence the propensity for women to do any casual wage labor. The new variable was not, however, significant, and the coefficients on the other variables were affected little.

References

Datt, Gaurav, and Martin Ravallion. 1994. "Transfer Benefits from Public Works Employment." *Economic Journal* 104: 1346–69.

Drèze, Jean, and Reetika Khera. 2011. "Employment Guarantee and the Right to Work." In *The Battle for Employment Guarantee*, edited by Reetika Khera. New Delhi: Oxford University Press.

Dutta, Puja, Rinku Murgai, Martin Ravallion, and Dominique van de Walle. 2012. "Does India's Employment Guarantee Scheme Guarantee Employment?" *Economic and Political Weekly* 48 (21): 55–64.

Gaiha, Raghav. 1997. "Rural Public Works and the Poor: The Case of the Employment Guarantee Scheme in India." In *Research in Labour Economics*, edited by S. Polachek. Greenwich, Connecticut: JAI Press.

Imbert, Clément, and John Papp. 2011. "Estimating Leakages in India's Employment Guarantee." In *The Battle for Employment Guarantee*, edited by Reetika Khera. New Delhi: Oxford University Press.

———. 2012. "Equilibrium Distributional Impacts of Government Employment Programs: Evidence from India's Employment Guarantee." Paris School of Economics Working Paper No. 2012-14.

Jha, Raghbendra, Sambit Bhattacharyya, Raghav Gaiha, and Shylashri Shankar. 2009. "'Capture' of Anti-Poverty Programs: An Analysis of the National Rural Employment Guarantee Program in India." *Journal of Asian Economics* 20 (4): 456–64.

Khera, Reetika, ed. 2011. *The Battle for Employment Guarantee*. New Delhi: Oxford University Press.

Lanjouw, Peter, and Martin Ravallion. 1999. "Benefit Incidence, Public Spending Reforms and the Timing of Program Capture." *World Bank Economic Review* 13 (2): 257–73.

Liu, Yanyan, and Christopher B. Barrett. 2013. "Heterogeneous Pro-Poor Targeting in the National Rural Employment Guarantee Scheme." *Economic and Political Weekly* 48 (10): 46–53.

Liu, Yanyan, and Klaus Deininger. 2013. "Welfare and Poverty Impacts of India's National Rural Employment Guarantee Scheme: Evidence from Andhra Pradesh." Policy Research Working Paper No. 6543, World Bank, Washington, DC.

Lokshin, Michael. 2006. "Difference-based Semi-parametric Estimation of Partial Linear Regression Models." *Stata Journal* 6 (3): 377–83.

National Sample Survey Organization (NSSO). 2009/10. "Socio-Economic Survey Sixty-Sixth Round Schedule 10: Employment and Unemployment." Government of India, New Delhi.

Niehaus, Paul, and Sandip Sukhtankar. Forthcoming. "Corruption Dynamics: The Golden Goose Effect." *American Economic Journal: Economic Policy.*

Ravallion, Martin. 2009. "How Relevant Is Targeting to the Success of an Antipoverty Program?" *World Bank Research Observer* 24 (3): 205–31.

———, Gaurav Datt, and Shubham Chaudhuri. 1993. "Does Maharashtra's 'Employment Guarantee Scheme' Guarantee Employment? Effects of the 1988 Wage Increase." *Economic Development and Cultural Change* 41: 251–75.

Shariff, Abusaleh. 2009. "Assessment of Outreach and Benefits of National Rural Employment Guarantee Scheme in India." *Indian Journal of Labor Economics* 52 (2): 243–68.

Witsoe, Jeffrey. 2012. "Everyday Corruption and the Political Mediation of the Indian State." *Economic and Political Weekly* 47 (6): 47–54.

2

Unmet Demand for Work on the Bihar Rural Employment Guarantee Scheme

In this chapter and the next, the survey data collected for Bihar are used to better understand the issues raised in the all-India analysis, including why the Bihar Rural Employment Guarantee Scheme (BREGS) falls so far short of meeting its promise of guaranteeing employment. Given that BREGS work is in short supply relative to demand, we ask, who gets BREGS jobs, and who is rationed out? Is it the poor who do not get the extra work they want? How do the answers to these questions vary by gender and caste? Does location matter? We first describe the panel household survey, representative of rural Bihar, that was fielded for this study and is the basis of the analysis that follows.

The BREGS Survey

The BREGS survey collected two rounds of data from 150 villages across Bihar. The first round of the survey was implemented between May and July of 2009 and the second during the same months one year later. Because both surveys included questions with recall periods of one year, we refer to them as covering 2008/09 and 2009/10.[1] The first of the survey periods included a time of severe floods during the monsoon (July–August of 2008) in six districts falling in the catchment area of the Kosi River. In contrast, rainfall was scant during the 2009 monsoons and drought was declared in 26 districts.[2]

A two-stage sampling design was followed, using the 2001 census list of villages as the sampling frame. In the first stage, 150 villages were randomly selected from two strata, classified by high and low BREGS coverage based on administrative data for the scheme for 2008/09. In the second stage, 20 households per village were randomly selected, drawing from three strata (proportions in parentheses)—those with at least one member who had been employed at public works in the past year (7 of 20), those with a member who had engaged in other (non-public-works) casual work (7 of 20), and all other households (6 of 20). This stratified approach ensured that the sample included both scheme participants and households with likely participants to ensure that we could compare their activities and outcomes, and assess the degree of demand and rationing. All results reported in the study are weighted with appropriate sample weights to reflect the sampling design and are representative for the state. The annex to this chapter describes the survey instruments and sampling design in more detail and provides definitions of key variables used in the analysis.

Data were collected through several survey instruments to bring together evidence on both the demand- and supply-side aspects of the scheme:

• *Household surveys.* These surveys collected information on a range of household-level characteristics, including demographics, socioeconomic status (including asset ownership and consumption), employment and wages, political participation and social networks, as well as information on BREGS participation and process-related issues. To collect information on consumption, the abridged consumption block of the Employment Schedules of the National Sample Survey was used.

• *Individual surveys.* Two individual household members (one male and one female) were also interviewed for information on individual participation in BREGS; experience of BREGS functioning at the most recent worksite; and perceptions of the program, the village labor market, the role of women, and so forth.

• *Village surveys.* In each village, key informants were interviewed to collect information on the physical and social infrastructure in the village and on access to government programs.

• *Gram Panchayat surveys.* A survey of Gram Panchayats (GPs), in which the sampled households lived, focused on the administrative capabilities of GPs as well as perceptions of implementation challenges by program functionaries (such as the panchayat rozgar sewak[3] and the Mukhiya) to generate insights into the institutional factors at the local level that contribute to program implementation and outcomes.

• *Block surveys.* This survey instrument collected basic information from block officials on the capabilities and perceptions of implementation challenges at the block level.

Whereas the household and individual questionnaires provided insights on program performance, the village, GP, and block questionnaires helped identify supply-side constraints on delivery. This information was supplemented by the following qualitative research: (1) detailed process assessments in purposively selected villages in six districts in north and south Bihar (Gaya, Khaimur, Kishanganj, Muzaffarpur, Purnea, and Saharsa) during February and August 2009;[4] and (2) in-depth case studies of the delivery mechanisms adopted in Andhra Pradesh, Madhya Pradesh, and Rajasthan.[5]

A pilot information campaign was conducted between the two survey rounds in February and March 2010 in 40 villages randomly selected from the BREGS sample. The campaign took the form of a movie on BREGS rights and entitlements, tailored to Bihar's specific context and program guidelines. We return to this in chapter 7.

In total, 3,000 households and approximately 5,000 individuals were interviewed in each of the two rounds. The panel comprises 2,728 households and 3,749 individuals. Table 2.1 summarizes the sample size in the two rounds. In the analysis that follows, the panel is used only when it is needed. In each case, the most observations possible are used, with the appropriate sample always determined by the question asked.

The overall attrition rate for households of 8 percent between the two rounds was not concentrated in any particular stratum. There were relatively few refusals; two-thirds of the attrition occurred because a household was away temporarily when the survey team visited the village during the second round. There is no significant attrition effect for household-level BREGS participation or when estimating the impacts of the pilot information campaign (see the annex to this chapter).

Table 2.1 Sample Sizes in Bihar Rural Employment Guarantee Scheme Survey

	R1	R2	Panel (R1, R2)
Households	3,000	3,000	2,728
Individuals	5,172	5,012	3,749
Males	2,399	2,230	1,586
Females	2,773	2,782	2,163

Note: R1 and R2 refer to rounds 1 and 2, respectively, of the Bihar Rural Employment Guarantee Scheme (BREGS) survey.

The questionnaire asked both surveyed households and individuals whether they engaged in casual work on "public works" (which could include BREGS, road-building programs, or other government public works schemes) and then whether this was BREGS work. In round 1 (R1), 14.4 percent of households and 12.6 percent of individuals who said they were employed in public works stated that they did not participate in BREGS. The equivalent percentages for round 2 (R2) were 16 percent and 11.8 percent of households and individuals, respectively. Some proportion of this work possibly really was BREGS although participants were not aware of it; however, we cannot be sure. For this reason, we will sometimes refer to public works and sometimes to BREGS in accordance with the terms used in the specific question being examined.

To estimate poverty measures for Bihar, we use the median per capita consumption level in R1 to delineate the poverty line and then update it using the consumer price index for agricultural laborers to get the R2 poverty line. This method yields poverty lines of 6,988 rupees (Rs) per person per year in R1 and Rs 7,836 in R2. The R1 poverty rate in Bihar is then 50 percent (by construction) and in R2, it is estimated to be 41.8 percent.

Performance in Meeting Demand for Work

As in the all-India results reported in the previous chapter, the participation rate, demand rate, and rationing rate are estimated for rural households in Bihar using the BREGS survey. Although we use the same concepts and definitions, three differences should be noted between estimates based on the National Sample Survey (NSS) and the BREGS survey. First, we expect to find differences in the estimates as the result of differences in how this information is captured through the two surveys. The NSS 66th round (Schedule 10.0) used in the cross-state analysis asks a single question on whether the household got work on the Mahatma Gandhi National Rural Employment Guarantee Scheme (MGNREGS) in the past year; this question is used to classify households into participants, excess demanders (those who wanted work but did not get it), and the rest. In contrast, the BREGS survey has two sources of information on participation: first, the household questionnaire has a module on BREGS participation (including the total number of days worked in the past year) for each household member; and second, the individual questionnaires have a detailed module on each episode of BREGS (and other public works) work for the two household members interviewed, one male and one female. These individuals were also asked whether they had wanted to work on BREGS in the past year but did not get work. We believe that a specialized survey with detailed questions on MGNREGS is more likely to capture this information than a single question in a general survey. This is particularly likely to be the case if awareness is low and the main household respondent is not entirely aware of the activities of other members. Second, the specialized individual questionnaires in the BREGS survey make it possible for us to estimate demand, participation, and rationing separately for men and women in each survey round. Third, using the BREGS survey, we can extend the demand analysis to also assess which participating households may be rationed with respect to days of work by asking if they received fewer days of employment than they desired. (Annex table 2A.3 provides a summary of the participation and excess demander variable definitions and their source at the individual and household levels in the BREGS survey.)

Table 2.2 reports the demand rate, participation rate, and rationing rate for households, and separately for men and women. Similar to results reported for Bihar in the previous chapter, the BREGS survey also indicates the presence of massive demand for BREGS employment in rural Bihar among both men and women; indeed, estimated demand for the scheme is higher when we use data from the BREGS survey, which, as noted, collected much more detailed information on program participation and demand than did the NSS questionnaire. In both rounds of the survey, nearly two-thirds

Table 2.2 Summary of Participation, Demand, and Rationing

	Households		Men		Women	
	Round 1	Round 2	Round 1	Round 2	Round 1	Round 2
Participation rate (percent)	22.4	17.6	23.6	16.8	5.7	6.8
Demand rate (percent)	65.5	64.4	68.1	64.1	38.3	44.1
Rationing rate (percent)	65.8	72.8	65.3	73.8	85.1	84.6

Source: Estimates based on the Bihar Rural Employment Guarantee Scheme (BREGS) survey.

Note: The participation rate is defined as the percentage of rural households that obtained work on the scheme. The demand rate is the percentage of rural households that were participants or excess demanders. The rationing rate is defined as the percentage of those who wanted work but did not get it.

of households stated that they would like to work on the scheme. Not surprisingly, demand was much higher among men than among women at 68 percent versus 38 percent in R1, and 64 percent versus 44 percent in R2. However, when seen in light of extremely low overall labor force participation rates for women in Bihar, female demand for BREGS employment is notable.[6]

The data indicate that BREGS meets only a fraction of the demand. In R1, only 22 percent of rural households secured any work on the scheme (table 2.2). Of those demanding work, only one-third got work—a rationing rate of 66 percent. The participation rate fell and the degree of unmet demand increased between the two surveys, with nearly three-quarters (73 percent) of the households rationed away from work in R2.

Women are less likely to demand work, and the rationing process is less favorable to them. In both rounds of the survey, fewer than 7 percent of women interviewed in the sampled households worked on the scheme. The vast majority (85 percent) of women who would like to get work on the scheme were rationed.

When we observe overall participation rates for different times, such as in table 2.2, we do not know whether the same people or different people are participating at each date. By exploiting the panel design of the survey, we can learn more about exits and entries, that is, the dynamics of participation.

We find high levels of churning, with households entering and exiting the program from year to year. Table 2.3 reports movement of households between the three categories—participants, excess demanders, and the rest—between the two survey rounds. Fewer than half (45 percent) of the R1 BREGS participants were

Table 2.3 Joint Distribution of Program Participation across the Two Survey Rounds

number of households

| | | Round 2 | | | |
		BREGS participants	*Excess demanders*	*The rest*	*Total*
	BREGS participants	279	291	50	619
Round 1	*Excess demanders*	162	685	333	1,179
	The rest	40	310	580	929
	Total	480	1,285	963	2,728

Source: Estimates based on the Bihar Rural Employment Guarantee Scheme (BREGS) survey.

Note: These are the weighted number of observations (calculated using household weights) in each cell in the subsample of panel households.

also participants in R2. Some 42 percent of participants in R2 were new entrants to the scheme. Only 10 percent of households were BREGS participants in both rounds of the survey. The degree of churning helps explain the similarity between participants and excess demanders that will be seen in chapter 3.

High levels of churning can be consistent with BREGS serving an insurance function, such that households seek employment on the scheme to cope with shocks and exit to the private labor market at other times. However, that interpretation is not consistent with the evidence already presented on the extent of rationing. Effective insurance requires that people can get the work when they want it.[7] It appears more plausible that withdrawals from the program are involuntary. Four of every five participants who exited the program expressed a desire to stay in it. About 72 percent of those in R1 who said they wanted work on BREGS but did not get it also expressed demand for work in R2. Only 19 percent of them actually got work in R2. Nearly a quarter of households wanted work but did not get it in both years. This is highly suggestive of unmet demand for work, in that the National Rural Employment Guarantee Act's (the Act's) stipulated guarantee of employment to anyone who wants it was not being fulfilled in Bihar.

Rationing can also take the form of fewer days of work than desired. Many households that participated may have been rationed in that they would have liked more days of work and still had fewer than the 100 days stipulated by the Act. This picture is confirmed in a comparison of the days of employment provided to days demanded under the scheme (table 2.4).

In 2008/09 (the year preceding R1), the scheme provided 24 days of employment to participating households, on average. However, 91 percent of these households reported that they would have liked additional days of work but were unable to get them. Satisfaction levels improved in R2—average employment rose to 37 days per participating household, but 82 percent of households continued to believe that they were rationed. If we truncate each individual's employment (participating days plus number of additional days desired) to 100 days, the average total extra days of desired employment across all participants in R2 was 44 days. Excess demanders (those not presently employed by the scheme) also reported high demand, at 79 days per household.

Household perceptions about why they did not get as much employment as they wanted on the scheme suggest possible reasons for rationing (table 2.5). Among participants, the overwhelming reason seems to be the lack of available BREGS work. This lack of work could reflect supply-side constraints (discussed in chapter 8)

Table 2.4 Days of Employment Provided and Demanded in
the Past Year

	Round 1	Round 2
Number of BREGS days worked		
Per household	23.5	36.8
Per female	4.7	8.1
Per male	18.4	27.4
Percentage of households that worked 100 days	2.1	9.0
Number of additional BREGS days wanted		
Per household	—	71.5
Per participating household	44.4	43.6
Per excess demander	—	79.2

Source: Estimates based on the Bihar Rural Employment Guarantee Scheme
(BREGS) survey.

Note: Average days are reported for the group of households that were BREGS
participants or excess demanders; households not interested in working on the program are not included. The number of days worked plus additional days desired is
truncated at 100. Information on days desired by nonparticipating households was
not collected in round 1 of the BREGS survey. — = not available.

Table 2.5 Household Perceptions about Why They Were
Rationed

percentage of respondents

Why did you not get (more) work on BREGS in the past year?	Participants		Excess demanders	
	Female	Male	Female	Male
Work is not available at worksite	70.2	77.4	26.1	24.4
I was not present when the work was available	2.4	2.9	6.5	7.6
Did not get work even after demanding	9.4	4.4	11.1	12.0
Do not have any facility for child care	4.2	0.0	n.a.	n.a.
Work not allotted to women	0.1	0.0	7.7	0.0
Do not have any personal contacts	2.0	0.7	4.0	3.9
Because of the 100-day limit of MGNREGS	0.5	2.5	n.a.	n.a.
Unable to work or disabled	n.a.	n.a.	3.2	4.5
Do not have job card	n.a.	n.a.	34.1	40.9
Other	11.2	12.1	7.3	6.8

Source: Estimates based on the Bihar Rural Employment Guarantee Scheme
(BREGS) survey.

Note: Table reports percentage of households that report stated option as the main
reason for why they did not get work (for excess demanders) or more days than they
actually worked (for participants). Results reported for round 2 of the BREGS survey
(the question was not asked in round 1). MGNREGS = Mahatma Gandhi National
Rural Employment Guarantee Scheme; n.a. = not applicable, as option not provided
to respondent.

that limit the ability of local administrators to open sufficient BREGS worksites in a timely manner. Among excess demanders, the lack of a job card was cited as the primary reason for lack of work. This reason is probably valid given that most participants did possess job cards (78 percent in R1 and 87 percent in R2), while a very large fraction of nonparticipants (79 percent in R1 and 68 percent in R2) did not. However, a small fraction of households without job cards were also able to get employment on the scheme (8 percent in R1 and 4 percent in R2), suggesting that other factors were also at play.

For instance, it is clear from the survey data and field reports that very few people were aware of how to apply for work, the first step toward registering demand. As documented later, the work application process was not yet in place. The vast majority of those who have worked report that work was "given to them" by the local authorities. Others who are interested in working wait passively for work to come their way. Despite growing public awareness (documented in chapter 7), few people understand that getting a job card is only the first step in obtaining employment on the scheme, which must then be followed by an application for work. In that sense, the fundamental principle of employment on demand has yet to sink in.

Of course, demanding work does not automatically translate into getting it—more than 10 percent of excess demanders state that they asked for work but were turned away. Households also perceived the need to have the right personal contacts and networks to be granted employment, a theme examined in more detail in the next chapter on who gets work and who is rationed out.

The extent of the rationing raises fundamental doubts about the scheme's effectiveness in reducing poverty, both now and in the future. We will return to these concerns throughout this volume. But first it is of interest to look more closely at how the available work is rationed, which we take up in the next chapter.

Annex 2A

The survey data for this study come mainly from two rounds of a panel survey administered to households, individuals (in the selected households), villages, Gram Panchayats, and blocks, with a gap of one year between survey rounds. The survey covered 150 villages across Bihar. In total, 3,000 households and approximately 5,000 individuals were interviewed in each of the two rounds. This annex describes the BREGS sampling design and provides definitions of key variables used in the analysis.

Sampling Design

The survey covered 150 villages spread across all 38 districts of Bihar. A two-stage sampling design was followed. In the first stage, 150 villages were selected; in the second stage 20 households from each of these villages were selected.

The BREGS sample recognized six explicit strata, defined by combinations of three household groups and two village groups. The three household strata (ST) were defined as follows:
ST1:   Households in which at least one member engaged in public works employment in the past year.
ST2:   Households in which at least one member engaged in other (non–public works) casual work (but no one engaged in public works employment in the past year).
ST3:   All other households.

Because of the program's wide variation in coverage and overall low coverage, two village strata (VS) were defined on the basis of program coverage (based on administrative data for 2008/09), as follows:
VS1:   Villages in districts with high BREGS coverage (10 districts).
VS2:   Villages in the remaining districts (28 districts).

The 2001 census frame of villages was used as the sampling frame. Urban areas as defined in the 2001 census were explicitly excluded from the study. The selection criteria for selection in R1 were as follows:

a. *First stage, village selection.* Half the sample villages (75 villages) were drawn from the high coverage stratum (VS1), and the remaining 75 villages from the remaining set of districts (VS2). Villages were selected within each stratum (as defined above) with probability proportional to village size.
b. *Second stage, household selection.* In villages of 150 households or fewer, a complete listing of all households was implemented and some basic information collected. Households were grouped into the three strata described above. Larger villages were divided into segments of roughly 75 households each, from which two segments were selected randomly to be completely listed. Twenty households were selected from all the households in the list using the following rule (where applicable or available): seven households from ST1, seven households from ST2, and six households from ST3. In villages in which there were insufficient households in a stratum,

households were taken from other strata, with probability proportional to size of the strata in the village.

c. *Individual selection.* From within each household, two individuals—one adult male and one adult female (ages 18–60)—were selected to respond to the individual-level questionnaire. Priority was given to individual members who had engaged in public works, if any:

  i. For households from ST2 or ST3 (no public works participants), the household questionnaire was administered to the (ideally male) main respondent, and the relevant individual questionnaire to the same person. An adult respondent of opposite gender for the other individual questionnaire was selected by simple random sampling from the household roster.

  ii. For households from ST1 (at least one public works participant), the household questionnaire was administered to the (ideally male) main respondent, and the individual questionnaire to the same person if he or she had participated in public works. If the main respondent had not participated in public works, the individual questionnaire was administered to a household member who had. Similarly, for the opposite gender, the individual questionnaire was administered to the person who had participated in public works. If no one of a particular gender had participated in public works, the individual questionnaire was administered to a person selected randomly from the household roster.

Note that because the BREGS program participants were purposively sampled within households in ST1, in the study we do not report any estimates that are representative of the male or female adult population in Bihar. In all cases, estimates are representative of rural households.

Table 2A.1 presents the distribution of households and individuals across strata.

R2 aimed to interview the same households and individuals as in R1. Village listing sheets were not updated in R2. In R2, the rules for substitution of households, and substitution or addition of individuals, were defined as follows:

a. *Household substitution.* If a household was not found (for example, because it had migrated out, or was temporarily unavailable when the survey team was in the village), the household was replaced by an adjacent household in the same stratum from the R1 list. A sample size of 3,000 households was retained in R2. For replacement households, the same rules of individual selection were followed as in R1.

Table 2A.1 Distribution of Households and Individuals across Strata (Round 1)

Stratum	Number of households	Percentage of households[a]	Number of individuals	Percentage of individuals[a]
ST1	922	27.1	1,650	29.2
ST2	1,137	40.4	1,929	39.6
ST3	941	32.5	1,593	31.2
Total	3,000	100.0	5,172	100.0

Source: Estimates based on the Bihar Rural Employment Guarantee Scheme (BREGS) survey.

Note: ST1 = worked on public works in 2008; ST2 = worked at other casual labor in 2008; ST3 = worked on neither public works nor casual labor in 2008.

a. With sample weights.

    b. *Individual substitution.* An attempt was made to interview the same individuals as in R1. If a person was not found or was not available, another adult (ages 18–60) of the same gender in the household was interviewed.

    c. *Individual addition.* For households from which only one individual was interviewed in R1 (for example, because no one from the other gender was resident in the household or available during the survey period), and a person of the missing gender was available during R2, that person was interviewed. Note that additions and substitutions were done from the updated household roster (that is, they need not be limited to those listed in the R1 household roster).

Sample Size and Attrition

In both survey rounds, 3,000 households and approximately 5,000 individuals were interviewed (see table 2A.2). In R2, 272 of the 3,000 households (8 percent) were new households. Of the 5,012 individuals interviewed in R2, 4,555 were from panel households and 3,749 had been interviewed in R1. The panel comprises 2,728 households and 3,749 individuals.

    The overall attrition rate for households was low at 8 percent. Household attrition was not concentrated in any particular stratum, and most of the replacements were taken from the same stratum except for 13 households (spread across 11 villages) for which replacement households were from different strata. There were relatively few refusals; two-thirds of the attrition was because the household was away temporarily when the survey team visited the village. However, the reasons for attrition do differ across strata.

Table 2A.2 Sample Size (Rounds 1 and 2)

	Cross-sections		Panel
	Round 1	*Round 2*	*(Round 1, Round 2)*
Households	3,000	3,000	2,728
Individuals	5,172	5,012	3,749
Males	2,399	2,230	1,586
Females	2,773	2,782	2,163

Source: Estimates based on the Bihar Rural Employment Guarantee Scheme (BREGS) survey.

Refusals were more likely in the third strata (ST3), while temporary or permanent migration was more likely in other strata, especially ST2 (casual labor other than public works).

The characteristics of those lost through attrition versus others suggest that households lost through attrition tend to have fewer adult males, to have younger household heads, and to be poorer. Households with the first two characteristics would be expected to be less likely to work on BREGS, while poorer households may be more likely to work on BREGS. However, probit regressions for household-level BREGS participation indicate no significant attrition effect. There also does not seem to be an attrition bias when estimating impacts of the movie (see chapter 7): (1) the attrition rate did not vary between treatment and control groups, and (2) the characteristics of those who were lost through attrition were similar between treatment and control groups.

Calculation of Weights

The raising factors (sampling weights) needed to extrapolate the results from the sample to rural Bihar are the inverses of their selection probabilities. Survey round–specific household and village weights were calculated using the 2001 census sampling frame and the R1 listing to reflect the probability of selection. There were some differences in household and individual weights between the two rounds resulting from the replacement of R1 households in R2 with households from different strata (13 cases spread across 11 villages). R1 weights were used for the analysis of the panel of households. Round-specific weights were used for the analysis of the two cross-sections.

Table 2A.3 Variable Definitions

Variable	Definition	Source
Participants (household)	At least one member worked on BREGS	Block 1 (individual questionnaire) and Block 19 (household questionnaire)
Excess demanders (household)	At least one member wanted work on BREGS but did not get it in the past year	Block 4 (individual questionnaire)
Participants (individual)	The individual worked on BREGS in the past year	Block 3 (individual questionnaire)
Excess demanders (individual)	The individual wanted to work on BREGS but did not in the past year	Block 4 (individual questionnaire)
BREGS days	Average days worked on BREGS in the past year by all household members combined	Block 19 (household questionnaire)[a]

Note: BREGS = Bihar Rural Employment Guarantee Scheme.
a. Total number of days for an individual was replaced by the response in the individual questionnaire if there were missing values in the household questionnaire.

Notes

1. However, because the interviews were spread over three months, there is some overlap in the recall periods between the two survey years.

2. Flood Management Information System, Water Resources Department, government of Bihar, available at http://fmis.bih.nic.in/history.html.

3. The panchayat rozgar sewak is hired on contract by the state government for implementing the scheme at the GP level.

4. Background notes were prepared by Development Alternatives (2009), Indian Grameen Services (2009), and Sunai Consultancy Pvt. Ltd. (2009).

5. A background note was prepared by MART (2010).

6. According to NSS 2009/10 data, only 10.6 percent of women ages 15–59 years were participating in the labor force in Bihar (including employed women and those seeking employment). Bihar's female labor force participation rate is the lowest across all major states and well below the nationwide average of 39.8 percent.

7. In R2, only 13 percent of men and 9 percent of women felt that BREGS work was available when they needed it in the past year.

References

Development Alternatives. 2009. "Report on Scoping Study for Design and Development of Alternative Implementation Model(s) on NREGS." Background note prepared for the BREGS study. Development Alternatives, Inc., New Delhi, India.

Indian Grameen Services. 2009. "Report on Scoping Study for Design and Development of Alternative Implementation Model(s) on NREGS and SGSY." Background note prepared for the BREGS study. Indian Grameen Services, Kolkata, India.

MART. 2010. "The Synthesis Report: Institutional Review of MGNREGS in Andhra Pradesh and Madhya Pradesh." Background note prepared for the BREGS study, NOIDA, India.

Sunai Consultancy Pvt. Ltd. 2009. "Process Qualitative Observation Report, Feb–Mar 2009, four blocks of Muzaffarpur and Saharsa districts of Bihar." Background note prepared for the BREGS study. Sunai Consultancy Pvt. Ltd., Bihar, India.

3

Who Gets Work?
Who Is Left Out?

The previous chapters show evidence of substantial unmet demand for work on the Mahatma Gandhi National Rural Employment Guarantee Scheme (MGNREGS). The extent of unmet demand is clear from survey responses in the National Sample Survey (for India as a whole, and especially in the poorer states) and in the specially designed survey for Bihar, the Bihar Rural Employment Guarantee Scheme (BREGS) survey. This unmet demand raises questions about how well the self-targeting feature of MGNREGS is working in practice. To understand whether the self-targeting mechanism is working despite significant rationing, this chapter examines who gets work and who gets left out. In the process, we will also learn more about how well the extra income gains from the scheme are "targeted" to poor families.

Table 3.1 summarizes the main characteristics of BREGS participating households in round 1 (R1) of the survey, and compares them to the characteristics of excess demanders, as well as to those of the "rest" who did not express interest in working on the scheme.

Participants generally belong to more-disadvantaged groups. For instance, only 31 percent of participant households own some land, compared with 64 percent of the "rest." They are much less likely to have a pucca roof[1] (21 percent versus 44 percent); to have a head of household who has completed class 8 of schooling or more (8 percent versus 36 percent); to rely on own-agriculture as their main income source (7 percent versus 33 percent); and much more likely to be dependent on casual labor, whether agriculture (33 percent versus 7 percent) or nonagriculture (51 percent versus 12 percent).

Table 3.1 Characteristics of Participants, Excess Demanders, and the Rest, Round 1

	BREGS participants (percent)	Excess demanders (percent)	Rest (percent)	Total (percent)
Main source of household income				
Own-agricultural activities	6.5	15.4	32.8	19.4
Own-nonagricultural activities	4.9	9.0	17.4	11.0
Casual farm labor	32.8	23.9	7.0	20.1
Casual nonfarm labor	51.2	40.1	12.4	33.1
Salaried job	0.3	1.7	8.9	3.9
Transfers from friends and family	3.5	9.6	20.0	11.8
Education and labor history				
Household head illiterate	69.3	60.0	42.1	55.9
Household head completed class 8 or higher	7.8	18.3	35.9	22.0
Household men engage in casual work	95.9	74.2	24.8	62.0
Household women engage in casual work	55.7	42.6	12.4	35.1
Male members ever migrated for work	47.7	48.7	31.3	42.5
Social identity				
Scheduled Tribe	3.1	2.5	1.1	2.2
Mahadalit	11.9	5.1	1.6	5.4
Scheduled Caste	30.4	25.9	8.6	20.9

Other Backward Class	51.0	55.6	64.5	57.6
Other caste	3.6	10.9	24.2	13.9
Hindu	95.7	88.5	83.8	88.5
Muslim	4.1	11.4	15.9	11.3
Living standards				
Has pucca roof	21.2	22.7	43.6	29.6
Has pucca floor	12.5	13.0	27.4	17.9
Has Below-Poverty-Line ration card	72.2	61.2	39.4	56.1
No ration card	13.2	20.0	24.9	20.2
Owns land (other than the homestead)	30.7	36.8	64.2	44.9
Monthly per capita expenditure (rupees)	625.7	716.0	828.4	734.6

Source: Estimates based on the Bihar Rural Employment Guarantee Scheme (BREGS) survey.

Note: The figures give the percentage of households with the specified characteristics in each group in round 1. Mahadalit is a subclassification of the poorest and most disadvantaged among Scheduled Castes, as notified by the government of Bihar. A pucca roof is made of materials such as timber, slate, corrugated iron, and the like. (The alternative, a kutcha roof, is made of materials such as bamboo or thatch.) Below-Poverty-Line (BPL) ration card refers to the card that defines the poverty status of rural households and determines entitlements to various government programs. We refer to the combined set of BPL (41 percent), Antyodaya (14 percent), and Annapoorna (less than 1 percent) cardholders as having a BPL card. Antyodaya cards are for the "poorest of the poor" (which was initially a subcategory of BPL households). Annapoorna cards are distributed to poor individuals 65 years or older who do not benefit from the Indira Gandhi National Old Age Pension. Note that the Mahatma Gandhi National Rural Employment Guarantee Scheme (MGNREGS) is not specifically targeted to BPL households.

In other respects as well, such as consumption levels, it is clear that participants are poorer than the rest.

Participation of disadvantaged social groups is high in comparison with that of other groups, a finding also corroborated by other field studies. About 45 percent of participating households were Scheduled Caste or Scheduled Tribe (SC/ST) in R1, which is well above the SC/ST share in the population (29 percent). This high relative level of participation is particularly true of Mahadalits, who in R1 comprised 5 percent of households but more than twice that as a share (12 percent) of participant households.[2] By round 2 (R2) of the survey, overall household participation rates fell, but SC/ST households were more likely to retain BREGS employment. Thus, in R2, more than 50 percent of BREGS participants were drawn from SC/ST groups. These patterns suggest that assignment of work on the scheme is pro-poor, despite very low levels of coverage and high unmet demand.

In many respects, as can be seen in table 3.1, excess demanders are not very different from participants. For example, the two groups have similar propensities to migrate for employment, and their housing is of the same quality. Excess demanders are better off than participants along some dimensions (for example, land ownership, monthly consumption per capita, lower dependence on casual labor), but in all characteristics are more similar to participants than they are to the rest. This is not surprising given the large degree of churning in the scheme reviewed in chapter 2, with households transiting between participant and excess demander categories from one year to the next.

Targeting

To assess targeting performance, table 3.2 reports participation, demand, and rationing rates by rural quintiles, defined by per capita consumption, from each round of the BREGS survey. The patterns for Bihar from the National Sample Survey data, described in chapter 1, are confirmed with the BREGS survey.

As expected, demand for work on BREGS declines with consumption; richer households are considerably less likely than the poorest 20 percent to want to do this work, although the gradient is flat between the 20th and 80th percentiles of the distribution. Even among the richest quintile, more than 50 percent of households express interest in working on the scheme, possibly because of its potential insurance function.

Participation rates also decline with consumption but more rapidly than do demand rates, showing that rationing of work among those

Table 3.2 Coverage of Bihar Rural Employment Guarantee Scheme across Consumption Quintiles of Rural Bihar

Quintiles	Participation rate	Demand rate	Rationing rate	Mean person days among participating households	Mean person days among all rural households	Share of days worked on BREGS (percent)
Round 1						
Q1 (Poorest)	0.333	0.830	0.599	20.6	6.8	27.2
Q2	0.199	0.651	0.694	22.2	4.4	16.7
Q3	0.284	0.698	0.592	28.5	8.1	31.2
Q4	0.221	0.645	0.658	23.0	5.0	14.5
Q5 (Richest)	0.134	0.529	0.747	21.7	2.9	10.4
All	0.224	0.655	0.658	23.5	5.2	100.0
Round 2						
Q1 (Poorest)	0.238	0.747	0.682	27.4	6.5	26.5
Q2	0.186	0.655	0.716	30.5	5.6	19.4
Q3	0.158	0.722	0.782	30.9	4.9	22.5
Q4	0.180	0.609	0.704	35.1	6.3	14.6
Q5 (Richest)	0.142	0.551	0.742	58.0	8.1	16.9
All	0.176	0.644	0.727	37.0	6.5	100.0

Source: Estimates from the Bihar Rural Employment Guarantee Scheme (BREGS) survey.

Note: The participation rate is the share of rural households working on BREGS. The demand rate is the share of rural households that want work on the program. The rationing rate is the share of those who wanted work but did not get it. Population is classified into quintiles based on per capita consumption in each round. Two outliers (with implausibly high weighted days worked) were dropped from round 2 and three from round 1.

who would like to work is pro-poor. The scheme is also pro-poor in its distribution of total days of employment. This pro-poor performance is achieved through both demand for work and the pro-poor rationing of work but not by the assignment of number of days of work actually received. The average days of work received by participants tends to increase with consumption, particularly in R2.

Patterns of coverage, demand, and rationing by social group (castes and tribes), reported in table 3.3, confirm the positive pro-poor targeting results. Disadvantaged social groups are more likely to participate, and face less (though not insignificant) rationing. In R1, a little more than 30 percent of SC (excluding Mahadalits) and ST households participated in the program. Participation was lower for Other Backward Classes (OBCs) at 20 percent and lowest for all others, at 6 percent. Mahadalits were much more likely to participate, with one of every two households securing some employment (on average, 25 days) on the scheme. In R2, the participation rates of Mahadalits fell, but likely because of the reclassification of other SC castes as Mahadalits in between the two survey rounds.

The targeting differential,[3] reported in table 3.4, provides a summary measure by which to compare targeting performance by consumption groups versus social groups.[4] It shows that the program is considerably more successful at targeting disadvantaged social groups (compared with others) than it is at targeting based on consumption poverty. The targeting differential for SCs, STs, OBCs, and Mahadalits together relative to "others" of 0.19 in R1 (0.16 in R2) compares favorably with the targeting differential based on poverty status of 0.06 in the same round. As shown in the next section, this good targeting performance likely relates to the fact that the rationing process in Bihar appears to rely heavily on indicators (or proxies) of poverty. Poor households that do not have the typical profile of the poor tend to be rationed out; conversely, groups that have been traditionally disadvantaged and have household characteristics (such as social group, Below-Poverty-Line [BPL] card) that are considered to be reasonable proxies of poverty status tend to be favored in the targeting process.

When participation and rationing probabilities are considered over the entire distribution (rather than across quintiles), the correlation with wealth is more complex than might at first be assumed. Figure 3.1 plots participation and rationing against three different indicators of wealth—an index of asset ownership, consumption per capita, and land area owned.[5] Although rationing of work tends to increase with all three indicators of wealth, the poorest of the poor (roughly the bottom 15 percent measured on the asset index or consumption) are more, not less, likely to be rationed out

Table 3.3 Coverage of the Bihar Rural Employment Guarantee Scheme across Social Groups of Rural Bihar

	Participation rate	Demand rate	Rationing rate	Mean person days among participating households	Mean person days among all rural households
Round 1					
Mahadalit	0.493	0.897	0.450	24.6	12.0
Scheduled Tribe	0.319	0.821	0.611	19.5	6.2
Scheduled Caste	0.325	0.858	0.621	31.1	10.0
Other Backward Class	0.198	0.613	0.677	19.4	3.8
Other	0.059	0.398	0.852	17.0	0.9
All	0.224	0.655	0.658	23.5	5.2
Round 2					
Mahadalit	0.291	0.863	0.663	56.8	16.5
Scheduled Tribe	0.206	0.836	0.753	21.6	4.5
Scheduled Caste	0.378	0.863	0.562	26.5	10.0
Other Backward Class	0.136	0.594	0.771	31.1	4.2
Other	0.039	0.411	0.904	45.8	1.7
All	0.176	0.645	0.727	36.9	6.5

Source: Estimates based on the Bihar Rural Employment Guarantee Scheme survey.

Note: The participation rate is the share of rural households working on BREGS. The demand rate is the share of rural households that want work on the program. The rationing rate is the share of those who wanted work but did not get it. Population is classified into quintiles based on per capita consumption in each round. Two outliers (with implausibly high weighted days worked) were dropped from round 2 and three from round 1.

Table 3.4 Targeting Differentials by Poverty Status and
Social Group

| | Participation rates | | Targeting differential |
	Poor	Nonpoor	
Round 1	0.257	0.201	0.056
Round 2	0.210	0.158	0.052
	SCsª/STs/OBCs	Others	
Round 1	0.251	0.059	0.192
Round 2	0.199	0.041	0.158

Source: Estimates based on the Bihar Rural Employment Guarantee Scheme survey.
Note: SCs/STs/OBCs = Scheduled Castes, Scheduled Tribes, and Other Backward
Classes.
a. Includes Mahadalits.

than households in the middle of the distribution. Adding controls
for household characteristics and village fixed effects[6] flattens the
gradient but the effect persists. These patterns are explored more
closely in the next section.

Determinants of Participation and Rationing

The summary statistics in table 3.1 are instructive, but there is an
interpretational issue because the identified characteristics linked to
participation are likely to be correlated with one another. For example, BPL card holders are more likely to participate in the scheme,
as are the landless; but the landless are more likely to be BPL card
holders. We need a multivariate regression model to separate out
the partial effects.

Table 3.5 reports the marginal effects of various household and
village characteristics on participation, demand, and rationing. To
ease interpretation of coefficients—so that higher values are positive and lower values negative for all three outcomes variables—we
replace rationing by its complement, namely, the *assignment of work*
among those who wanted work. (Assignment is, in effect, 1 minus
rationing.) There are two regressions for each independent variable:
the first case incorporates explicit village characteristics available in
the data, whereas the other includes a complete set of village dummy
variables to represent village fixed effects.

To investigate potential heterogeneity by wealth level, we also
estimate these regressions for different wealth groups (defined using
the asset index), namely, the richest 50 percent and the poorest
15 percent. The detailed results for R1 are given in table 3A.1 in the
annex to this chapter. The following discussion notes cases in which

the effect of characteristics differ significantly across wealth groups, in particular, for the poorest 15 percent because this is the group for whom targeting is perverse (as illustrated by figure 3.1).

The regressions include a cubic function of the asset index as well as a quadratic function of landholding.[7] (Consumption was not used given the potential endogeneity concerns.) The pattern of the wealth effects is similar between actual participation and demand. Higher wealth as measured by the asset index is associated with lower demand for this work, and lower actual participation. For landholding, participation falls as landholding increases for 99 percent of the data. (The turning point, at 5.7 acres of land, is at the 99th percentile of the land distribution. This could be due to measurement errors.) However, participation depends on many other factors, to which we now turn.

Household Characteristics

Given that physically demanding outdoor work is required on BREGS, one expects a family's demographic characteristics to matter to household demand for work. The regression results show that, controlling for wealth and other factors, a higher share of adult males in the household increases the probability that a household will demand work, and get it. The effect is stronger (in both size and significance) for demand for work than for actual participation or assignment of work. Households with a female head were less likely either to want to participate or to participate; they were also less likely to be assigned work when they did want it. This echoes the findings of a study in Andhra Pradesh (AP) that also finds a lower likelihood of participation for female-headed households (Liu and Deininger 2013). Some households headed by women may have a remitting male migrant member, others may lack labor, and yet others may be denied work even if they want it. There is no sign of a "life cycle" effect, as measured by age of the household head. However, households with more old people are less likely to want this work, but no less likely to get it.

Controlling for wealth (including land) and other factors, households with heads who have completed secondary and higher levels of schooling are less likely to participate or to want to do so compared with those with less-educated heads. Note that illiterate heads are the excluded group. However, the negative effect of higher education is stronger (in size and significance) for actual participation than for demand and strongest for being assigned work. This outcome is consistent with a rationing mechanism that excludes educated households even when they may want work for some reason.

Figure 3.1 Participation and Rationing as a Function of
Wealth

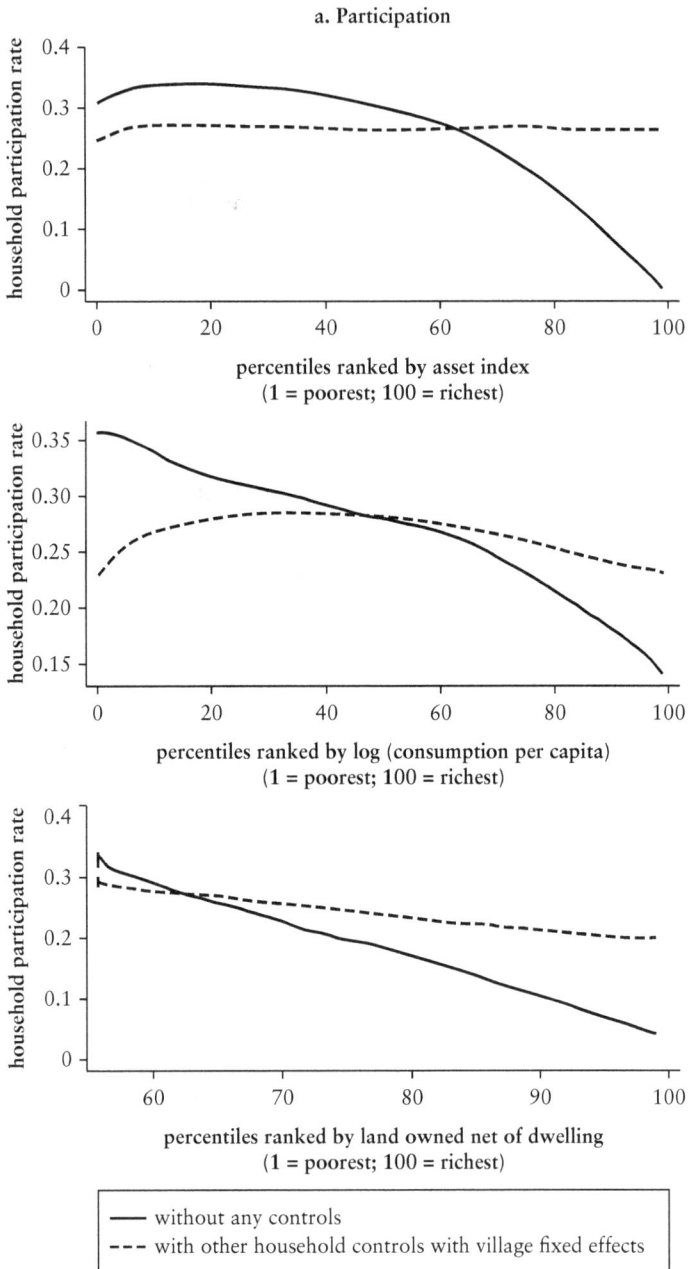

a. Participation

b. Rationing

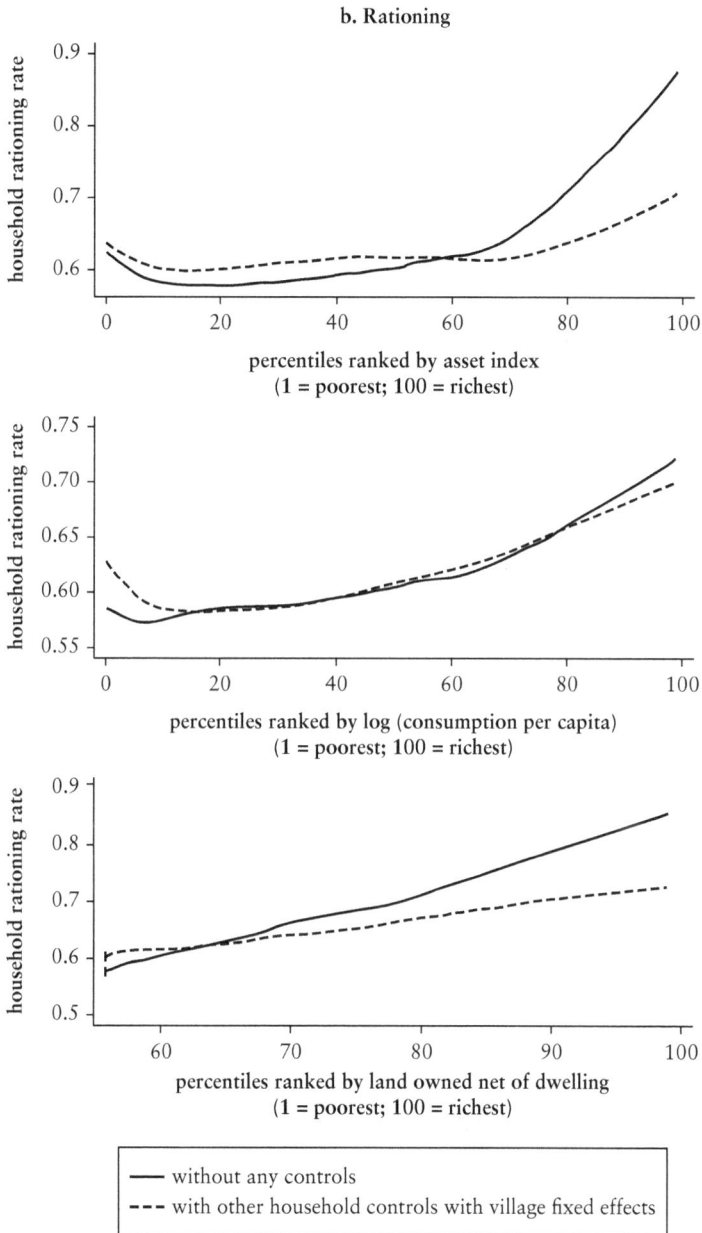

Source: Estimates based on the Bihar Rural Employment Guarantee Scheme (BREGS) survey.

Table 3.5 Regressions for Household Participation, Demand, and Assignment of Work

	Participation		Demand		Assignment of work	
	(1)	(2)	(3)	(4)	(5)	(6)
Household characteristics						
ln (household size)	0.116	0.143	-0.058	-0.070	0.166	0.146
ln (household size) squared	-0.023	-0.034	0.045	0.048	-0.036	-0.032
Share of male adults	0.161**	0.153**	0.235***	0.274***	0.218**	0.198*
Share of female adults	-0.048	-0.061	-0.165**	-0.185**	-0.042	-0.062
Share of elderly	-0.062	-0.115	-0.293***	-0.239**	0.046	-0.074
Share of children (younger than age 6)	0.059	0.060	-0.066	-0.050	0.132	0.128
Gender of head (male = 1)	0.069***	0.081***	0.090***	0.103***	0.091**	0.096**
Age of head (years)	0.004	0.006	0.000	-0.000	0.007	0.007
Age of head (years), squared	-0.000	-0.000	-0.000	-0.000	-0.000	-0.000
Maximum education in household						
Literate (< class 5)	0.011	-0.003	0.012	0.008	0.017	0.011
Class 5 pass (primary)	-0.016	-0.024	-0.016	-0.016	-0.013	-0.000
Class 8 pass (middle)	-0.014	-0.023	-0.046	-0.025	-0.007	-0.014
Class 10 pass (secondary)	-0.089***	-0.090***	-0.089**	-0.072*	-0.125***	-0.114**
Class 12 pass (higher secondary)	-0.061*	-0.077***	-0.099*	-0.133**	-0.049	-0.053
More than higher secondary	-0.126***	-0.159***	-0.021	-0.083	-0.233***	-0.258***
Social group						
Scheduled Caste	0.009	0.072	0.086**	0.111***	-0.015	0.058
Mahadalit	0.111**	0.358***	0.121***	0.134***	0.122*	0.358***

	(1)	(2)	(3)	(4)	(5)	(6)
Other Backward Class	-0.060*	-0.014	0.007	0.029	-0.099*	-0.044
Scheduled Tribe	0.019	0.037	0.031	0.085	0.023	0.025
Hindu	0.082***	0.042	0.096**	0.069	0.114***	0.050
Asset-house index	-0.015**	-0.014*	-0.032***	-0.034***	-0.012	-0.007
Asset-house index squared	-0.005**	-0.004*	-0.006***	-0.004*	-0.004	-0.005
Asset-house index cubed	0.000	0.000	0.001***	0.001**	0.000	0.000
Land owned	-0.068***	-0.087***	-0.036**	-0.056***	-0.102***	-0.128***
Land owned squared	0.006***	0.007***	0.002	0.004**	0.011**	0.013**
BPL ration card	0.063***	0.087***	0.054**	0.051**	0.079***	0.099***
Know Mukhiya or Sarpanch	0.052**	0.061**	-0.004	0.013	0.075**	0.084**
Know ward member or panch	0.005	0.007	0.065***	0.066***	-0.020	-0.022
Know program officer or block development officer	0.213**	0.200	0.000	0.014	0.431***	0.422***
Know any political worker	0.021	0.007	-0.070	-0.093	0.050	0.044
Cast vote in panchayat election	0.092***	0.117***	0.002	0.004	0.158***	0.192***
Household shock in past year						
Accident	0.015	0.005	0.030	0.026	0.010	-0.012
Illness	0.000	-0.002	0.026	0.025	-0.016	-0.028
Job loss	0.037	0.069*	-0.011	0.004	0.062	0.090*
Natural disaster	0.024	0.021	0.034	0.047	0.025	0.003
Other	0.010	0.036	0.015	0.014	0.026	0.052
Men do casual work	0.217***	0.247***	0.272***	0.276***	0.247***	0.286***
Women do casual work	0.071***	0.079***	0.142***	0.158***	0.073***	0.070**
No male migration	0.020	0.036*	-0.016	-0.016	0.028	0.050*
Regular-salaried worker in household	-0.067*	-0.084**	-0.142***	-0.158***	-0.059	-0.054

(Continued on the following page)

Table 3.5 *(Continued)*

	Participation		Demand		Assignment of work	
	(1)	*(2)*	*(3)*	*(4)*	*(5)*	*(6)*
GP characteristics						
GP has a panchayat bhawan	0.005		−0.023		0.015	
Mukhiya's characteristics						
Age (years)	0.000		0.002		−0.000	
Lives in village	0.035*		−0.028		0.065**	
Gender (male = 1)	−0.007		−0.043*		0.006	
Completed class 5	−0.000		−0.013		0.005	
Main occupation is farming	0.014		0.017		0.025	
Held a GP post in the past	0.079***		−0.049		0.130***	
Family held GP post	−0.008		0.015		−0.006	
Is a contractor	0.111*		−0.000		0.149*	
Village characteristics						
Share of Scheduled Caste households	−0.046		0.038		−0.107	
Share of OBC households	0.039		−0.052		0.060	
Predominant religion (Hindu = 1)	0.022		0.005		0.034	
Is electrified	−0.026		0.004		−0.042	
Has a pucca road	0.045**		−0.039*		0.075***	
Within 5 km of bus stop	−0.033		−0.053**		−0.046	
Within 5 km of GP	−0.085***		−0.094***		−0.089**	
Within 5 km of town	−0.024		0.005		−0.035	

	(1)	(2)	(3)	(4)	(5)	(6)
Within 5 km of block headquarters	0.037*		0.011		0.055*	
Post office in village	0.016		0.047**		0.019	
Nonagricultural enterprises within 5 km	0.039		0.043		0.060	
ln of mean asset index in village	0.025		0.135*		0.009	
Asset inequality in village	−0.246		−0.398**		−0.159	
Share of households with kutcha house	−0.003		0.009		−0.004	
Share of households with BPL card	0.058		0.027		0.111	
Flood in past year	0.034*		0.021		0.047	
Drought in past year	0.010		0.034		0.009	
Any shock past year	−0.031		−0.003		−0.053	
Good relations between social groups	0.027		0.000		0.050	
Self-help group in village	−0.032		0.012		−0.054*	
Civil society organization in village	0.023		−0.018		0.038	
BREGS group in village	0.019		0.056*		0.010	
Other group in village	−0.028		0.053*		−0.049	
Village fixed effects?	No	Yes	No	Yes	No	Yes
Observations	2,815	2,633	2,815	2,933	1,947	1,867
Pseudo R^2	0.248	0.283	0.316	0.361	0.155	0.197

Source: Estimates based on the Bihar Rural Employment Guarantee Scheme (BREGS) survey.

Note: Household, village, and GP variables observed in round 1. Land owned is net of dwelling. The omitted education category is illiterate. Probit marginal effects are reported. BPL = Below Poverty Line; GP = Gram Panchayat; OBC =Other Backward Class; km = kilometers.

*, **, and *** indicate significance at the 10 percent, 5 percent, and 1 percent levels, respectively, based on robust standard errors.

There is strong evidence that group identities or "poor credentials" play an important role in explaining participation, and that these identity effects exist independently of non-land wealth or landholding. Mahadalits are significantly more likely to participate than are other social groups but only among the richer half of households (see table 3A.1). However, this effect reverses when we look at demand for work, in that the poorest Mahadalit households are significantly more likely to desire this work than are the richest. Being a Mahadalit from the wealthier half of the Mahadalit population is a strong correlate of participation but not of demand, suggesting a role is played by group identities in the rationing process: being a Mahadalit is treated as a proxy for poverty status when allocating work.

In contrast, SC households that were not classified as Mahadalits at the time of the R1 survey were at a disadvantage. They were more likely to demand work than general category households, but no more likely to get it. There are weak effects of OBC status on overall participation rates in the sample. Both OBC and ST status variables become very significant *negative* determinants of participation among the poorest 15 percent (see table 3A.1 in the annex to this chapter). However, this negative effect arises because OBC and ST households were no more likely to want work than general category households.

Being a Hindu (as opposed to a Muslim) household increases both demand and participation.[8] However, the household religion effect is much smaller and becomes statistically insignificant when we focus on the impact of religion on household participation *within* villages by adding village fixed effects. Thus, the religion effect seems to be stemming from village attributes correlated with the religious composition of the village, rather than from whether the village is majority Hindu or Muslim.

There are strong signs that households with local political connections—as indicated by reported connections to village leaders (for example, the Mukhiya or Sarpanch) or administrative officials (for example, the block development officer [BDO])[9]—are more likely to get BREGS work, even though their demand for work is not any higher. The pattern is reversed, however, for self-reported connections to the ward member, which increases demand but not participation. We can only speculate on why. Ward members may be important sources of village information about the scheme, while the assignment of work lies under the control of the Mukhiya and others (such as the panchayat rozgar sewak [PRS]).

However, focusing on the poorest 15 percent, we find notable differences in the effects of political connections on participation.

Knowing the Mukhiya discriminates well among the rich, but matters little among the poor. Connections to administrative officials
(such as the BREGS program officer or the BDO) have a significant
effect for the poorest 50 percent but again, matter little to the poorest 15 percent. This result may be a reflection of the "quality" of the
political connections of the poor. However, political participation
(as indicated by voting in local elections) is a more significant covari-
ate with a larger effect for the poorest 15 percent than for any other
group (see table 3A.1).

Having a BPL ration card is strongly correlated with securing
employment on the scheme.[10] BPL households are twice as likely to
be BREGS participants as other households—a pattern that persists
even after controlling for wealth, landholding, and other household
characteristics. However, disaggregating by wealth, this result holds
only among richer households. Among the richest 50 percent, BPL
card holders do not demand more work than other households,
but are significantly more likely to get it (table 3A.1). In contrast,
having a BPL card significantly increases demand for work by the
poorest 15 percent, but has no effect on these households being
assigned work.

The BPL effect could be picking up some dimension of poverty
omitted from the regressions. However, problems of inclusion and
exclusion errors in the allocation of BPL cards are well known, and
Bihar is no exception. In the sample, BPL card distribution among
households is only mildly progressive. Whereas 68 percent of households in the bottom per capita consumption quintile have a BPL
card, almost half (49 percent) of those in the top quintile also possess
one. Using the median consumption per capita level as the poverty
line, we find that 61 percent of Bihar's poor households are in possession of BPL cards versus 52 percent of nonpoor households. These
patterns may also possibly indicate that the BPL effect in the upper
end of the distribution is picking up not poverty, but privilege—the
same factors that determine why a household (among the relatively
better off) receives a BPL card may also result in its being assigned
work under BREGS.

It also may be that in a context of supply constraints, a BPL card
is used by scheme functionaries as a mechanism for allocating what-
ever work becomes available. Holding a BPL card is not an eligibility
criterion stipulated by the National Rural Employment Guarantee
Act (the Act). However, knowledge of this fact is low: 62 percent
of interviewed women (47 percent of men) reported that they did
not know that BREGS employment is also available to households
that lack a BPL card. That said, when asked why they thought they
did not get work despite wanting it, only a miniscule percentage

(fewer than 0.5 percent) mentioned not having a BPL card as the main determinant. The lack of available work (23 percent in R1 for both men and women) or of a job card (33 percent for women and 42 percent for men) were perceived to be more pertinent. However, BPL status was seen to play a role in acquiring a job card in the first place. In R1, 11.2 percent of households without a job card and who made no effort to get one said one reason for not even applying was not being BPL. Some 3.9 percent of households without job cards and that did make an effort to get one said that they were not granted one because they were not BPL. Of course, as one might expect, almost all Mukhiyas and PRSs report in both rounds that non-BPL households can also get work as per the scheme's guidelines. (See chapter 7 for further discussion of household awareness of BREGS rules and procedures.)

We find little to suggest that the scheme is providing insurance benefits not otherwise captured by the other explanatory variables. Households reporting shocks did not have either higher demand for work or higher participation (although a mildly significant effect of job loss appears when one allows for village fixed effects).

Labor market history clearly matters. If the household includes either men or women who have previously engaged in casual labor it is more likely that they will both demand and get this work. Having a household member who had a regular salaried job in the past year makes it less likely that the household will want to work on public works; there is a considerably weaker effect on actually doing this work.

Panchayat and Village Characteristics

GP and village-level characteristics are also driving participation levels.[11] The Mukhiya is important to the scheme's functioning. Villages in which the Mukhiya has held a GP post in the past have higher levels of participation and assignment of work, though, not surprisingly, this village attribute has no effect on the demand for work. Villages in which the Mukhiya resides are more likely to have work, as are villages in which the Mukhiya is a contractor.

Better village infrastructure in the form of a pucca road has opposite effects on demand and participation, increasing participation while lowering demand for work. Other accessibility indicators also suggest that more-remote villages (farther from a bus stop, farther from the GP headquarters) have higher demand for work, and less participation. Having a post office in the village increases demand for this type of work but has no significant effect on actually getting the work.

Higher wealth inequality within the village is associated with significantly lower demand for work, and, less strongly, lower participation.[12] This effect is particularly strong for the poorest. Possibly the same factors that create high inequality in a village lessen the knowledge of one's rights under the Act as well as a poor household's ability to demand those rights.[13] (Chapter 7 points to some evidence consistent with this view.) Power relations in high-inequality villages may mean that the scheme gets very little attention.

One of the most notable differences in the participation model for the poorest 15 percent versus the rest of the population is in the coefficient of having "good relations among different groups within the village." This village attribute emerges as a significant positive correlate of participation, consistent with the hypothesis that the job-rationing process favors the poor in more cohesive, cooperative village environments.

However, there is clearly some unexplained variance in village characteristics: the pseudo R^2 is typically about 0.04 higher in the model with a complete set of village fixed effects, which can be interpreted as indicating that about 4 percent of the variance is attributable to omitted village characteristics. Undoubtedly some village-specific factors, such as the extent to which local officials share the aims of the scheme or their capacity to deliver, are hard to capture empirically.

Several other GP-level characteristics (other than the characteristics of the Mukhiya) can also be expected to matter to participation. The survey included a module on GP characteristics. However, a sizable share of these data were incomplete, resulting in a marked reduction in sample size—600 households from the full sample used for modeling participation were lost—when these variables are included as predictors of participation. Annex table 3A.2 shows regression results with GP characteristics included, but they should be treated as highly tentative given the potential sample selection bias. (The regressions also included all the variables listed in annex table 3A.1, but we do not report them in their entirety because there were few differences of any note.)

The level of safety (as measured by responses to a question about whether it was safe to move around after dark) in the GP attracts a significant and positive coefficient in the participation regression, particularly for the poorest. Certain characteristics of the PRS, the main program functionary at the local level, also emerge. Having a lower caste PRS makes participation less likely for the poor, as does the PRS living outside the GP. Another seemingly puzzling finding is that having a PRS responsible for more than one GP (implying a higher workload) is associated with higher participation rates. However, qualitative research suggests it is the Mukhiya rather than the PRS who influences participation. The former is the local elected leader, whereas the latter may often be an outsider to the GP.

An important supply-side variable is whether the GP has a shelf of projects ready to start up for BREGS work. This is a stronger predictor of participation among the poor. In the absence of an approved shelf of works, GPs may be constrained in providing work in response to demand (see chapter 8).

Determinants of Individual Participation, Demand, and Rationing

So far we have only looked at which households participated or wanted to do so. Focusing on the individual level, as in results reported in annex table 3A.3, highlights the particular constraints to participation faced by women in the scheme.

The most notable observation is the significant gender effect on participation, favoring men. Men also had a higher demand for work. But it is telling that they were more likely to get work, given that they wanted it, and that this holds controlling for other individual, household, and village characteristics. There is marked unmet demand for work by women that exists independently of other characteristics, which corroborates much anecdotal evidence.

Other points of note are that demand for work is higher among household heads. Women with stronger self-efficacy, as measured by the Pearlin scale, are also more likely to express demand for this type of work, but they are no more likely to get work.[14] A man's Pearlin scale does not make a difference to his demand for work or participation in BREGS.

Days of Employment

Rationing can take two forms. Households can either be rationed by not getting any employment on the scheme, or they may receive fewer days of employment than they desire. Chapter 2 documents that both forms of rationing are prevalent. The preceding analysis has explored who gains entry into the scheme. This section explores the correlates of the number of days of employment received, to better understand this dimension of rationing. Table 3.6 reports regressions of the number of days of employment at the individual level. The sample consists of participants 18–65 years old, and results are

Table 3.6 Individual-Level Determinants of Days Worked on the Bihar Rural Employment Guarantee Scheme in Round 1

	Whole sample		Women		Men	
	(1)	(2)	(3)	(4)	(5)	(6)
Individual characteristics						
Age	0.308	0.328	3.980	8.086	0.743	0.564
Square of age	-0.001	-0.002	-0.030	-0.073	-0.006	-0.005
Education						
Literate (< class 5)	1.609	2.347	-5.208	-6.931	2.922	3.386
Class 5 pass (primary)	-5.156***	-2.506	-1.894	7.298	-4.711**	-2.707
Class 8 pass (middle)	-0.604	0.300	-5.034	4.552	1.318	1.757
Class 10 pass (secondary)	-0.167	2.857	—	—	1.142	5.952
Class 12 pass (higher secondary)	5.081	2.686	—	—	7.226	3.041
More than higher secondary	-9.384*	-6.105	—	—	-6.895	-0.734
Head of household	-5.493	-3.601	-44.591	-60.130	-6.487*	-1.219
Spouse of head	-10.204**	-9.113*	47.665	67.963	-8.987	-9.798
Married or gauna	-0.687	0.580	—	-0.719	-1.328	0.467
Widowed or divorced	-0.929	1.760	-13.929*	—	-5.573	-0.441
Gender (male = 1)	-6.153	-5.334	n.a.	n.a.	n.a.	n.a.
Female Pearlin scale	-0.111	-0.436	-2.163*	-3.035*	n.a.	n.a.
Male Pearlin scale	0.187	-0.404	n.a.	n.a.	0.235	0.037
Household characteristics						
ln (household size)	3.574	4.436	5.686	-1.289	9.941	8.275
ln (household size) squared	-1.363	-1.468	-4.202	-1.148	-2.963	-2.333

(Continued on the following page)

Table 3.6 (Continued)

	Whole sample		Women		Men	
	(1)	(2)	(3)	(4)	(5)	(6)
Share of male adults	-3.370	2.450	-19.415*	-7.780	3.161	7.304
Share of female adults	-7.328	-9.932*	-8.542	-24.652	-8.962	-6.241
Share of elderly	-7.434	-11.295	-8.146	-53.400***	-6.020	-3.314
Share of children younger than age 6	-1.113	-3.899	-17.825*	-4.188	-0.290	-0.624
Gender of head (male = 1)	7.033***	7.490*	-79.847	-110.771	7.614	6.008
Age of head (years)	-0.090	-0.843	-2.843	-6.458	-0.285	-0.918
Age of head, squared	0.000	0.009	0.015	0.051	0.003	0.011
Maximum education in household						
Literate (< Class 5)	-3.956**	-2.815	-1.243	4.056	-3.865*	-2.950
Class 5 pass (primary)	-2.914	-3.965**	-6.026	-9.079	-3.264	-3.353
Class 8 pass (middle)	-1.413	-2.205	-2.184	5.485	-2.934	-3.286
Class 10 pass (secondary)	-3.914	-4.018	-6.061	2.426	-5.549	-6.717*
Class 12 pass (higher secondary)	-2.190	-2.842	0.200	-4.071	-5.885	-6.584
Social group						
Scheduled Caste	0.970	6.312**	7.074	1.748	0.398	6.838*
Mahadalit	2.405	6.097	11.837	-0.099	0.425	4.261
Other Backward Class	-2.206	0.575	4.750	1.557	-2.902	0.720
Scheduled Tribe	-0.947	4.170	-7.901	-9.624	0.427	6.307
Hindu	0.261	-3.378	15.320*	2.830	-1.153	-3.697
Asset-house index	2.493***	1.947**	4.562*	4.675	2.524**	1.964**
Asset-house index squared	0.473*	0.398*	1.346*	0.988	0.370	0.322
Asset-house index cubed	-0.265**	-0.213**	-0.233	-0.314	-0.266**	-0.188*
Land owned except dwelling	3.889	3.952	-9.693	8.162	5.369	6.512**

	(1)	(2)	(3)	(4)	(5)	(6)
Land owned, squared	-0.821*	-0.689*	13.748	-5.601	-1.028**	-1.036**
BPL ration card	-0.366	-1.744	1.231	-9.671**	-0.859	-1.018
Know Mukhiya or Sarpanch	5.361***	3.209**	7.375*	4.868	4.747***	3.523*
Know ward member or panch	-3.630***	-2.180	2.909	8.408	-4.355**	-3.176*
Know program officer or block development officer	3.849	1.898	14.939	9.650	3.095	3.076
Know any political worker	-1.574	3.615	3.674	19.376	0.744	5.430
Household voted in panchayat election	2.584	4.510	10.489	24.080**	1.554	1.140
Household shock in past year						
Accident	-0.397	-1.255	-4.330	-3.554	1.324	-0.316
Illness	1.947	0.313	0.269	-4.095	4.249	2.148
Job loss	3.593	2.241	0.573	3.825	1.875	-0.719
Natural disaster	1.170	1.493	-0.413	1.173	0.756	1.761
Other	4.075	4.312	10.630	14.446	3.429	2.276
Men do casual work	-0.192	-2.405	-14.410***	-10.260*	5.550**	1.528
Women do casual work	3.313**	3.767**	4.035	-4.358	2.709*	4.281***
No male migration	3.065**	3.510***	8.250***	9.307*	2.229	2.725*
Regular-salaried worker in household	3.214	8.469	—	-0.245	4.788	11.252*
Constant	34.625**	18.930	85.583*	66.340	12.166	-1.320
Village fixed effects?	No	Yes	No	Yes	No	Yes
Observations	727	760	194	198	533	562
R^2	0.200	0.423	0.560	0.745	0.181	0.433

Source: Estimates based on the Bihar Rural Employment Guarantee Scheme (BREGS) survey.

Note: Data from round 1 on individuals ages 18–65. All specifications include controls for village characteristics or village fixed effects. The omitted education category is illiterate. Gauna is the point in an arranged marriage at which a wife begins to live with her husband. BPL = Below Poverty Line; n.a. = not applicable; — = not available.

*, **, and *** indicate significance at the 10 percent, 5 percent, and 1 percent levels, respectively, based on robust standard errors.

reported separately for men and women, using R1 data. Focusing on individuals (rather than the total household days of employment) allows us to explore the potential role of gender, and of other individual characteristics, in determining days of employment.

Household composition and gender effects are strong correlates of the intensity of participation, as measured by the number of days worked. Households with a male head get 7 more days on average than households with female heads, and the spouse (almost always a woman) of the household head gets 10 fewer days of employment than the head. Both these effects are consistent with the fact that women tend to have fewer days of employment than men. This effect is further reinforced by the fact that households with a greater share of adult women get fewer days, and (focusing on the regression for women) that women get fewer days of employment if the share of adult males in their household increases, or if men in their households tend to do casual labor. Similar to the patterns seen in table 3.5, we find that even after controlling for other household and village characteristics, richer households (based on the asset index or land ownership) get more days of employment, if they participate. Connections (to the Mukhiya or Sarpanch) matter, positively, to participation and to the intensity of participation. Caste and education attributes, or having a BPL card, are not strong or consistent correlates of days of employment, unlike their strong association with household participation. Household shocks are uncorrelated with days received. Finally, note that the predictive power of the regression (R^2) doubles when village fixed effects are added, suggesting that village-level effects are very important in explaining the intensity of employment.

In summary, we find clear signs that the scheme is reaching the poor, despite the rationing of work. The rationing process appears to rely heavily on indicators of poverty, meaning that poor households that do not have the typical profile of the poor tend to be rationed out. We also find signs that the poorest of the poor are underrepresented, as are households led by women or with a high share of female members. The rationing process is likely to undermine BREGS' insurance benefits. Consistent with that expectation, we find that neither participation nor the number of days of employment provided is responding to shocks.

Annex 3A

Table 3A.1 Participation and Demand for Work by Household Asset Group

	Participation			Demand for work		
	Richest 50 percent	Poorest 50 percent	Poorest 15 percent	Richest 50 percent	Poorest 50 percent	Poorest 15 percent
Household characteristics						
ln (household size)	0.114	0.187	−0.019	0.030	−0.013	0.062
ln (household size) squared	−0.030	−0.035	0.047	0.036	0.006	−0.023
Share of male adults	0.133**	0.264**	0.002	0.319***	0.138	0.012
Share of female adults	−0.079	0.038	−0.076	−0.134	−0.192**	−0.116
Share of elderly	0.006	−0.026	−0.087	−0.332*	−0.226*	−0.087
Share of children younger than age 6	0.066	0.067	0.094	0.002	−0.100	−0.131
Gender of head (male = 1)	0.024	0.121***	0.089	0.109**	0.079**	0.041
Age of head	0.003	0.010	−0.002	0.000	0.003	0.010*
Age of head squared	0.000	0.000	0.000	0.000	0.000	−0.000**
Maximum education in household						
Literate (< Class 5)	0.029	−0.022	0.020	−0.045	0.019	−0.027
Class 5 pass (primary)	−0.009	−0.038	−0.099	0.002	−0.037	−0.106
Class 8 pass (middle)	0.006	−0.048	−0.118	−0.106	−0.011	−0.007
Class 10 pass (secondary)	−0.044*	−0.163***	−0.172**	−0.105	−0.098*	0.053
Class 12 pass (higher secondary)	−0.044*	−0.033	0.083	−0.154*	−0.079	−0.475*
More than higher secondary	−0.055*	—	—	−0.061	0.012	−0.016
Social group						
Scheduled Caste	0.002	0.000	−0.118	0.083	0.080**	0.012
Mahadalit	0.127*	0.079	−0.106	0.088	0.105***	0.016

(Continued on the following page)

Table 3A.1 (Continued)

	Participation			Demand for work		
	Richest 50 percent	Poorest 50 percent	Poorest 15 percent	Richest 50 percent	Poorest 50 percent	Poorest 15 percent
Other Backward Class	-0.038	-0.075	-0.328***	-0.012	0.026	-0.067
Scheduled Tribe	0.039	-0.008	-0.209***	0.061	0.015	0.004
Hindu	0.056***	0.123***	0.181***	0.105*	0.070	0.054
Asset-house index	-0.007	0.178	-4.571	-0.056*	0.121	0.204
Asset-house index squared	-0.005	0.144	-1.598	-0.002	0.086	0.029
Asset-house index cubed	0.000	0.029	-0.177	0.001	0.016	0.001
Land owned except dwelling	-0.040**	-0.118	-0.566*	-0.043*	-0.022	0.151
Land owned squared	0.003***	0.019	0.109	0.003	-0.001	-0.110
BPL ration card	0.038**	0.076***	0.048	0.035	0.048**	0.077**
Know Mukhiya or Sarpanch	0.062**	0.041	0.058	0.016	-0.010	0.005
Know ward member or panch	-0.017	0.031	0.108	0.036	0.069***	0.068**
Know program officer or block development officer	0.135	0.443**	—	-0.044	—	—
Know any political worker	-0.010	0.114	0.032	-0.116	-0.026	-0.400*
Household voted in panchayat election	0.033	0.158***	0.226***	0.058	-0.018	-0.025
Household shock in past year						
Accident	0.042**	-0.019	0.010	0.074**	-0.010	0.049*
Illness	0.004	-0.005	-0.139*	-0.031	0.045	-0.007
Job loss	0.000	0.079	0.038	-0.019	0.006	-0.005
Natural disaster	-0.017	0.066	-0.021	-0.025	0.060**	-0.005
Other	0.017	-0.005	0.059	0.059	-0.044	-0.006

Men do casual work	0.194***	0.206***	0.194***	0.345***	0.190***	0.202***
Women do casual work	0.043**	0.110***	0.047	0.228***	0.084***	0.043
No male migration	0.016	0.037	-0.114**	-0.062*	0.011	-0.043
Regular-salaried worker in household	-0.056**	-0.048	0.005	-0.106	-0.232**	-0.291
Village and GP characteristics						
GP has a panchayat bhawan	0.013	-0.023	0.068	-0.009	-0.027	0.017
Mukhiya's age	0.000	-0.001	-0.004	0.000	0.002**	0.003*
Mukhiya lives in village	0.013	0.065*	-0.041	-0.010	-0.036	-0.082**
Mukhiya is male	0.002	0.007	-0.077	-0.046	-0.029	-0.067*
Mukhiya completed class 5	-0.001	0.006	0.006	-0.026	0.004	-0.047
Mukhiya is a farmer	0.022	0.000	-0.044	0.036	0.012	-0.001
Mukhiya held GP post in past	0.070**	0.096**	0.182**	-0.065	-0.032	0.034
Mukhiya family held a GP post	-0.012	0.008	-0.011	0.033	0.009	-0.017
Mukhiya is a contractor	0.043	0.234**	0.579***	-0.009	0.006	-0.142
Listing: share of SC households	-0.116**	0.047	-0.191	0.086	0.025	0.237***
Listing: share of OBC households	0.041	0.056	0.003	-0.072	-0.021	0.085
Village is predominantly Hindu	-0.019	0.046	-0.003	0.030	-0.010	-0.017
Village is electrified	-0.017	-0.030	0.036	-0.004	0.007	0.095**
Village has a pucca road	0.053**	0.038	0.012	-0.032	-0.032	-0.099**
Within 5 km of bus stop	-0.001	-0.062*	-0.027	-0.033	-0.055**	-0.031
Within 5 km of GP	-0.040	-0.107**	-0.140	-0.093*	-0.073***	-0.103***
Within 5 km of town	-0.029	0.000	-0.019	-0.021	-0.017	-0.142
Within 5 km of block headquarters	0.035	0.022	-0.010	0.015	0.006	-0.034
Post office in village	-0.003	0.043	-0.074	0.043	0.039	0.110***

(Continued on the following page)

Table 3A.1 (Continued)

	Participation			Demand for work		
	Richest 50 percent	Poorest 50 percent	Poorest 15 percent	Richest 50 percent	Poorest 50 percent	Poorest 15 percent
Nonagricultural enterprises within 5 km	−0.023	0.093*	0.079	0.055	0.045	0.138**
ln of mean asset index in village	0.021	0.026	0.098	0.172	0.141*	0.375***
Asset inequality in village	−0.103	−0.349	0.125	0.096	−0.664***	−0.612**
Listing: share of households with kutcha house	0.051	−0.085	0.013	0.095	−0.031	0.091
Listing: share of BPL households	0.035	0.159*	0.210	0.000	0.037	−0.032
Flood in village in past year	0.062***	0.005	0.123*	0.036	0.019	0.028
Drought in village in past year	−0.003	0.026	0.014	0.015	0.033	0.048
Any shock in past year	−0.067*	−0.032	−0.012	0.025	−0.037	−0.084***
Good relations among village social groups	−0.029	0.119***	0.188***	0.004	0.017	0.201
Self-help group in village	0.014	−0.052	0.036	0.014	0.016	0.088**
Civil society organization in village	0.045*	0.003	0.125*	−0.022	−0.005	−0.017
BREGS group in village	−0.045	0.073**	−0.009	0.082*	0.032	0.047
Other group in village	−0.003	−0.063	−0.079	0.029	0.061*	0.057
Observations	1,396	1,402	421	1,396	1,415	425
Pseudo R^2	0.329	0.198	0.272	0.329	0.275	0.425

Source: Estimates based on the Bihar Rural Employment Guarantee Scheme (BREGS) survey.

Note: Household, village, and selected GP variables observed in round 1. The omitted education category is illiterate. Probit marginal effects are reported. BPL = Below Poverty Line; GP = Gram Panchayat; km = kilometers; OBC = Other Backward Class; SC = Scheduled Caste; — = not available.

*, **, and *** indicate significance at the 10 percent, 5 percent, and 1 percent levels, respectively, based on robust standard errors.

Table 3A.2 Effects of Gram Panchayat Attributes on Participation by Asset Group

	All	Richest 50 percent	Poorest 15 percent
Safe to move around after dark?	0.067***	0.005	0.223***
PRS lives outside the GP at more than 5 km away	-0.009	0.005	-0.143*
PRS is Scheduled Caste or Mahadalit	-0.061*	-0.009	-0.288***
PRS is Scheduled Tribe	0.026	0.017	—
PRS is Other Backward Class	-0.019	-0.020	-0.245*
PRS is responsible for more than one GP	0.066**	0.016	0.178
Years PRS has spent at this GP post	0.023	0.009	0.011
GP has a shelf of works	0.044	0.014	0.249***
Adequate BREGS staff in past year	-0.042	-0.013	-0.129
Adequate BREGS funds in past year	0.021	0.002	-0.000
PRS and Mukhiya are same caste	0.006	0.011	0.061
Works hard to do at certain times of year	-0.008	-0.006	0.087
Observations	2,223	1,082	330
Pseudo R^2	0.266	0.358	0.344

Source: Estimates based on the Bihar Rural Employment Guarantee Scheme (BREGS) survey.

Note: Regressions also contains round 1 household, village, and other selected GP variables listed in table 3.5. Probit marginal effects are reported. GP = Gram Panchayat; km = kilometers; PRS = panchayat rozgar sewak; — = not available.

*, **, and *** indicate significance at the 10 percent, 5 percent, and 1 percent levels, respectively, based on robust standard errors.

Table 3A.3 Individual-Level Participation, Demand, and Assignment of Work

	Participation		Desired participation		Assignment of work	
	(1)	(2)	(3)	(4)	(5)	(6)
Individual characteristics						
Age	0.000	-0.001	0.002	0.002	0.000	-0.002
Square of age (/1,000)a	0.002	0.003	-0.018	-0.026	0.008	0.013
Education						
Literate (< class 5)	0.006	0.013	-0.095***	-0.107***	0.022	0.038
Class 5 pass (primary)	-0.007	-0.010	-0.017	-0.007	-0.015	-0.020
Class 8 pass (middle)	-0.024*	-0.017	-0.115**	-0.096**	-0.028	-0.015
Class 10 pass (secondary)	-0.039***	-0.050***	-0.050	-0.093**	-0.072**	-0.086***
Class 12 pass (higher secondary)	-0.024	-0.017	-0.058	-0.058	-0.034	-0.008
More than higher secondary	0.944***	0.938***	-0.006	-0.053	0.859***	0.849***
Household head	0.010	0.034	0.050	0.054	0.025	0.067
Spouse of head	-0.041*	-0.016	-0.022	-0.012	-0.081*	-0.036
Married or gauna	-0.048	-0.040	-0.082	-0.070	-0.075	-0.064
Widowed or divorced	-0.010	0.006	-0.107	-0.054	-0.026	0.003
Male gender	0.082***	0.117***	0.477***	0.535***	0.123***	0.181***
Male Pearlin scale	-0.000	-0.001	-0.010	-0.012	0.000	-0.001
Female Pearlin scale	-0.003	-0.004	0.022***	0.024***	-0.008	-0.009
Household characteristics						
ln (household size)	0.050	0.040	-0.015	-0.003	0.123	0.073
ln (household size) squared	-0.018	-0.016	0.004	0.009	-0.044	-0.028

Share of male adults	0.014	0.001	−0.097	−0.056	0.039	0.019
Share of female adults	−0.080**	−0.078*	−0.119	−0.145	−0.139*	−0.144*
Share of elderly	−0.040	−0.128	−0.185	−0.092	−0.064	−0.278
Share of children younger than age 6	0.017	−0.002	−0.028	−0.007	0.040	0.003
Male head	0.007	−0.004	−0.051	−0.088**	0.010	−0.010
Age of head	0.000	0.000	−0.004	−0.002	0.000	0.001
Age of head, squared (/1,000)[a]	−0.004	0.002	0.026	0.005	−0.007	−0.001
Maximum education in household						
Literate (< Class 5)	0.001	−0.006	0.037	0.029	0.000	−0.007
Class 5 pass (primary)	−0.016	−0.014	−0.005	−0.019	−0.031	−0.019
Class 8 pass (middle)	−0.002	−0.007	−0.016	−0.008	−0.002	−0.013
Class 10 pass (secondary)	−0.018	−0.007	−0.065	−0.053	−0.031	−0.018
Class 12 pass (higher secondary)	−0.018	−0.029	−0.074	−0.126**	−0.012	−0.027
More than higher secondary	−0.098***	−0.101***	−0.069	−0.128*	−0.180***	−0.186***
Social group						
Scheduled Caste	0.003	0.039	0.165***	0.187***	−0.015	0.037
Mahadalit	0.084**	0.255***	0.226***	0.238***	0.129**	0.314***
Other Backward Class	−0.031*	−0.001	0.065*	0.073**	−0.066**	−0.020
Scheduled Tribe	0.080*	0.092*	0.093	0.174***	0.122*	0.113
Hindu	0.037***	0.017	0.072**	0.092**	0.068***	0.034
Asset-house index	−0.007***	−0.007***	−0.038***	−0.040***	−0.008*	−0.007
Asset-house index cubed (/1,000)[a]	—	—	0.254	0.268	—	—
Land owned	−0.019*	−0.026**	−0.042***	−0.057***	−0.033*	−0.046**
BPL ration card	0.028***	0.031***	0.059***	0.053***	0.046***	0.047***
Know Mukhiya or Sarpanch	0.020**	0.019*	0.002	0.020	0.036*	0.036*
Know ward member or panch	−0.001	0.001	0.051**	0.041*	−0.013	−0.010

(Continued on the following page)

Table 3A.3 (Continued)

	Participation		Desired participation		Assignment of work	
	(1)	(2)	(3)	(4)	(5)	(6)
Know program officer or block development officer	0.037	0.029	-0.004	0.008	0.103	0.120
Know any political worker	0.038	0.047	-0.021	-0.016	0.084	0.100
Household voted in panchayat election	0.032***	0.044***	0.006	0.014	0.065***	0.090***
Household shock in past year						
Accident	0.011	0.007	0.021	0.012	0.014	0.008
Illness	-0.014	-0.005	0.028	0.030	-0.034	-0.021
Job loss	0.032*	0.040**	-0.024	-0.028	0.065**	0.074**
Natural disaster	0.008	0.010	0.014	0.019	0.007	0.005
Other	0.006	0.005	0.037	0.007	0.017	0.012
Men do casual work	0.068***	0.083***	0.214***	0.234***	0.082***	0.108***
Women do casual work	0.060***	0.062***	0.159***	0.183***	0.098***	0.092***
No male migration	0.009	0.015*	-0.036*	-0.033*	0.022	0.027*
Regular-salaried worker in household	-0.051***	-0.030*	-0.187***	-0.166***	-0.088**	-0.032
Village and GP characteristics						
GP has a panchayat bhawan	-0.005		-0.002		-0.007	
Mukhiya's age	0.000		0.000		0.000	
Mukhiya lives in village	0.006		-0.004		0.020	
Mukhiya is male	-0.011		-0.064***		-0.012	
Mukhiya completed class 5	-0.021**		0.006		-0.038*	
Mukhiya is a farmer	-0.016		0.011		-0.025	

Mukhiya held GP post in the past	0.037***	-0.018	0.073***
Mukhiya's family held a GP post	-0.006	0.002	-0.012
Mukhiya is a contractor	0.054	0.073	0.072
Listing: share of SC households	-0.011	0.193***	-0.045
Listing: share of OBC households	0.011	-0.095*	0.026
Village is predominantly Hindu	0.018*	0.047	0.032
Village is electrified	-0.025***	0.013	-0.050***
Village has a pucca road	0.016*	-0.021	0.032*
Within 5 km of bus stop	-0.012	-0.044*	-0.024
Within 5 km of GP	-0.039**	-0.159***	-0.052**
Within 5 km of town	0.004	-0.004	0.007
Within 5 km of block headquarters	0.006	0.034	0.013
Post office in village	0.019**	0.023	0.032*
Nonagricultural enterprises within 5 km	0.013	0.086**	0.025
ln of mean asset index in village	0.023	0.210***	0.016
Asset inequality in village	-0.141**	-0.567***	-0.160
Listing: share households with kutcha house	0.010	0.187***	0.009
Listing: share BPL households	0.067***	-0.031	0.131***
Flood in village in past year	0.003	0.028	0.009
Drought in village in past year	0.013	0.051**	0.022

(Continued on the following page)

Table 3A.3 (Continued)

	Participation		Desired participation		Assignment of work	
	(1)	(2)	(3)	(4)	(5)	(6)
Any shock in past year	-0.006		-0.051		-0.011	
Good relations among village social groups	0.010		0.009		0.018	
Self-help group in village	-0.026***		-0.007		-0.055***	
Civil society organization in village	0.025**		0.017		0.045**	
BREGS group in village	0.016*		0.056**		0.017	
Other group in village	-0.018		0.038		-0.038	
Safe to move around after dark	0.031***		0.086***		0.060***	
Village fixed effects?	No	Yes	No	Yes	No	Yes
Observations	4,057	4,131	4,063	4,699	2,965	3,076
R^2	0.280	0.319	0.304	0.355	0.226	0.270

Source: Estimates based on the Bihar Rural Employment Guarantee Scheme (BREGS) survey.

Note: Individual-level regressions on round 1 data for individuals ages 18–65. If individual reports not having heard of BREGS, observations are set to missing. The omitted education category is illiterate. Gauna is the point in an arranged marriage at which a wife begins to live with her husband. BPL = Below Poverty Line; GP = Gram Panchayat; km = kilometers; OBC = Other Backward Class; SC = Scheduled Caste; — = not available.

a. Variables rescaled to reveal at least one significant figure for their coefficients.

*, **, and *** indicate significance at the 10 percent, 5 percent, and 1 percent levels, respectively, based on robust standard errors.

Notes

1. *Pucca* refers to a solid, permanent, or proper structure and is often contrasted to *kutcha,* meaning crude or temporary. A pucca roof is made of materials such as timber, slate, corrugated iron, or the like. The alternative, a kutcha roof, is made of materials such as bamboo or thatch.

2. As mentioned in chapter 1, four broad categories are typically used to classify households into social groups—Scheduled Castes (SCs), Scheduled Tribes (STs), Other Backward Classes (OBCs), and others. In Bihar, Mahadalits, comprising the poorest and most disadvantaged among SCs, have been notified as a separate subcategory by the state government.

3. See chapter 1 for an explanation of the targeting differential.

4. As in chapter 1, for consumption groups, the targeting differential is defined as the difference between the BREGS participation rates of the poor and the nonpoor. For social groups, we estimate it as the difference between the weighted average participation rate of SCs, STs, OBCs, and Mahadalits, and the participation rates for "others." Tables 1.4 and 1.5 report the all-India results.

5. The asset index is the first principal component of an index that combines data on household ownership of durables and dwelling characteristics as a proxy for household wealth (following Filmer and Pritchett [2001]). As in the corresponding figure in chapter 1 (figure 1.5 for all-India results), the x-axis is the percentile of the wealth distribution.

6. The controls are entered linearly, giving a "partial linear regression" in which the wealth effect is nonparametric.

7. These parametric functional forms appeared to offer a reasonably good approximation over the bulk of the data to the nonparametric functional forms shown in figure 3.1, though naturally they still have less flexibility in representing the data.

8. Fewer than 1 percent of households were neither Hindu nor Muslim.

9. The Mukhiya, in Bihar, is the elected leader of the GP and is responsible for implementation of development programs at the panchayat level. The Sarpanch is the elected leader of the panchayat judicial body. The BDO is a civil servant responsible for the administration of a block. GPs are typically divided into a number of wards, each of which is represented by the elected ward member in the Gram Panchayat body.

10. BPL cards, used to target a number of social assistance schemes, are meant for poor households that are identified based on a periodic BPL Census. Note that we refer to the combined set of BPL, Antyodaya, and Annapoorna cardholders as BPL households (see note to table 3.1).

11. The explanatory power of the regression models increases with the inclusion of village fixed effects or village characteristics compared with specifications with household characteristics only.

12. We measure inequality of wealth within a village using the mean log deviation from the village household mean of the asset index. This is a standard inequality measure, known to have a number of desirable properties.

13. Galasso and Ravallion (2005) report such an effect of land inequality on the performance of an antipoverty program in Bangladesh.

14. The Pearlin Mastery scale is a measure of the extent to which individuals perceive themselves to be in control of factors that affect their lives (Pearlin and Schooler 1978; Pearlin and others 1981).

References

Filmer, Deon, and Lant Pritchett. 2001. "Estimating Wealth Effects without Expenditure Data—Or Tears: An Application to Educational Enrollments in States of India." *Demography* 38 (1): 115–32.

Galasso, Emanuela, and Martin Ravallion. 2005. "Decentralized Targeting of an Anti-Poverty Program." *Journal of Public Economics* 85: 705–27.

Liu, Yanyan, and Klaus Deininger. 2013. "Welfare and Poverty Impacts of India's National Rural Employment Guarantee Scheme: Evidence from Andhra Pradesh." Policy Research Working Paper No. 6543, World Bank, Washington, DC.

Pearlin, Leonard, Elizabeth Menaghan, Morton Lieberman, and Joseph Mullan. 1981. "The Stress Process." *Journal of Health and Social Behavior* 22 (4): 337–56.

Pearlin, Leonard, and Carmi Schooler. 1978. "The Structure of Coping." *Journal of Health and Social Behaviour* 19: 2–21.

4

Wages

The National Rural Employment Guarantee Act (the Act) stipulates a minimum wage rate for the Mahatma Gandhi National Rural Employment Guarantee Scheme (MGNREGS). In 2009, an all-India uniform wage of 100 rupees (Rs) per day was notified for the scheme, but adjusted subsequently for state-specific inflation. Five main reasons indicate why the actual net income gain received by workers may end up being less than these stipulated wages for the scheme:

• Workers may be unable to meet the productivity norms required for earning the minimum wage if the norms are very stringent or if the scheme attracts workers with lower-than-average physical ability.

• There may be delays in payment (random or purposeful).

• Corruption may be present, whereby local leaders or officials take a cut, possibly as a "fee" for their services, such as providing wages in advance or collecting wages against "ghost workers." Or there may be collusion between officials and village residents such that wages are collected and shared against work not done.

• There may be exploitation stemming from the monopsony power of the village leader acting as a contractor.

• There may be forgone income, that is, some opportunity cost to the worker from some forgone economic activity.

This chapter examines wages paid by the Bihar Rural Employment Guarantee Scheme (BREGS): specifically their levels and trends, in relation to the stipulated wage rate for the scheme, the wages paid in the casual labor market, and the total wage bill as reported in the administrative data. The next chapter focuses on forgone income.

Payment of Wages

According to the scheme's guidelines, wages are to be paid either on a time- or piece-rate basis. The time rates are based on the scheme's notified state daily minimum wages, and the implementing agencies are supposed to ensure that productivity norms are met. An individual worker who does not attain the productivity norms should be paid less than the scheme wage. During the survey period, Bihar's notified MGNREGS wage started at Rs 89 per day, rising to Rs 102 on June 16, 2009, and to Rs 114 on May 18, 2010. The piece-rate wages are based on the rural district-level Schedule of Rates (SoR), which specifies the wages to be paid based on the type of work done. The productivity norms in the SoRs are supposed to be such that an able-bodied worker is capable of earning the scheme-notified wages.

Several states have modified the SoRs specifically for the MGN-REGS following detailed time and motion studies. We found that, although different SoRs exist for different parts of Bihar, scheme functionaries typically apply a single set of productivity norms. The qualitative research also suggested differences between workers and scheme functionaries in their understanding of the SoRs.

In Bihar, qualitative research and the BREGS survey suggest that the time-rate system is common (see also Pankaj 2008). As noted, in this case, too, scheme functionaries are required to ensure that productivity norms are being met by measuring the work done at the worksite. Yet, nearly half of the men and women workers interviewed reported seeing no one measuring work at the most recent worksite at which they worked. When measurement was undertaken, among those aware of the process, the majority (83 percent of the male and 75 percent of the female workers interviewed) reported equal payments to all workers at the site. These equal payments indicate that wages were estimated on the basis of the work done at the entire worksite rather than that done by individual groups based on measurement against productivity norms. It is of interest that when we asked Mukhiyas why workers reported not being paid the stipulated BREGS wage, they typically responded that workers had not performed to the SoR standards and hence were not owed the stipulated wage. They also noted that workers did not understand this.

Since April 2008, in an effort to promote financial inclusion of the poor and to improve transparency in wage payments, all wages are supposed to be paid through beneficiary bank or post office accounts rather than as direct cash payouts.[1] Practice, based on responses to our survey, is unclear. Panchayat rozgar sewaks (PRSs) report that the majority of wage payments are made through beneficiary bank or post office accounts. In contrast, workers report that wage payments are often made in cash at the worksite. For 2009/10, the time period covered by round 2 of the BREGS survey (R2), more than half of the workers interviewed—52 percent of women and 56 percent of men—reported receiving wages in cash from the Mukhiya, the contractor, the mate, or another official at the most recent worksite at which they worked. In round 1 of the BREGS survey (R1), the shares were 78 percent and 64 percent for female and male workers, respectively. Thus, there is evidence of a decline over time, particularly for women, but the share of total workers getting cash at worksites remains high. This may reflect, in some cases, partial initial cash payments to workers by the Mukhiya while funds are being transferred to worker accounts.

Mukhiyas or their spouses or close family members often act as money lenders as well as contractors, making advance payments to workers.[2] The reasons given for them doing so include delays in work measurement, delays in obtaining post office or bank accounts, and delays in the flow of funds to the workers' post office or bank accounts.[3] In principle, the scheme should move toward financial inclusion and full reliance on accounts with financial institutions rather than cash. But practice is still a long way from that ideal. Weaknesses in the flow of funds or administration of accounts, leading to delays in payment, create scope for the Mukhiya or other intermediaries to profit by being able to provide advance cash payments to needy workers.[4] Fieldwork for this study indicated that some local officials also take a cut from the wages due the worker, possibly in the process of making advance payments.

There are many qualitative reports from the field of partial payments and long delays in receiving wages owed. Our survey corroborates these findings. We asked sample households whether BREGS participants had received wages owed in full. Some 72 percent of our households' female participants in R1 and 67 percent in R2 had been paid in full by the time of the survey, while this was the case for 66 percent and 72 percent of participating men. Women who had not been fully paid were still owed 58 percent and 75 percent of wages, on average, in R1 and R2, respectively. Unpaid men were still waiting for 64 percent and 57 percent of their earned wages. The amount owed is likely to decline with increases in time since participation. The data confirm that the share of wages received is higher for participants for whom more time has elapsed since they participated in BREGS. This can be seen in figure 4.1, which plots the share of total wages owed that were actually received by months since the work was completed for the sample of participants who have not received their full wages. The mean share of wages paid rises with

Figure 4.1 Delays in Bihar Rural Employment Guarantee
Scheme Wage Payments

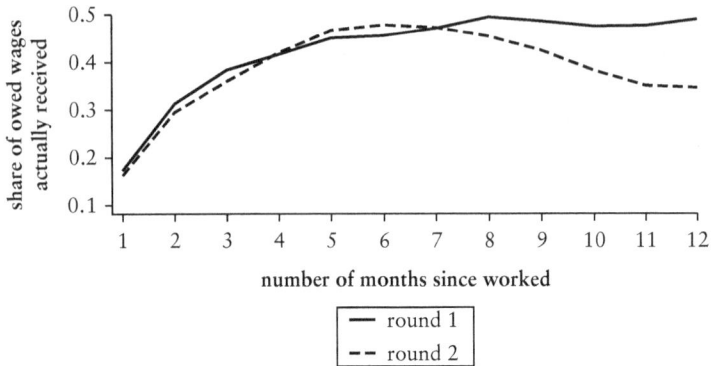

Source: Estimates based on the Bihar Rural Employment Guarantee Scheme
(BREGS) survey.
Note: Based on Block 1 from the individual questionnaire. Sample restricted to
participants who have not been fully paid BREGS wages owed to them.

time up to six months, then stabilizes (R1) or falls (R2). However,
even at its peak, the share of wages received among those receiving
less than they felt they were due was no more than 50 percent.

Advocates have hoped that the scheme would reduce the exploitation of rural workers in local labor markets that stems from the
labor market power of large farmers and contractors. This might
have been wishful thinking given that the local leaders in charge of
implementing the scheme often overlap with the set of people who
have been employers in the past. For example, the Mukhiya, acting
as a contractor directly or via a close ally, can maintain similarly
exploitative relations in implementing the scheme. The scheme offi-
cially bans contractors, but we found that they are common, with
half or more of the responding workers reporting that contractors
were present at worksites (chapter 8).

The next section discusses how the actual wages reported by
workers in the survey compare with the stipulated wages for BREGS.

Wages Received by Households

The BREGS survey includes two sources of information on wages
received. The household questionnaire (Block 23) asks about wage
earnings and days worked as casual labor in the week preceding the
survey for each adult household member.[5] It differentiates between
public works and other (agricultural or nonagricultural) casual wage

work, but does not differentiate between BREGS and other public works employment. Wage earnings include cash payments and the value of in-kind payments. In addition, for each work episode, the questionnaire records information separately on wages that were owed and wages that had already been received at the time of the interview. We expect recall to be excellent, but the data have the disadvantage of covering employment for one week and thus provide relatively few observations.[6] Because the survey was fielded during May, June, and July, wage information from this block pertains only to these months.

The second source of information about wages is from the individual-level questionnaire (Block 1) which asked (up to) one male and one female adult in each household about their involvement in public works, including type (whether BREGS or other), days worked, wages owed, and wages received, separately for each episode of public works employment during the past year. These data have already been referred to above with respect to delays in wages paid. In addition to providing details specifically about BREGS, this source has the advantage of giving us far more observations. The drawback is that there may be mismeasurement caused by the long recall period and by the fact that this does not give wages for non–public works (non-PW) work.[7] Given that each source has different pros and cons, we make use of both.

Wages in the Last Week

Table 4.1 provides summary statistics on casual labor wages reported for the week preceding the survey. In R1, median public works wages were nearly 30 percent higher than the prevailing casual wage. Wages were higher for men than for women in both segments of the labor market, but for women, PW paid much better than the private sector. Between 2009 and 2010, average PW wages maintained value in real terms (increasing by 14.6 percent in nominal terms, compared with a 12 percent rate of inflation),[8] but the gap between public works and labor market wages narrowed because mean casual wages rose by 21 percent, and median casual wages rose by 43 percent. Women, however, still earned significantly higher wages under BREGS in R2 than in the casual labor market ($t = 3.91$ in R1 and $t = 4.85$ in R2).

Figure 4.2 and table 4.2 provide a closer look at PW and market wages for casual labor in relation to the stipulated BREGS wage, and their evolution. First, it can be seen that wages owed, as reported by participants on the scheme, are lower than the stipulated BREGS wage rate (top panels of figure 4.2). Summary statistics and statistical

Table 4.1 Daily Wage Rate for the Week before Interview
rupees

		Mean	Standard deviation	Median	Number of observations
Round 1					
All	Public works	82.7	27.4	89.0	54
	Other casual labor	72.2	31.2	70.0	1,031
Men	Public works	85.8	25.2	89.0	41
	Other casual labor	79.1	29.2	80.0	815
Women	Public works	73.0	32.6	80.0	13
	Other casual labor	46.0	23.6	45.0	216
Round 2					
All	Public works	94.8	22.3	100.0	118
	Other casual labor	87.2	42.0	100.0	796
Men	Public works	99.4	18.2	100.0	75
	Other casual labor	97.9	39.3	100.0	574
Women	Public works	86.8	26.6	100.0	43
	Other casual labor	59.4	35.2	50.0	222

Source: Estimates based on the Bihar Rural Employment Guarantee Scheme survey.
Note: Based on Block 23. We treat wages of more than Rs 200 or less than Rs 10 per day as missing values. Wage data are in nominal terms, and reported as unweighted means and medians from the sample.

tests reported in table 4.2 show that, on average, workers received Rs 10 less per day than the stipulated wage for much of the recall period. Note that this gap is not due to payment delays, because the wages summarized are total wages *owed* to the individual, not the amount actually received by the time of the survey interview.

Second, the evidence about whether BREGS has been placing pressure on the private labor market for unskilled labor is not clear. On the one hand, comparing the average wage gaps in R1 and R2 shows that market wages started catching up with PW wages in R2, consistent with labor market tightening, possibly *because of* the scheme. On the other hand, non-PW wages do not respond in a predictable pattern to changes in the BREGS stipulated wage. In R1, other (non-PW) wages did not rise after the BREGS wage was increased; and in R2, non-PW wages actually fell even as the BREGS wage was raised during the reporting period. (Note that these are nominal wage rates, so the trend increase in wages in part reflects inflation.)

Wage trends do show that the gap between non-PW and PW wages narrowed, though more for men than for women, even though women began in R1 with a larger gap between the two sets of wages.

Figure 4.2 Wages over Time

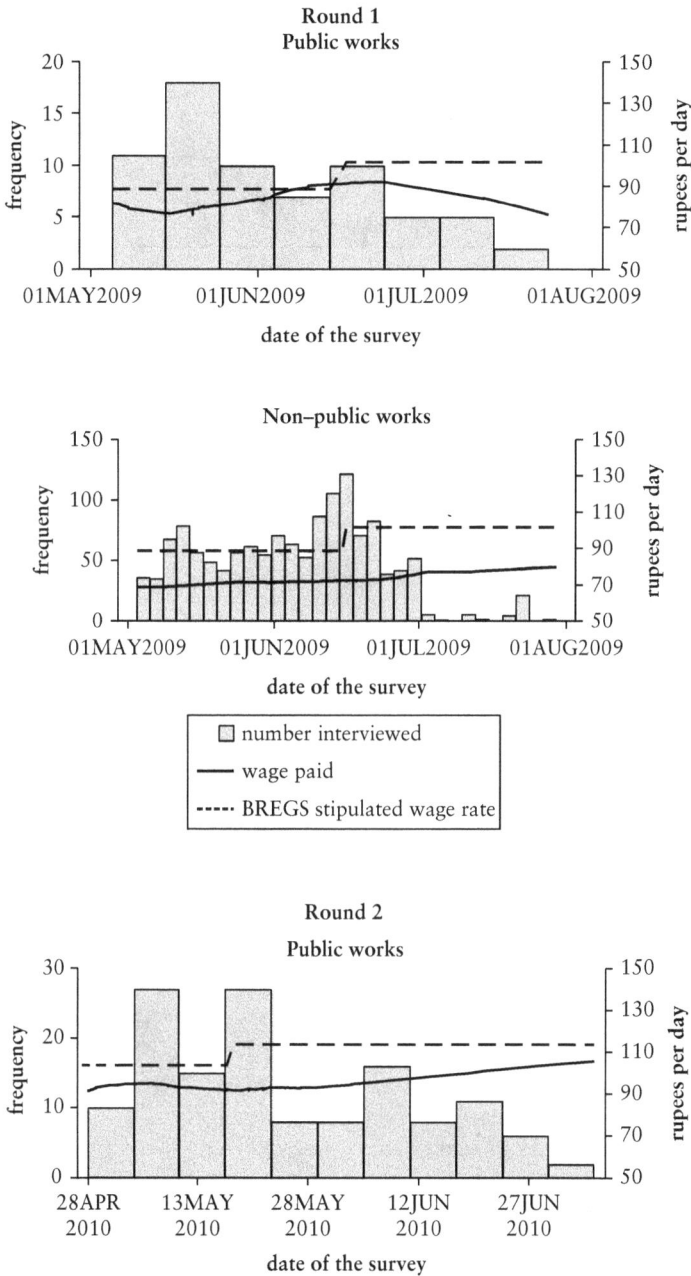

Round 1
Public works

Non–public works

Round 2
Public works

(*Continued on the following page*)

Figure 4.2 (Continued)

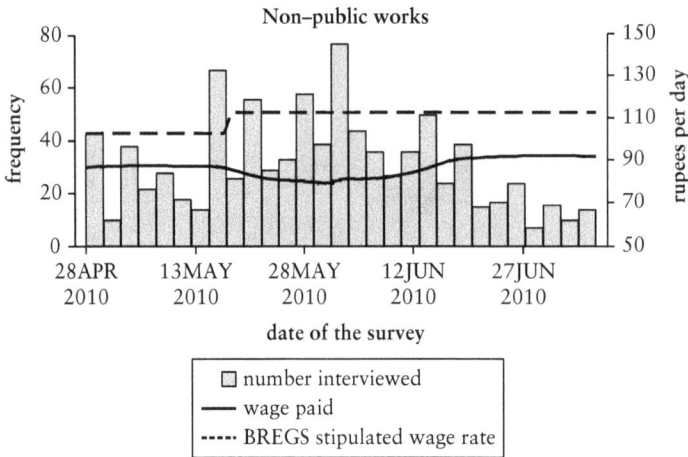

Non–public works

Source: Estimates based on the Bihar Rural Employment Guarantee Scheme (BREGS) survey.

Note: The figure reports data on wages owed, based on Block 23 for casual labor done in the week preceding the survey. Wages are nominal.

The view that the scheme has tightened up the labor market and increased wage rates is also hard to reconcile with the evidence of considerable rationing of BREGS work (chapter 2). However, recall that there is far more rationing in some states than in others. The scheme may be having larger impacts on private sector wages in states with less rationing.

Wages in the Past Year from the Public Works Module

Turning to the second source of data on wages on BREGS from the survey, figure 4.3 plots the mean wage rate by month for both men and women based on Block 1. The figure also gives total days of work, and it identifies the survey periods.

There is a marked seasonality in days of employment, although perhaps exaggerated by recall problems. As before, we see a persistent absolute gap between the stipulated wage rate for BREGS and the wage actually reported by respondents. The absolute gap is roughly unchanged over time. There is some sign of convergence in male and female wages, but this outcome is possibly deceptive, given that there were very few observations in the early months, when the

Table 4.2 Average Wage Rates before and after Increases in the Bihar Rural Employment Guarantee Scheme Stipulated Wage

		Round 1			Round 2		
		Public works wage	Non-public works wage	Stipulated BREGS wage	Public works wage	Non-public works wage	Stipulated BREGS wage
Before increase of stipulated wage	Mean	80.7	71.4	89.0	93.8	91.5	104.0
	Standard deviation	20.4	30.6	n.a.	24.8	39.8	n.a.
	Observations	46	946	n.a.	54	226	n.a.
t-test: Hypothesis: Mean actual wage = stipulated wage (probability)		−2.8 (0.008)	−17.8 (0.000)	n.a. n.a.	−3.0 (0.004)	−4.7 (0.000)	n.a. n.a.
After increase of stipulated wage	Mean	92.2	74.7	102.0	95.5	83.9	114.0
	Standard deviation	32.8	30.1	n.a.	24.3	39.2	n.a.
	Observations	20	377	n.a.	81.0	649.0	n.a.
t-test: Hypothesis: Mean actual wage = stipulated wage (probability)		−1.3 (0.199)	−17.6 (0.000)	n.a. n.a.	−6.9 (0.000)	−19.6 (0.000)	n.a. n.a.

Source: Estimates based on the Bihar Rural Employment Guarantee Scheme (BREGS) survey.

Note: The wage was increased to 102 rupees (Rs) on June 16, 2009, in round 1, then to Rs 104, and to Rs 114 on May 18, 2010, in round 2. *T*-tests use only daily wages greater than Rs 10 per day and lower than Rs 200 per day. The number of observations differs from that in table 4.1 because in this table we use observations even when a valid gender identifier is missing and drop those with missing survey dates. Wage data are unweighted. n.a. = not applicable.

Figure 4.3 Evolution of Bihar Rural Employment Guarantee Scheme Wages and Days Worked over the Entire Survey Period

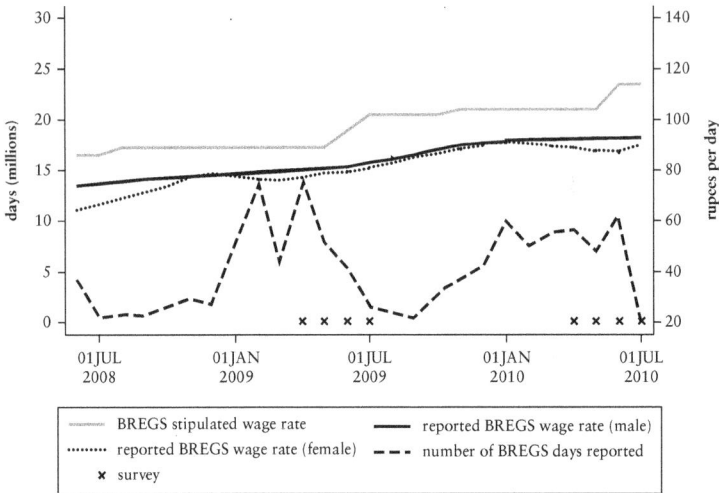

Source: Estimates based on the Bihar Rural Employment Guarantee Scheme (BREGS) survey.

Note: Based on Block 1 of the BREGS survey, individual questionnaire with recall over past year. Reported wage data are household-weighted wages owed to the worker.

female wage was lower. The longer recall periods required by this source of wage data also raise doubts about the reliability of the early data points.

Wages from the National Sample Survey 2009/10

A third source of wage data for Bihar is the National Sample Survey (NSS) for 2009/10. Table 4.3 gives estimates of the mean and median wage rate by subrounds, essentially spanning the period between R1 and R2 of the BREGS survey. Here too we see an increase in agricultural wages, notably between subrounds 2 and 3, corresponding to the last quarter of 2009 and first quarter of 2010, respectively. BREGS activity typically picks up in the first quarter of every year, so this agricultural wage increase does coincide with BREGS activity. However, also note that there was an even steeper increase in manual nonagricultural wages during the year.

Table 4.3 Daily Wages for Farm and Nonfarm Casual Labor in Bihar from the 2009/10 National Sample Survey, by Subround

rupees

| | Agricultural work | | | | Manual nonagricultural | |
| | All operations | | Cultivation | | | |
Subround	Mean	Median	Mean	Median	Mean	Median
1. July–Sept 2009	74.8	77.5	72.4	73.3	86.9	80.0
2. Oct–Dec 2009	72.8	80.0	67.6	70.0	103.4	95.0
3. Jan–Mar 2010	84.6	80.0	80.2	80.0	97.1	90.0
4. Apr–June 2010	86.0	81.4	78.9	80.0	120.7	100.0
Total	79.0	80.0	74.4	76.7	100.2	90.0
Percentage change between subrounds 1 and 4	15	5	9	9	39	25

Source: Calculations from National Sample Survey 66th round.

Comparing PW and Non-PW Wages for BREGS Participants, Excess Demanders, and the Rest

Figure 4.4 gives the density functions for daily casual work wage rates for R1 and R2 (in the week preceding the survey) for public works (PW) and three comparators: (1) the non-PW wages for BREGS participants; (2) the non-PW wages for the excess demanders; and (3) the non-PW wages of the others (the "rest"). The wage rates were calculated by taking total wage earnings by type of work in the week before the interview and dividing by the total number of days of such work reported.

Two points are worthy of note. First, as already discussed, PW wages are higher than other casual wages earned by BREGS participants, for both men and women. We can reject the null hypothesis of equality between the PW wage and the non-PW wage distributions for both men and women in R1 (probability less than 0.0005 in both cases). This situation is true for other comparator groups as well: the people who said they wanted work on BREGS but did not get it (the excess demanders) were typically earning less than those working on PW.

Second, the difference between PW wages and casual wages earned by other (nonparticipant) workers does not appear to be due to different abilities of the workers who are participating in PW.

Figure 4.4 Density of Daily Casual Wages, by Bihar Rural Employment Guarantee Scheme Participation Status

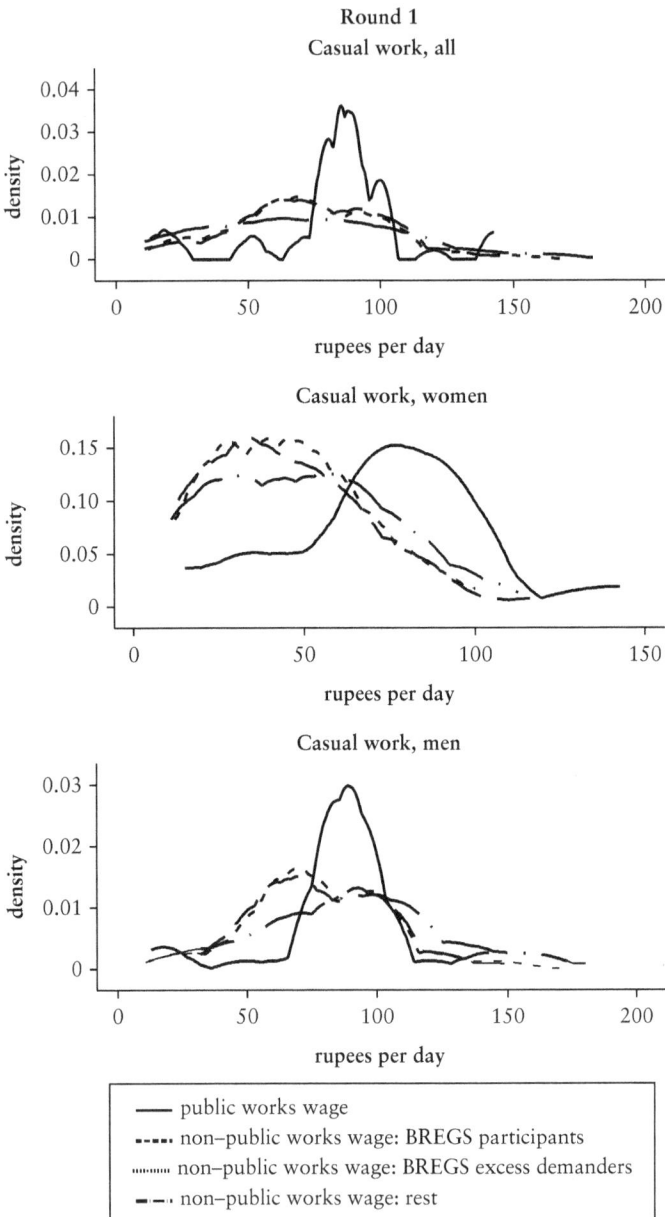

Round 1

Casual work, all

Casual work, women

Casual work, men

—— public works wage
▪▪▪▪▪ non–public works wage: BREGS participants
▪▪▪▪▪▪ non–public works wage: BREGS excess demanders
▪ ▪ ▪ non–public works wage: rest

(Continued on the following page)

Figure 4.4 (Continued)

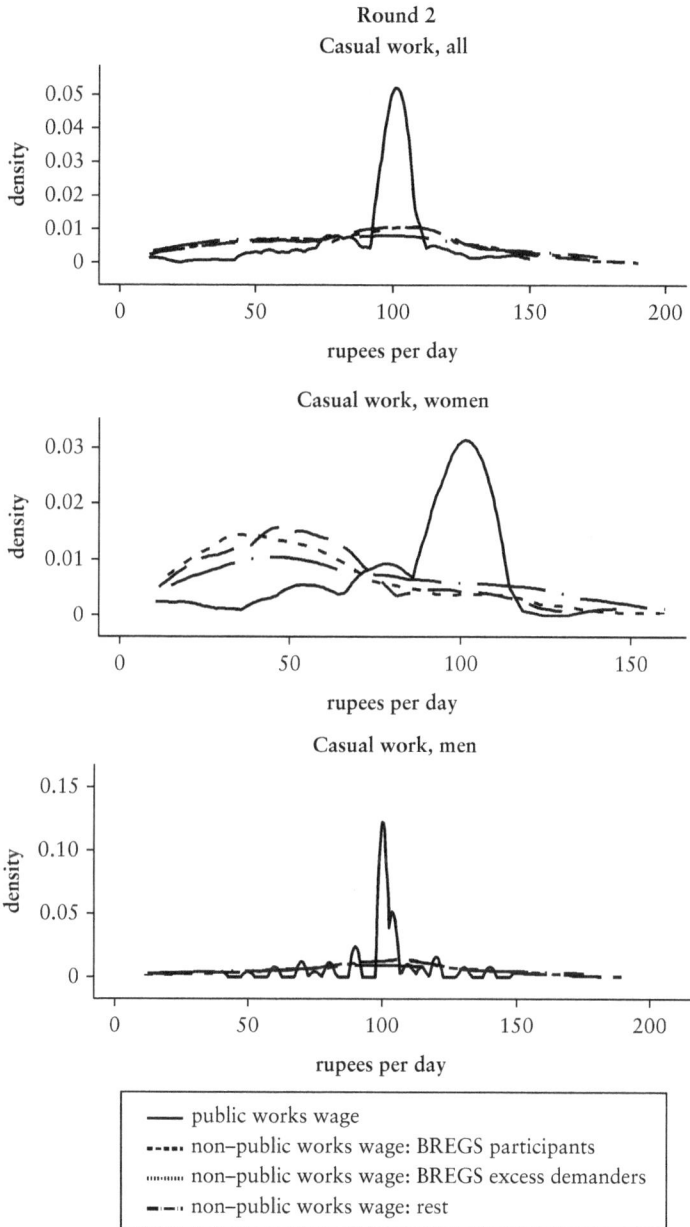

Round 2
Casual work, all

Casual work, women

Casual work, men

——— public works wage
▪▪▪▪▪ non–public works wage: BREGS participants
▪▪▪▪▪▪ non–public works wage: BREGS excess demanders
▪—▪ non–public works wage: rest

Source: Estimates based on the Bihar Rural Employment Guarantee Scheme (BREGS) survey.
Note: Based on Block 23 and questions about casual work done in the last week. Wage data are unweighted.

It could be possible that piece work schedules such as used by BREGS reward physically stronger workers. However, this explanation does not seem to hold, given that we also see that BREGS participants were earning significantly less in non-PW work than in PW. In fact, there is no statistically significant difference between the wage distributions of the three comparators for either women or men.[9] And there is essentially no difference between the wage distribution for the "excess demanders" and the non-PW wage distribution of those who also do PW. Those who get the jobs on PW are essentially drawn from the same wage distribution as those who do not get that work, but want it. This is again suggestive of unmet demand for work stemming from some form of rationing in the assignment of jobs on PW.

Impact of BREGS on Wages

If BREGS provided an unconditional guarantee of work to anyone who wanted it at a wage equal to or above the wage for alternative work, the BREGS wage rate would become binding on the casual (farm and nonfarm) labor market. Nobody would be willing to work at less than the BREGS wage rate. Lags may be present in the adjustment process, but we would expect to see casual wages catching up to BREGS wages.[10]

There are intuitive reasons to doubt whether BREGS would be putting upward pressure on wages in the casual labor market. The guarantee is only conditional, up to 100 days, and in practice the work is confined largely to the lean season, when there is less likelihood of a spillover effect on agricultural wages.[11] But, probably more important, chapter 1 has shown for all of India and chapter 2 for Bihar that there is substantial unmet demand for work on the scheme even among those with fewer than 100 days of work. With so much rationing, the scheme driving up other wages in Bihar does not seem plausible. The option value of BREGS in wage bargaining in the casual labor market depends critically on employers believing that the scheme is available. The bargaining value might not require a strict guarantee of employment under BREGS; the scheme might still help workers bargain up their non-BREGS wages as long as there is a reasonably good chance of obtaining BREGS work. However, it is hard to believe that this would be the case with the degree of rationing in BREGS jobs observed in the survey data. We cannot rule out the possibility that the scheme is causing a tightening of the agricultural labor market, but the extent of the unmet demand for BREGS work does introduce skepticism.

Could the tightening of the casual agricultural labor market have come instead from the expansion of nonfarm work opportunities other than BREGS? Table 4.4 reports the count of person days in all types of non-PW operations from the Bihar sample of the 2009/10 NSS (as used in table 4.3). We see substitution between casual labor (on someone else's farm) and own-farm work between subrounds 2 and 3, whereas the total amount of agricultural work remained roughly constant. What increased between these two subrounds was the amount of manual nonfarm work. This fact is at least suggestive of the possibility that the increasing availability of this work was driving up the agricultural wage rate in this period, not BREGS.

Respondent perceptions that improvements in both wages and employment opportunities are unconnected to BREGS (see chapter 6) are also consistent with this reading of the evidence. Workers can be expected to know whether BREGS is enhancing their bargaining power in the labor market, but they do not think so overall. Also, recall that for women the gap between public works and non–public works wages was much less affected than that for men over the period. The fact that men are generally more likely than women to be engaged in casual off-farm work gives added weight to this interpretation.

Note that there may be larger impacts on wages in states where there is less rationing (chapter 1). Indeed, Imbert and Papp (2012) present evidence that in states with more effective implementation, the scheme has had a greater impact on casual wages.

A Fuzzy Wage Floor?

If the scheme guaranteed employment at the stipulated wage rate, it would provide a binding wage floor across all casual work, including in the private sector. However, given the extensive rationing we have documented, we would not expect to find this wage floor. But how close does the scheme come in practice to providing a wage floor even for PW labor?

To answer this question we need to examine the distribution of the wage rates received relative to the stipulated BREGS wages. To see how the wages reported in the survey compare with the stipulated wages for MGNREGS in Bihar, the survey wage rate (for the week before the interview) is divided by the stipulated wage rate in Bihar for that week. In R1 the unweighted mean of this ratio is 0.88 (standard deviation = 0.16), and in R2 the mean is 0.86 (standard deviation = 0.21). The corresponding medians are 0.91 and 0.88.

It is evident from the medians that about half the workers on PW earned less than 90 percent of the stipulated wage rate.

Table 4.4 Sample Total Person Days of Non–Public Works Work by Operation and Subround, 2009/10

Subround	Manual agricultural	Manual nonagricultural	Nonmanual nonagricultural	Missing operation code	All operations	Household own-farm enterprise
1. July–Sept 2009	1,340.0	440.0	150.0	21.0	1,951.0	2,354.0
2. Oct–Dec 2009	1,284.5	473.0	324.0	32.0	2,120.5	2,406.0
3. Jan–Mar 2010	973.0	577.0	235.0	7.0	1,792.0	2,728.0
4. Apr–June 2010	1,035.0	399.5	297.0	7.0	1,759.5	2,280.5
Total	4,632.5	1,889.5	1,006.0	67.0	7,623.0	9,768.5

Source: Calculations from National Sample Survey 66th round.
Note: Public works excluded. The total for all operations includes some minor omitted categories.

Figure 4.5 shows the full distributions of this ratio; in each case, both the densities and the cumulative distribution are provided, to show more clearly how many workers were earning less than the stipulated wage rate. For R1 we see that about the same percentage of PW workers were earning less than the stipulated wage rate as were non-PW workers. For R2, we find a slightly *higher* proportion of workers on PW earn less than the stipulated wage rate than do workers on non-PW work. However, this comparison is deceptive, given the greater compression of PW wages. This illusion becomes clear if we calculate the proportion of workers earning less than 75 percent of the stipulated wage rate. For example, in R1, only 14 percent of PW workers earned less than 75 percent of the stipulated wage rate, as compared with 46 percent of non-PW workers. In R2, the corresponding proportions were 21 percent and 45 percent.

Figure 4.5 Wages Relative to the Bihar Rural Employment Guarantee Scheme Stipulated Wage Rate

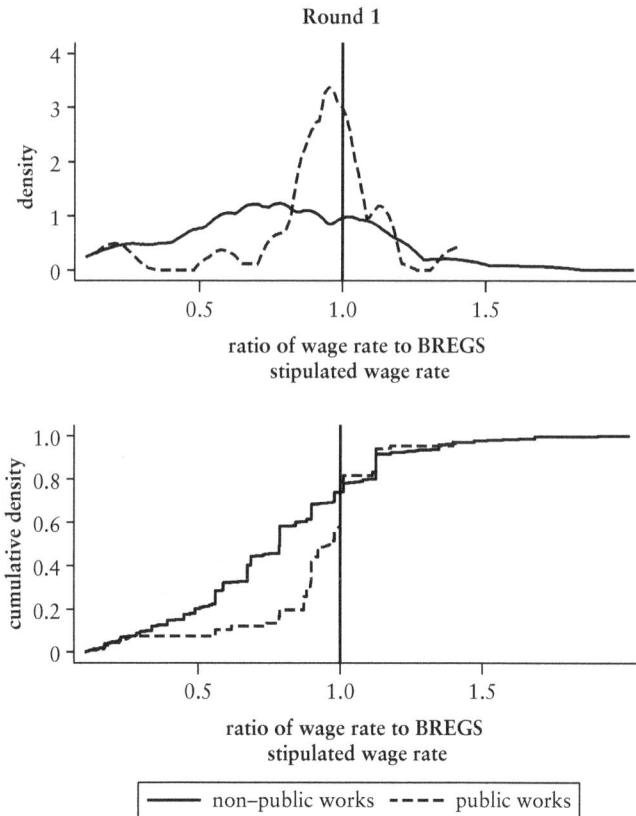

(*Continued on the following page*)

Figure 4.5 (Continued)

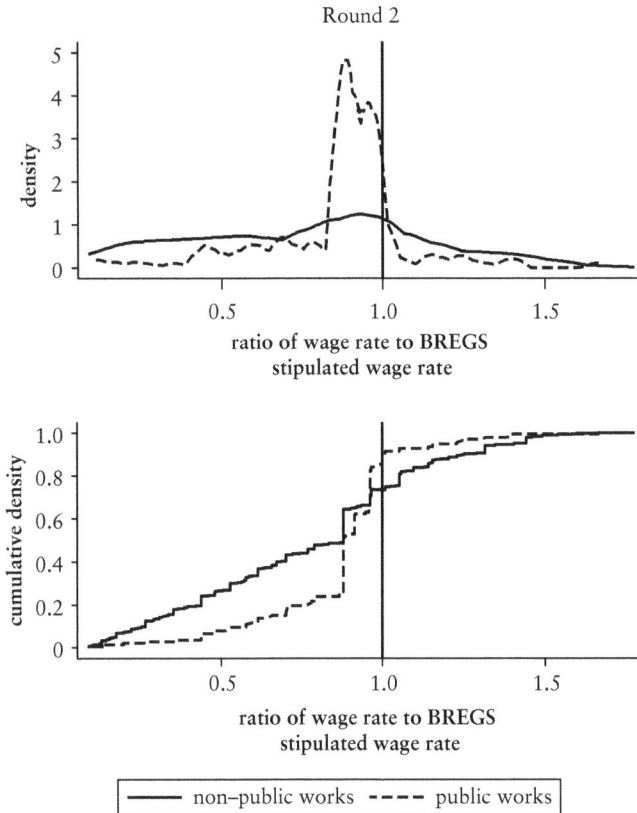

Round 2

ratio of wage rate to BREGS
stipulated wage rate

ratio of wage rate to BREGS
stipulated wage rate

——— non–public works – – – – public works

Source: Estimates based on the Bihar Rural Employment Guarantee Scheme (BREGS) survey.
Note: Based on Block 23 and questions about casual work done in the last week. Wage data are unweighted.

It appears that BREGS is able to provide a "fuzzy wage floor" to participants that is not available for other (non-PW) casual work.

Figure 4.6 examines whether there is a difference in the wage floor for men versus women. We use data from Block 1 in the individual questionnaire, which is based on one-year recall and therefore has more observations for a gender-wise disaggregation. In means and medians, the ratio of the BREGS wage rate to the stipulated wage rate for both men and women was similar in both rounds.[12] However, the gap widens at lower proportions of the stipulated wage rate (as is evident from the cumulative distributions in figure 4.6).

The proportion of women earning considerably less than the stipulated wage rate is markedly higher than for men in both rounds. In R1, 19 percent of women were earning less than 75 percent of the stipulated wage rate, as compared with 13 percent of men. The gap narrowed slightly in R2, with 15 percent of women earning less than 75 percent of the stipulated wage rate, versus 11 percent of men. It is clear that BREGS is even less effective in providing a wage floor for women than for men.

Determinants of Wages

Wages are stipulated by the scheme, though compliance is clearly another matter. A piece rate schedule identifies wages for specific tasks, such that a person working with "normal" effort will attain the stipulated minimum wage rate under the scheme. By contrast, wages for other casual labor (primarily in agriculture) are determined by

Figure 4.6 Actual BREGS Wages Relative to the BREGS Stipulated Wage Rate, by Gender

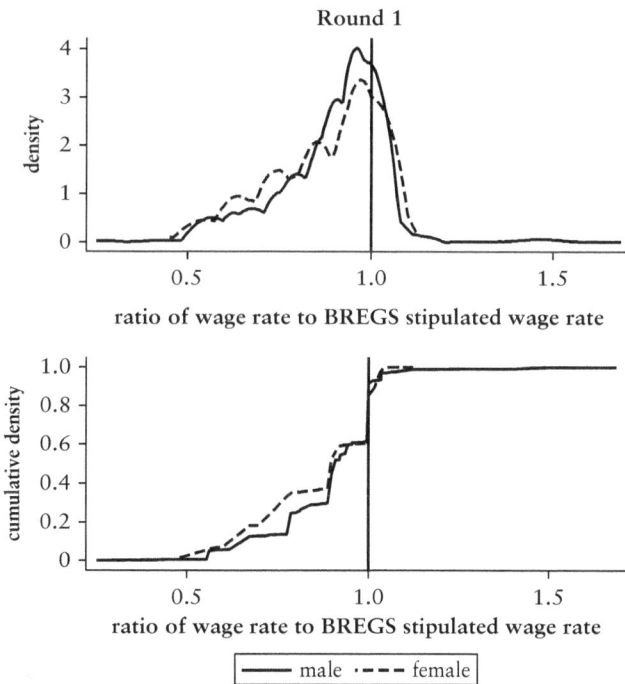

(*Continued on the following page*)

Figure 4.6 (Continued)

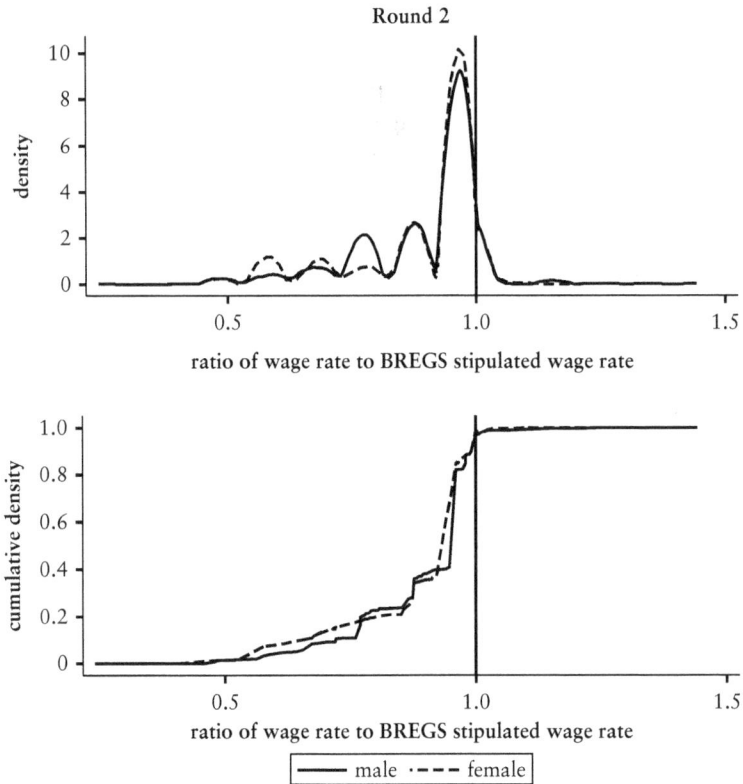

Round 2

ratio of wage rate to BREGS stipulated wage rate

ratio of wage rate to BREGS stipulated wage rate

——— male · - - - female

Source: Estimates based on the Bihar Rural Employment Guarantee Scheme (BREGS) survey.

Note: Based on Block 1, individual questionnaire with recall over the past year. Concerns BREGS only.

market conditions and local idiosyncratic institutional factors, such as longer-term agreements between specific employers and employees (possibly tied to other transactions, such as in credit markets). It should be noted that village labor markets for casual labor operate differently from the standard competitive labor market, and are arguably much more complex, involving interlinkage and sometimes complex reciprocal arrangements, including for risk sharing. Local employers can often exercise a degree of monopsony power. In this setting, it is likely that household characteristics as well as worker characteristics will matter to wages.

It is of interest to see how the determinants of wages differ between BREGS and the casual labor market. Annex table 4A.1 reports results from regressions of wages on a set of individual, household, and village characteristics. Some practical data issues must be noted.

In particular, we obtained casual (non-PW) wages from the previously mentioned one-week recall segment of the questionnaire (Block 23). As noted, this source provided an adequate number of observations for non-PW wages but not PW wages. For PW wages, we relied on the special segment of the questionnaire that used one year recall (Block 1), and is likely to be subject to greater measurement error.

What is most striking in this comparison is how dissimilar the factors determining wages are between the PW scheme and the casual labor market. The PW wage regressions have higher explanatory power than the casual labor regressions for women but not for men. The PW wage regression with village fixed effects explains a remarkable 90 percent of the variance in wages, though almost 20 percentage points of this is due to the strong village effects that are not being captured by the included village variables.

Strikingly, the strong gender effect on casual wages in agriculture and other non-PW activities—whereby the coefficient on being male implies a difference in log wage rates of about 0.3 (0.4 with complete village effects)—vanishes in the PW wage regressions; controlling for other worker characteristics, there is no evidence of women earning less than men in public works. There is still a gender gap, but it is on account of the differences in worker characteristics. Although there are signs of wage discrimination against women in the casual labor market, we find no evidence of such discrimination in setting PW wages. This is clearly a positive achievement of BREGS. In fact, lower rationing in BREGS may also reduce discrimination in the casual labor market.

Comparing Survey Aggregates with Administrative Data

The analysis presented thus far shows that wages received by BREGS workers are less than what they should be paid if they are meeting productivity norms. The wage gap is evidently not caused by any differences in BREGS workers (for example, less physically able) to the extent that lower wages than received by other workers would be warranted. Although we are unable to comment on whether the Schedule of Rates in Bihar is too exacting for a normal worker to achieve the stipulated wage (in piece-rate work), the majority of payments are made on a time basis or on group (rather than individual) productivity. On the positive side, we find that, controlling for worker characteristics, there is no evidence of wage discrimination against women on BREGS.

Another reason that wages may be lower than stipulated wages is corruption, or "leakage." As noted earlier, leakage can take various forms, including workers receiving less than their due for work done, or ghost workers (who are on the books but not employed) drawing wages.

Because the survey is representative of rural Bihar, we can scale up the survey-based estimates (using the appropriate weights) to obtain an estimate of the gross wages and employment received by households. The total estimated wage bill can then be compared with the wages recorded as being paid in the administrative data. This process has been used in the literature as a method of assessing leakages in MGNREGS (Bhalla 2011; Himanshu 2010; Imbert and Papp 2011). The shortfall in estimated total employment relative to days of employment recorded in the administrative data is, however, a crude estimate of the number of days accruing to ghost workers. This interpretation depends, of course, on the accuracy of the survey-based estimates and of the administrative data. Although the sampling error will be negligible with our sample size (and relatively simple two-stage design), we cannot rule out nonsampling errors in the survey or errors in the administrative data.

Table 4.5 provides the results of this comparison, including employment as well as wages. The survey aggregates account for 80 percent of the employment claimed in the administrative data for 2008/09, rising to 86 percent in 2009/10. The survey aggregates account for a slightly lower share of the administrative data on wages paid—75 percent in the first year and 80 percent in the second. These proportions compare favorably with the estimated leakage from another large antipoverty program, the Public Distribution System (PDS), that distributes subsidized food to poor households. One study matches administrative data on the off-take of grain by state governments from the Food Corporation of India (FCI) with NSS data on household purchases from PDS shops for 2007–08. Khera (2011b) estimates that in Bihar, as much as 90 percent of the grain off-take from the FCI does not reach households. The corresponding all-India figure is 43.9 percent.

These estimates are in reasonably close accord with Himanshu's (2010) estimates for India as a whole, which are based on comparing administrative records with the NSS data for 2007/08. However, Imbert and Papp (2011) obtained larger discrepancies between NSS aggregates and administrative data on MGNREGS. For Bihar, Imbert and Papp can only account for about 30 percent of the administrative amount of employment using the scaled-up estimate based on the 2007/08 NSS. We would conjecture that our survey instrument is doing a better job than the NSS in picking up spells of work on BREGS. In addition, the BREGS survey includes various questions asked both at the household and individual levels that probe respondents about participation from different angles and with various recall periods. Such a specialized survey is likely to capture actual levels of participation and remuneration in the scheme much more accurately than surveys with single questions about MGNREGS.

Table 4.5 Wages and Employment Comparison between Survey Data and Administrative Data

	2008/09			2009/10		
	Administrative data	Survey data	Survey data as percentage of administrative data	Administrative data	Survey data	Survey data as percentage of administrative data
Employment (million person days)						
Person days generated	99	79	80	114	98	86
Wage earnings (million Rs)						
Total wages paid and owed	8,396	6,310	75	11,087	8,910	80
Total wages paid and received	8,396	5,310	63	11,087	7,850	71

Source: Estimates based on the Bihar Rural Employment Guarantee Scheme (BREGS) survey.

Note: Totals computed by multiplying survey averages by projected population from census. The estimates are based on a combination of data from Block 1 of the household questionnaire and Block 19 of the individual questionnaire of the BREGS survey.

Annex 4A

Table 4A.1 The Determinants of BREGS and Non-BREGS Casual Wages at the Individual Level

	ln BREGS wages				*ln non-BREGS casual wages*			
	All		*Women*	*Men*	*All*		*Women*	*Men*
	(1)	(2)	(3)	(4)	(5)	(6)	(7)	(8)
Age	-0.001	0.002	-0.012	0.011	-0.000	-0.007	0.016	0.012
Square of age	0.064	0.038	0.086	-0.111	0.016	0.055	-0.022	-0.087
Literate (< class 5)	0.023	-0.000	0.074	0.006	0.065	0.077	0.087	0.029
Class 5 pass (primary)	-0.009	-0.016	0.055	-0.040	0.069	0.025	-1.688*	0.076
Class 8 pass (middle)	-0.055	-0.114**	0.095	-0.088	0.089	0.126	0.447	0.008
Class 10 pass (secondary)	-0.029	0.052	—	-0.017	0.063	0.058	—	-0.001
Class 12 pass (higher secondary)	-0.023	-0.066	—	-0.095	-0.103	-0.088	—	-0.150
More than higher secondary	0.011	0.053	—	0.371***	-0.395	0.193	—	-0.294
Household head	-0.095**	-0.096*	0.135	-0.065	-0.118	-0.016	-0.600	-0.205
Spouse of head	-0.012	-0.044	-0.369	-0.239*	-0.168	-0.004	0.032	-0.132
Married or gauna	0.187***	0.128*	-0.080	0.131**	0.208**	0.202**	-1.859**	0.194**
Widowed or divorced	0.177**	0.131*	—	0.156*	0.081	0.151	-2.197***	0.169
Male gender	0.047	0.076			0.314**	0.382***		
Male Pearlin scale	0.015**	0.005		0.009	-0.007	-0.009		-0.010
Female Pearlin scale	0.002	0.006	0.023**		-0.020	-0.016	-0.066***	
ln (household size)	0.032	-0.048	0.392	-0.078	-0.251	-0.051	-0.524	-0.036

ln (household size) squared	0.001	0.023	-0.108	0.030	0.037	-0.012	0.176	-0.035
Share of male adults	0.092	0.063	0.173	0.035	-0.254*	-0.215*	0.696**	-0.188
Share of female adults	0.255***	0.154*	0.147	0.269**	-0.344**	-0.268*	-0.537	-0.417**
Share of elderly	-0.190	-0.160	0.089	-0.335*	0.012	0.162	0.560	0.053
Share of children younger than age 6	0.042	0.013	-0.161	0.093	0.090	0.020	0.135	0.060
Gender of head	-0.042	-0.022	0.481	-0.142	0.141*	0.117	-0.831*	0.250
Age of head	0.003	-0.001	0.019*	-0.009	0.006	0.008	0.007	-0.006
Age of head squared	-0.081*	-0.046	-0.150***	0.093	-0.086	-0.089	-0.168	0.021
Maximum education in household								
Literate (< class 5)	-0.016	-0.008	-0.112***	0.009	0.009	0.015	-0.024	0.023
Class 5 pass (primary)	-0.033	-0.037	-0.103	-0.011	-0.033	-0.017	-0.056	-0.062
Class 8 pass (middle)	-0.080**	-0.044	-0.156***	-0.039	0.036	0.040	-0.278*	0.104
Class 10 pass (secondary)	-0.000	0.002	-0.084	0.016	0.107	0.109	0.128	0.172**
Class 12 pass (higher secondary)	-0.063	-0.035	-0.386*	-0.020	0.042	0.001	-0.182	0.116
More than higher secondary	0.223**	-0.008	0.049	—	-0.034	-0.108	—	-0.060
Social group								
Scheduled Caste	-0.097*	-0.033	-0.028	-0.096*	-0.015	-0.159*	-0.599*	-0.018
Mahadalit	-0.102*	-0.015	-0.018	-0.088	0.088	-0.013	-0.514	0.089
Other Backward Class	-0.090*	-0.031	-0.123	-0.081	0.016	-0.092	-0.564*	0.029
Scheduled Tribe	-0.111*	-0.054	0.016	-0.136**	-0.174*	-0.258**	-0.714**	-0.072
Hindu	-0.061	-0.035	-0.145	-0.013	-0.161**	-0.046	0.207	-0.254***

(Continued on the following page)

Table 4A.1 (Continued)

	In BREGS wages				In non-BREGS casual wages			
	All		Women	Men	All		Women	Men
	(1)	(2)	(3)	(4)	(5)	(6)	(7)	(8)
Asset-house index	-0.012**	-0.009	-0.016	-0.016**	0.014	-0.001	-0.002	0.019
Land owned	0.008	0.006	0.170**	0.001	-0.002	0.127	-0.525*	0.041
BPL ration card	-0.032	-0.032*	0.006	-0.027	0.049	0.013	0.059	0.043
Know Mukhiya or Sarpanch	0.026	0.030	0.002	0.027	0.005	-0.052	0.133	-0.021
Know ward member or panch	0.038**	0.003	0.059	0.049**	0.030	0.015	-0.099	0.060
Know program officer or block development officer	0.064	0.084*	—	0.024	0.502***	0.723***	—	0.349***
Know any political worker	0.062**	0.036	-0.129	0.061**	0.020	0.019	1.605	-0.012
Household voted in panchayat election	-0.037	-0.047	-0.120	-0.057	0.057	0.050	0.218*	0.036
Household shock in the past year								
Accident	0.029*	0.044***	-0.041	0.042**	-0.054	-0.019	-0.241**	-0.022
Illness	0.044	0.052*	-0.014	0.012	0.048	0.016	0.035	0.101
Job loss	0.036	0.046*	0.170***	0.021	0.070	0.069	-0.141	0.112**
Natural disaster	0.008	0.008	0.046	0.018	-0.042	-0.057	-0.184*	-0.061
Other	-0.022	-0.008	0.016	-0.020	-0.115	-0.112	-0.363***	-0.017

Men do casual work	0.011	0.009	−0.006	−0.016	0.086	0.047	−0.149	0.366***
Women do casual work	0.010	0.019	0.020	0.006	−0.052	−0.073*	−0.137	−0.025
No male migration	−0.038**	−0.020	−0.030	−0.032*	0.074***	0.040	0.134	0.065**
Regular-salaried worker in household	0.118	0.011		0.138*	0.068	−0.012	−0.090	0.001
GP has a panchayat bhawan	−0.026		−0.056	0.000	0.112***		0.149	0.098***
Mukhiya's age	0.001		0.001	0.001	−0.001		−0.003	−0.000
Mukhiya lives in village	−0.022		−0.189***	0.025	0.022		0.019	0.026
Mukhiya is male	0.004		0.022	−0.010	0.120**		0.114	0.096*
Mukhiya completed class 5	0.023		−0.007	0.032	0.208***		0.276*	0.162***
Mukhiya is a farmer	0.016		0.016	0.007	−0.075*		0.116	−0.146***
Mukhiya held a GP post	−0.004		−0.064	0.009	0.087*		−0.066	0.121**
Mukhiya's family in GP post	−0.020		−0.044	−0.017	−0.051		0.059	−0.084*
Mukhiya is a contractor	0.134**		0.106	0.150**	0.050		−0.134	0.006
Listing: share of SC households	0.168***		0.181	0.101	−0.018		−0.153	0.015
Listing: share of OBC households	0.130***		0.382***	0.059	0.069		−0.101	0.046
Village is predominantly Hindu	0.042		0.072	0.028	−0.041		−0.158	−0.002
Village is electrified	0.025		0.071	0.009	0.001		0.081	−0.022
Village has a pucca road	0.060***		0.079*	0.055**	0.015		0.099	−0.007
Within 5 km of bus stop	0.048**		−0.039	0.057***	−0.012		0.090	−0.032

(Continued on the following page)

Table 4A.1 (Continued)

	In BREGS wages				In non-BREGS casual wages			
	All		Women	Men	All		Women	Men
	(1)	(2)	(3)	(4)	(5)	(6)	(7)	(8)
Within 5 km of GP	-0.020		-0.015	-0.011	0.095**		-0.231	0.115**
Within 5 km of town	0.022		-0.077	0.040	0.127***		0.125	0.167***
Within 5 km of block headquarters	0.019		0.076	-0.000	-0.084**		0.248*	-0.144***
Post office in village	0.002		-0.019	0.008	-0.007		-0.027	0.026
Access to nonagricultural enterprises	-0.116***		-0.064	-0.100***	0.062		-0.104	0.141**
ln of mean asset index in village	0.181***		0.216*	0.137**	-0.186		0.948**	-0.211*
Asset inequality in village	-0.470***		-0.504	-0.377*	0.200		-1.010	0.286
Share of households with kutcha house	-0.019		-0.083	0.010	-0.022		0.774***	-0.095
Share of BPL households	0.073		0.144	0.073	-0.196*		-0.142	-0.108
Flood in village in past year	-0.076***		-0.088**	-0.073***	-0.040		-0.064	-0.025
Drought in village in past year	-0.041**		-0.078	-0.028	-0.035		0.002	0.011
Any shock in past year	0.014		0.153**	-0.010	-0.001		0.036	0.016
Good relations among village groups	-0.055		-0.083	-0.068	0.011		0.072	-0.011

	(1)	(2)	(3)	(4)	(5)	(6)	(7)	(8)
Self-help group in village	0.010		-0.036	0.033	0.067*		0.124	0.035
Civil society organization in village	0.034		0.006	0.011	-0.023		-0.050	-0.005
BREGS group in village	0.027		0.170***	-0.030	-0.059		-0.219	-0.028
Other group in village	0.007		-0.033	-0.014	-0.007		-0.148	-0.004
Constant	3.841***	4.285***	3.332***	4.226***	4.269***	4.114***	5.684***	4.253***
Village fixed effects?	No	Yes	No	No	No	Yes	No	No
Observations	858	898	214	644	992	1,021	183	809
R^2	0.348	0.507	0.686	0.378	0.404	0.532	0.605	0.292

Source: Estimates based on the Bihar Rural Employment Guarantee Scheme (BREGS) survey.

Note: Based on round 1 data and sample of all participants in BREGS or in casual work. Observations for which wages are recorded as greater than 200 rupees or less than 20 rupees are trimmed. Gauna is the point in an arranged marriage at which a wife begins to live with her husband. The omitted education category is illiterate. BPL = Below Poverty Line; GP = Gram Panchayat; km = kilometers; — = not available.

*, **, and *** indicate significance at the 10 percent, 5 percent, and 1 percent levels, respectively, based on robust standard errors.

Notes

1. Exceptions are allowed in certain isolated areas that have no banking facilities.

2. As in other states, one-third of elected positions are reserved for women in Bihar. Thus, elected Mukhiyas are sometimes female. However, once the election is over, a male surrogate, frequently a husband or father, often takes on the job. When we refer to the Mukhiya we mean either the elected or surrogate one.

3. Also see the discussion in Khera (2011a).

4. This is not confined to Bihar; Vanaik (2009) reports the same practice in Rajasthan—thought to be among the best performing states in implementing MGNREGS.

5. Block 23 is a modified version of the standard weekly block module in the National Sample Survey Employment-Unemployment (Schedule 10.0) surveys.

6. Because of the scant number of observations, we do not weight the wage data from Block 23.

7. To reduce sensitivity to measurement errors, we treat recorded wages of more than Rs 200 per day or less than Rs 10 from both sources as missing values.

8. The inflation rate is based on the consumer price index for agricultural laborers in the state.

9. The Kolmogorov-Smirnov test does not reject the null hypothesis that the distributions are identical in the three binary comparisons between the three comparison wage distributions for either men or women.

10. This is not, of course, a bad thing, because it could make the employment guarantee a very effective policy for fighting poverty by bringing all wages up to the minimum wage. Doing so, however, does not mean that it will be more effective than other policy options. For further discussion, see Murgai and Ravallion (2005a, 2005b).

11. Zimmerman (2012) finds evidence of wage gains for women when MGNREGS work is provided in the main agricultural season, but not for men.

12. The mean ratio was 90 percent for men in both rounds; for women the means were 87 percent and 89 percent in R1 and R2, respectively. Medians were similar, with half the workers (of both genders) earning less than 91 percent of the stipulated wage rate in R1 and 96 percent in R2.

References

Bhalla, Surjit. 2011. "Does NREGA Really Work?" *Business Standard*, March 27.

Himanshu. 2010. "Five Heady Years of MGNREGA." *Livemint* website. August 31. http://www.livemint.com/Opinion/j679CUhM1MM qfBDdFYSmCL/Five-heady-years-of-MGNREGA.html.

Imbert, Clément, and John Papp. 2011. "Estimating Leakages in India's Employment Guarantee." In *The Battle for Employment Guarantee*, edited by Reetika Khera. New Delhi: Oxford University Press.

———. 2012. "Equilibrium Distributional Impacts of Government Employment Programs: Evidence from India's Employment Guarantee." Paris School of Economics Working Paper No. 2012 – 14, Paris School of Economics, Paris.

Khera, Reetika, ed. 2011a. *The Battle for Employment Guarantee*. New Delhi: Oxford University Press.

———. 2011b. "Trends in Diversion of Grain from the Public Distribution System." *Economic and Political Weekly* 46 (21): 106–14.

Murgai, Rinku, and Martin Ravallion. 2005a. "Employment Guarantee in Rural India: What Would It Cost and How Much Would It Reduce Poverty?" *Economic and Political Weekly*, July 30, pp. 3450–55.

———. 2005b. "Is a Guaranteed Living Wage a Good Anti-Poverty Policy?" Policy Research Working Paper No. 3460, World Bank, Washington, DC.

National Sample Survey Organization (NSSO). 2009/10. "Socio-Economic Survey Sixty-Sixth Round Schedule 10: Employment and Unemployment." Government of India, New Delhi.

Pankaj, Ashok K. 2008. "Processes, Institutions and Mechanisms of Implementation of NREGA: Impact Assessment of Bihar and Jharkhand." Institute of Human Development, New Delhi.

Vanaik, Anish. 2009. "Accounts of Corruption." *Frontline*, January 16, p. 21.

Zimmerman, Laura. 2012. "Labor Market Impacts of a Large-Scale Public Works Program: Evidence from the Indian Employment Guarantee Scheme." IZA Working Paper No. 6858, Institute for the Study of Labor (IZA), Bonn, Germany.

5

Forgone Employment and Income

Some loss of income from other sources is bound to occur for at least some of those who take up public works (PW) employment. Given that the wage rate is higher than that for other work, some people will naturally be attracted to the Bihar Rural Employment Guarantee Scheme (BREGS) for the wage gain. Others will no doubt be unable to find other work, and for them the wage gain is also the net income gain from BREGS. The literature on the impacts on poverty of public works schemes has emphasized the importance of assessing the forgone income (see, among others, Ravallion 1999; Murgai and Ravallion 2005; Jha, Gaiha, and Pandey 2012). However, advocates of such schemes have typically ignored this issue, implicitly assuming that there is no displacement of other employment opportunities.[1]

The BREGS survey asked counterfactual questions of actual participants to obtain their assessments of how many days they would have otherwise worked and what they think they would have earned if they had not been doing the BREGS work during that period. All survey participants were asked for their expectations of employment and income from that employment if they did not have the BREGS job at the time.

This method is unusual in the literature on the impact evaluation of antipoverty programs.[2] Standard methods rely heavily on comparing means between those in a "treatment group" and in a "comparison group" of nonparticipants deemed to reveal the counterfactual. Various observational and experimental methods are used to derive the comparison group under maintained identifying assumptions. A number of evaluations of the Mahatma Gandhi National Rural Employment Guarantee Scheme (MGNREGS) in various states adopt this approach (for example, Ravi and Engler 2013; Liu and Deininger 2013; Imbert and Papp 2012; and Berg and others 2012).

As described in the overview, we adopt a different approach. Our method relies instead on asking participants themselves what they think they would have done in the absence of the program. If they said that they would have worked, we asked them how many days and at what wage. This approach is similar to widely used expectations surveys, in which respondents are asked for their point expectation for some event or number at some point in the future, which cannot be directly observed at present. Here we are also asking about an unobserved state—the outcome in the absence of the intervention. The difference is that we are asking about a concurrent counterfactual state rather than a future state.

This aspect of our methodology comes with both a benefit and a cost. The benefit is that we obtain individual-specific data on impacts. By contrast, standard impact-evaluation methods only deliver mean impacts, or at best conditional mean impacts. This benefit of our methodology facilitates quite fine distributional analysis, as required for assessing impacts on poverty. The cost is that counterfactual subjective questions are not always easy for respondents, although we found that, with appropriate training for interviewers, high response rates could be obtained. The overall nonresponse rates to our questions on forgone income were 8 percent in the first round of the survey (R1), falling to 2 percent in the second round (R2).[3] There may also be some double-counting of forgone work opportunities if different respondents have in mind the same forgone job.

One of the options for respondents was "housework or own-enterprise" (typically the own-farm). For this category (grouped into one option), forgone income was assumed to be zero, on the plausible assumption that such work can be readily reallocated in time to ensure little or no forgone income. Questions about forgone work and incomes were asked for each episode of BREGS work, for each individual. The gender-specific median was then used as the household value. Missing values for forgone income were replaced with the median for the household's stratum or the village median if it was still missing.

Forgone Opportunities

The nature of forgone opportunities varies considerably across workers and between men and women. Table 5.1 summarizes the types of activities that BREGS participants identified as being displaced by

Table 5.1 Forgone Work Opportunities Identified by Bihar
Rural Employment Guarantee Scheme Participants

	Round 1		Round 2	
Alternative to BREGS Work	Men (percent)	Women (percent)	Men (percent)	Women (percent)
Migrated for work	10.7	2.9	14.0	1.0
Worked at paid work, by type				
Casual work (agricultural)	22.4	24.8	19.4	23.6
Casual work (nonagricultural)	23.8	5.7	25.7	5.0
Other	1.0	0.8	2.1	0.0
Searched for work or remained unemployed	44.0	35.7	37.6	13.2
Worked on own land or house	8.8	33.1	14.9	58.2
Total	100.0	100.0	100.0	100.0

Source: Estimates based on the Bihar Rural Employment Guarantee Scheme
(BREGS) survey.

Note: The questions were asked of BREGS participants by work episode. The
means are formed over all work episodes such that an individual who worked more
than once is also counted more than once. Would-be migrants are included in totals
according to the type of activity they would have done. Data are household weighted.

their BREGS work; we give results for both survey rounds and both
genders. For men, about 14 percent in R2 (fewer in R1) said they
would have migrated if not for BREGS; the same was true of only
1 percent of women in R2. With regard to activity, casual work in
agriculture was identified as the forgone work opportunity for about
22 percent of men and 25 percent of women in R1. Casual nonfarm
work was more important for men than for women. Not surprisingly, work on own land or in the house was the most common
answer given by women.

Forgone Income

In estimating income from these forgone opportunities, one concern emerged about the responses to the questions about reported
income during the period of BREGS work. About 10 percent of
respondents reported forgone earnings greater than their reported
earnings from public works. This is implausible, and most likely
reflects a misunderstanding of the question, which is clearly not an

easy one because it requires a counterfactual response. We truncated the data such that whenever the reported forgone income exceeded the earnings from PW, the forgone income was set equal to the PW earnings.

However, the survey design also allows for a test of the reliability of reported forgone incomes for the main relevant activity, that is, casual work. We compare the reported month-specific forgone wage for casual work with the mean wage rate actually received by casual workers (in the week before the survey) for that same month. Sample sizes mean that the test is only feasible for May and June of 2009 and 2010.

Table 5.2 gives the results. We find a fairly close correspondence between the means, and more so in R2 than R1, suggesting that there may have been some learning. (Recall also that the response rate was higher in R2.) The variance is greater for actual than for counterfactual wages. These results give us greater confidence that the counterfactual questions were understood and that the answers are sensible.

Forgone Employment and Income as a Result of BREGS

On average, workers had to give up work days equivalent to 40–45 percent of the total BREGS employment received. Although BREGS provided the sampled households with 18,900 person days of employment in R1, we calculate that 7,700 days of other employment were given up to take on this BREGS work. In R2, 20,400 person days of employment were provided, but 9,300 days had to be given up. Forgone employment is higher for men than for women. In R1 the share of gross employment that was accounted for by forgone work was 0.42 for men, versus 0.36 for women. In R2, the corresponding ratios were 0.51 and 0.31.

Averages mask three distinct types of BREGS participants in relationship to forgone employment and income. The density functions of the ratio of self-assessed forgone days to PW days, in the left-hand panel of figure 5.1, have three distinct modes. One is around zero, which is the overall mode. These participants would not have had any days of work had they not worked on BREGS. A second mode is around 0.6, and the third and smallest mode is about 0.9. The latter beneficiaries would have worked almost as many days in non-BREGS work, possibly for a much lower wage.

Forgone income tends to be slightly lower than forgone employment, reflecting the lower wages from casual work on the

Table 5.2 Forgone Wages for Casual Work Compared with Actual Wages for Those Working in the Same Month

		Reported forgone wage for those working on BREGS (rupees/day)				Casual wage received for those not working on BREGS (rupees/day)			
		Mean	Median	Standard deviation	Observations	Mean	Median	Standard deviation	Observations
All individuals									
R1	May 2009	67	70	21	49	71	70	30	418
	June 2009	68	70	17	32	72	70	30	571
R2	May 2010	85	85	33	45	87	100	38	361
	June 2010	81	100	27	31	83	90	41	337
Men only									
R1	May 2009	71	70	20	38	78	75	29	325
	June 2009	68	70	17	32	79	80	27	454
R2	May 2010	96	100	29	29	96	100	36	260
	June 2010	90	100	23	18	95	100	37	240

Source: Estimates based on the Bihar Rural Employment Guarantee Scheme (BREGS) survey.
Note: The right-hand panel is based on responses to the question about wages actually received by casual workers in the week preceding the survey for all non-BREGS work (which could include other public works). R1 = round 1; R2 = round 2.

Figure 5.1 Distribution of the Ratio of Self-Assessed
Forgone Days to Public Works Days and Ratio of Forgone
Wages to Public Works Wages

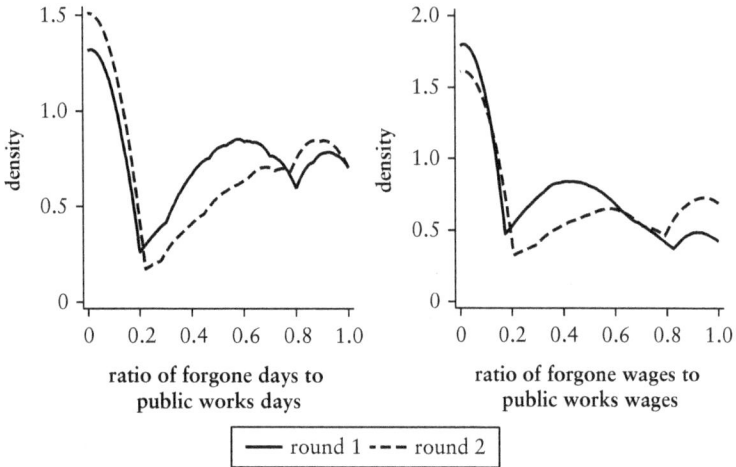

ratio of forgone days to   ratio of forgone wages to
public works days   public works wages

——— round 1 - - - round 2

Source: Estimates based on the Bihar Rural Employment Guarantee Scheme
(BREGS) survey.
Note: Distributions are estimated for all public works at the household level.

labor market as compared with working on BREGS. The mean
ratio of forgone income to PW wages is 0.35 (standard deviation = 0.344; observations = 930) in R1, rising to 0.39 (standard
deviation = 0.392; observations = 774) in R2.[4] The corresponding medians are 0.30 and 0.31. Density functions of the ratio of
forgone income to PW wages (right-hand panel in figure 5.1) also
have three distinct modes. As with days, one is around zero and
is the overall mode. This represents the BREGS participants who
stated that they would not have been earning income had they not
worked on PW. A second mode is around 0.5, where participants
would have earned about half of the earnings on PW, and the third
and smallest mode is around 0.9. The latter beneficiaries would
have earned an amount close to the amount earned on BREGS
but possibly would have had to migrate and bear costs to do so.
There may also be unobserved nonpecuniary benefits to PW that
make them more desirable than alternative equally remunerated
casual work.

In summary, these observations suggest that forgone income is
significant, though it varies considerably between workers. There
are three distinct groups of participants—those for whom there is

no likely income loss from joining the program, those for whom there is only a small net income gain from joining the program, and an intermediate group for whom about half of the BREGS wage represents a net income gain.

Impacts on Migration

Table 5.1 shows that BREGS has some impact on reducing migration. In R2, 14 percent of male BREGS workers stated that in the absence of that work, they would have migrated elsewhere. Combined across men and women, 13 percent of BREGS households said they would have migrated. These responses are a clear sign of some impact, but how big is the impact? How does it compare with the total amount of migration in Bihar?

In R1, 22 percent of households had at least one member who migrated for work in the year preceding the survey. Factoring in the *extra* migration implied by the fact that some households that did not have any migrants would have otherwise migrated in the absence of the program, we estimate that the proportion of households with migrants would have risen to 23.3 percent (see table 5.3). In R2, the proportion of households with a migrant would have risen from 23.7 percent to 24.9 percent.

We estimate that a total of 1.6 million days of migration did not occur because of BREGS, rising to 2.3 million days in R2. Thus, without BREGS, total migration days would have risen by 0.5 percent in

Table 5.3 Migration Impact of Bihar Rural Employment Guarantee Scheme

	Round 1	Round 2
Households with at least one member who migrated in the past year (percent)	22.2	23.7
Households that did not migrate in the past year, but had at least one member who would have migrated in the absence of BREGS work (percent)	1.1	1.2
Total number of days of migration among all household members (millions)	312.7	382.0
Total number of *additional* days of migration that would have occurred in the absence of BREGS work (millions)	1.6	2.3

Source: Estimates based on the Bihar Rural Employment Guarantee Scheme (BREGS) survey.

Note: Household weighted. Based on BREGS participant responses to question about whether they would have migrated if not for BREGS work.

R1 and 0.6 percent in R2. These estimates suggest that although the program is reducing migration, it is not having an impact on a large enough scale to significantly stem the flow of migrants who travel to look for work outside Bihar.

Notes

1. For example, in a compilation of popular writings in broad support of the Mahatma Gandhi National Rural Employment Guarantee Scheme in Khera (2011), there is only one passing reference in a footnote to the possibility of forgone income.

2. For a survey of the methods found in practice, see Ravallion (2008).

3. Exploiting our survey design, we can also confirm the reliability of reported forgone incomes for the main relevant activity, that is, casual work. This is discussed later in this chapter.

4. The corresponding means without truncation are 0.63 (standard deviation = 2.31) and 0.63 (standard deviation = 2.73). However, these means are distorted by some very large outliers (reaching a forgone income of 68 times actual wage receipts from PW) that are clearly measurement errors.

References

Berg, Erlend, Sambit Bhattacharyya, Rajasekhar Durgam, and Manjula Ramachandra. 2012. "Can Rural Public Works Affect Agricultural Wages? Evidence from India." Center for the Study of African Economies Working Paper 2012-05, University of Oxford, U.K.

Imbert, Clément, and John Papp. 2012. "Equilibrium Distributional Impacts of Government Employment Programs: Evidence from India's Employment Guarantee." Paris School of Economics Working Paper No. 2012 - 14. Paris School of Economics, Paris.

Jha, Raghbendra, Raghav Gaiha, and Manoj K. Pandey. 2012. "Net Transfer Benefits under India's Rural Employment Guarantee Scheme." *Journal of Policy Modeling* 34 (2): 296–311.

Khera, Reetika, ed. 2011. *The Battle for Employment Guarantee*. New Delhi: Oxford University Press.

Liu, Yanyan, and Klaus Deininger. 2013. "Welfare and Poverty Impacts of India's National Rural Employment Guarantee Scheme: Evidence from Andhra Pradesh." Policy Research Working Paper No. 6543, World Bank, Washington, DC.

Murgai, Rinku, and Martin Ravallion. 2005. "Employment Guarantee in Rural India: What Would It Cost and How Much Would It Reduce Poverty?" *Economic and Political Weekly*, July 30, pp. 3450–55.

Ravallion, Martin. 1999. "Appraising Workfare." *World Bank Research Observer* 14: 31–48.

———. 2008. "Evaluating Anti-Poverty Programs." In *Handbook of Development Economics*, Volume 4, edited by Paul Schultz and John Strauss. Amsterdam: North-Holland.

Ravi, Shamika, and Monika Engler. 2013. "Workfare as an Effective Way to Fight Poverty: The Case of India's NREGS." Available at SSRN: http://ssrn.com/abstract=1336837.

6

Impacts on Poverty

We can now bring together the main elements from the preceding chapters to derive our estimate of the impact of Bihar Rural Employment Guarantee Scheme (BREGS) earnings on the incidence of rural poverty in Bihar. We focus mainly on quantifying the income gains to households through their participation as workers. When comparing the actual impact with simulated impacts under different scenarios, it is evident that there is a large "lost impact" on poverty from BREGS. We investigate the extent of this lost impact that is due to the unmet demand for work and due to the gap between the actual wages received and the stipulated wages. We also make some observations from the survey on respondents' perceptions of the scheme that are relevant to its poverty impacts.

Impacts on Poverty of the Extra Earnings from BREGS

In estimating the impacts on poverty, we use the household-specific estimates of forgone income for men and women. The post–public works (PW) distribution of consumption is that actually observed in the data. The pre-PW distribution is derived from this by subtracting the net gains from PW, as given by gross wages less the estimated forgone income.

As mentioned in Chapter 2, in estimating poverty measures for Bihar, we use the median per capita consumption level from round 1 of the survey (R1) as the poverty line and update it over time using the consumer price index for agricultural laborers to get the round 2 (R2) line. This gives poverty lines of 6,988 rupees (Rs) per person per year in R1 and Rs 7,836 in R2. However, recognizing that any poverty line is bound to be somewhat arbitrary, we also provide estimates of the poverty impacts over a wide range of potential lines.

We estimate that the poverty rates (proportion of the population of Bihar living below the poverty line) *among BREGS participants* would have been 62.2 percent in R1 and 52.6 percent in R2 without the program. By contrast, what we observe in the data (including, of course, net earnings from the scheme) are corresponding poverty rates of 56.8 percent and 50.2 percent. Thus, we estimate that the extra earnings from the scheme reduced poverty among participants by 5.4 percentage points in R1 and 2.4 percentage points in R2.

There is no reason to consider just one poverty line. The upper panel of figure 6.1 gives the observed (post-BREGS) cumulative distribution function and the estimated counterfactual distribution of consumption in R1 for PW participants only. The difference between the distribution functions is plotted in the lower panel. Thus, the lower panel plots the impact on the poverty rate at a given poverty line. We call this the "poverty impact graph." The peak reduction in the poverty rate is (coincidentally) near the R1 median.[1] At about two-thirds of the median, poverty falls by about 1 percentage point, and at one-third above the median, it falls by more than 3 percentage points. (Naturally, impacts go to zero at the extremes.)

Of course, the average impact is lower for the population of rural Bihar as a whole. We find that without the program, the poverty rate would have been 51.4 percent and 42.3 percent for R1 and R2, respectively. The estimated postprogram poverty rates are 50.0 percent (by construction) and 41.8 percent, respectively. Therefore, we conclude that the scheme reduced the poverty rate in rural Bihar as a whole by 1.4 percentage points in R1 and 0.5 percentage points in R2.

Figure 6.2 reproduces the poverty impact graph from the lower panel of figure 6.1 but compares it with the corresponding graph for the sample as a whole for R1 (top panel) and R2 (bottom panel). In the full sample, the impact on poverty in R1 peaks near the median, but falls off quickly on either side. In R2, the impacts on poverty peak just above the median.

As noted in the previous chapter, it is possible that we have over-estimated forgone incomes, to the extent that there are overlaps in the self-reported opportunities forgone. The unemployment rate provides a clue. The Labour Bureau's estimate of the unemployment rate for rural Bihar in 2009/10 was 18 percent, comprising 16 percent for men and 32 percent for women (Ministry of Labour and Employment 2010). While the true rate is likely to be higher in the lean season and in the absence of BREGS, a reasonably conservative upper bound is 50 percent. Therefore, as a sensitivity test, we reestimate the poverty impacts after halving reported forgone incomes on the grounds that, if the true unemployment rate were as high as 50 percent, there would only be half the number of job options available to BREGS workers as

Figure 6.1 Impacts on Participants' Poverty in Round 1

cumulative distributions of consumption with and without earnings from public works

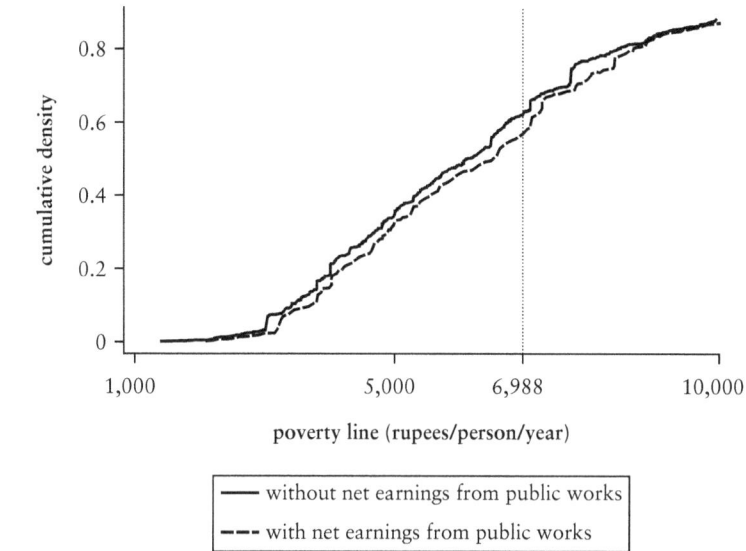

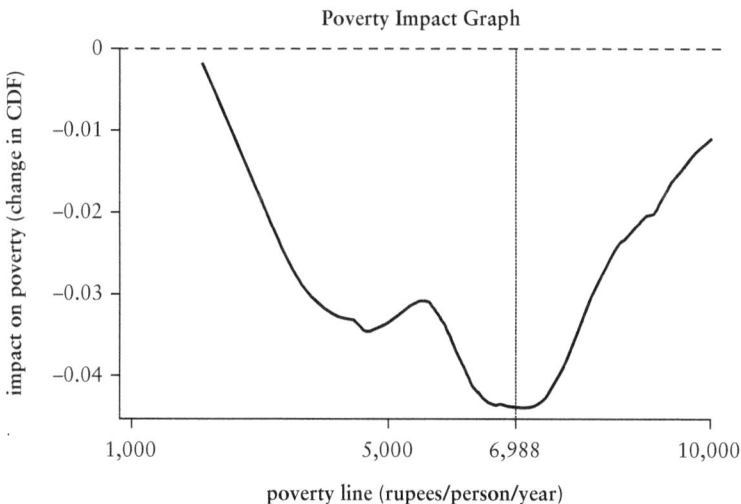

Source: Estimates based on the Bihar Rural Employment Guarantee Scheme (BREGS) Survey.

Note: A smoothing parameter of 0.3 is used for all figures in this chapter. The poverty impact graph is estimated as the difference between the cumulative distribution functions of consumption with and without the program. CDF = cumulative distribution function.

Figure 6.2 Poverty Impact Graph for Public Works
Participants and the Whole Population

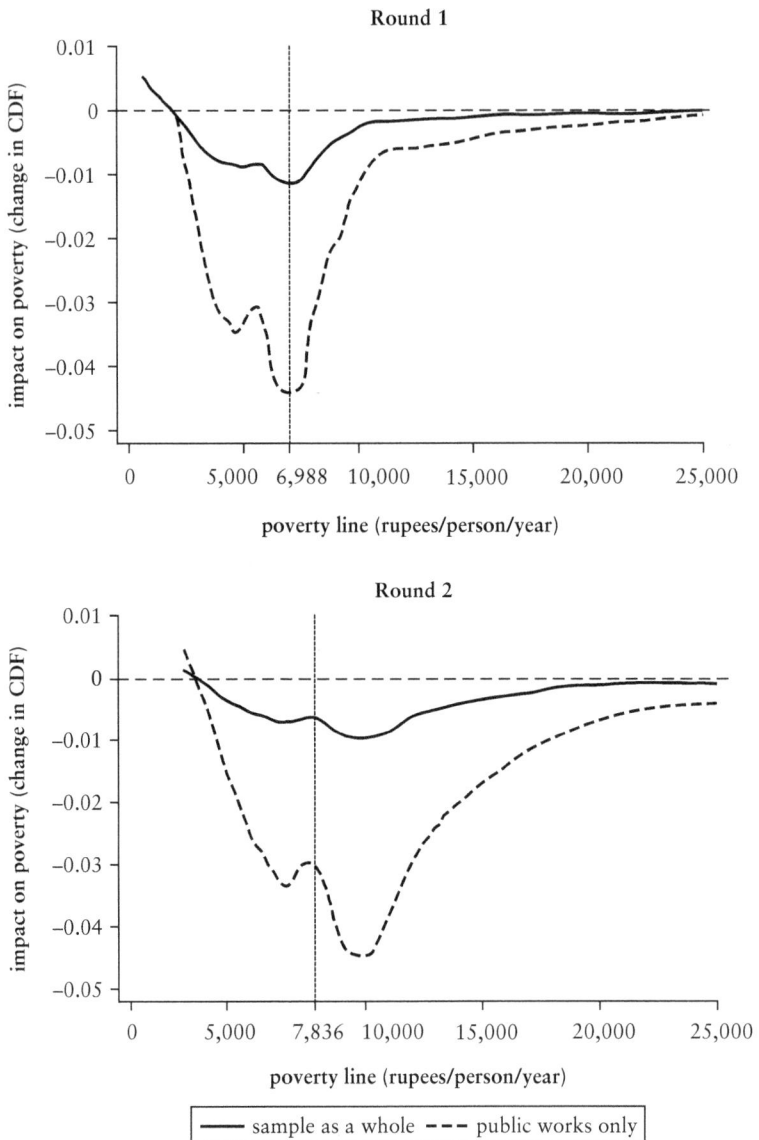

Source: Estimates based on the Bihar Rural Employment Guarantee Scheme
(BREGS) survey.

Note: CDF = cumulative distribution function.

predicted by adding up their idiosyncratic reports on forgone work. Poverty impacts, illustrated in figure 6.3, are greater (as one would expect), but the difference is not large. In R1, the impact among PW participants at the median rises by less than 1 percentage point. The extra impact at the median is even lower in R2, but larger impacts—an extra 1–2 percentage points—are found within the region of one-third below the median to one-third above.[2]

Naturally, eliminating all forgone income yields even higher poverty impacts. This sensitivity test (see figure 6.4) indicates that BREGS reduced the poverty rate for R1 PW participants from 63.1 percent to 56.8 percent; instead of an impact of 5.4 percentage points with full forgone income, we estimate an impact of 6.3 percentage points. For the rural population as a whole, the R1 poverty rate fell by 1.7 percentage points instead of 1.4 percentage points with full forgone income. In R2, without any forgone income the poverty rate for PW participants would have fallen by 6.2 percentage points (from 56.4 percent to 50.2 percent) whereas it would have fallen by 1.4 percentage points in the rural population as a whole, from 43.2 percent to 41.8 percent.

So even if we have substantially overestimated forgone incomes using the individual survey responses, the poverty impacts for the rural population as a whole are not considerably greater.

Comparisons with Other Simulated Impacts

We started this book by noting the potential for the scheme to substantially reduce poverty—by 14 percentage points in 2009. More precisely, recall that we calculate that the poverty rate in the absence of the extra earnings from BREGS would have been 51.4 percent. Giving all households that want work on the scheme 100 days at the stipulated wage rate would have brought the poverty rate down to 37.6 percent—a drop of 13.8 percentage points. This stylized version of the scheme would have had an even larger impact in R2. We estimate that the poverty rate (again using the 2009 median as the poverty line adjusted for inflation) in R2 would have fallen from 42.3 percent without the scheme to 27.3 percent—a 15 percentage point decline.

This calculation is, of course, stylized. It assumes that every household that said it wanted work on the scheme (those who actually worked on the scheme *plus* the excess demanders) got the full 100 days of work allowed under the legislation, no participant had to give up any other source of income to take on this work, and every participant was paid the stipulated wage rates. It also assumes that other wages are unaffected. As noted in the introduction, the 100-day limit on employment means that the complete general equilibrium effects of

Figure 6.3 Poverty Impact Graph with 50 Percent Lower Forgone Income

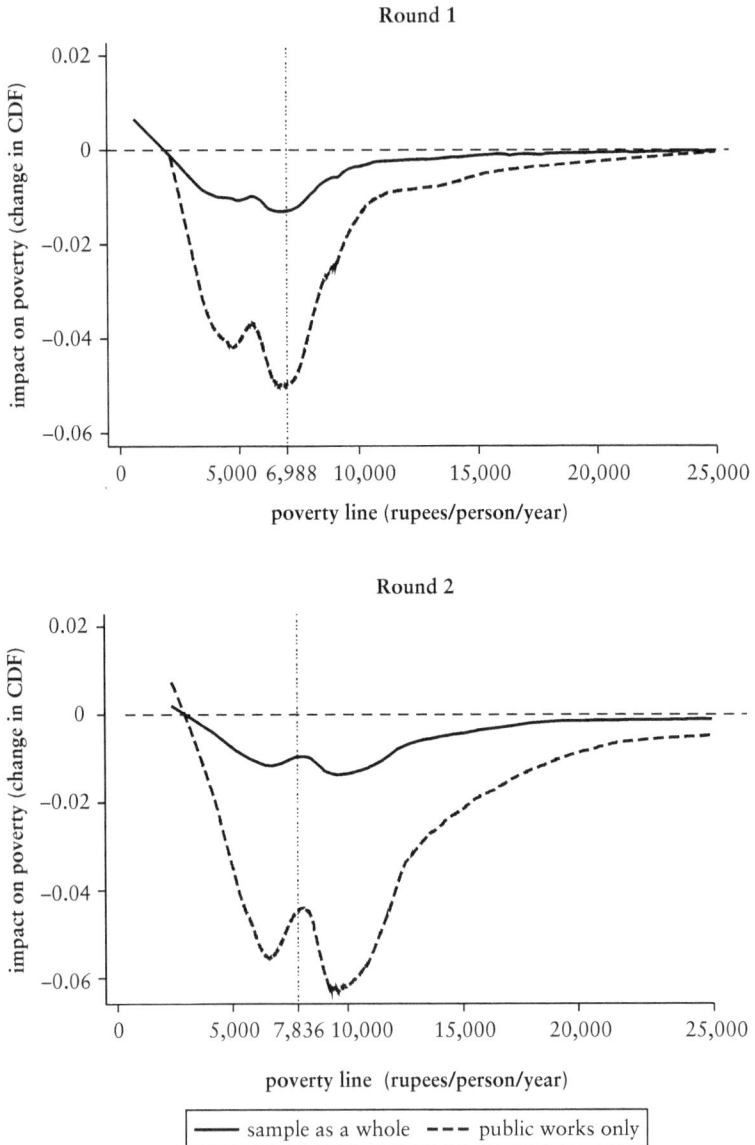

Round 1

Round 2

| | sample as a whole | ‐ ‐ ‐ public works only |

Source: Estimates based on the Bihar Rural Employment Guarantee Scheme (BREGS) survey.

Note: CDF = cumulative distribution function.

Figure 6.4 Poverty Impact Graph without Forgone Income

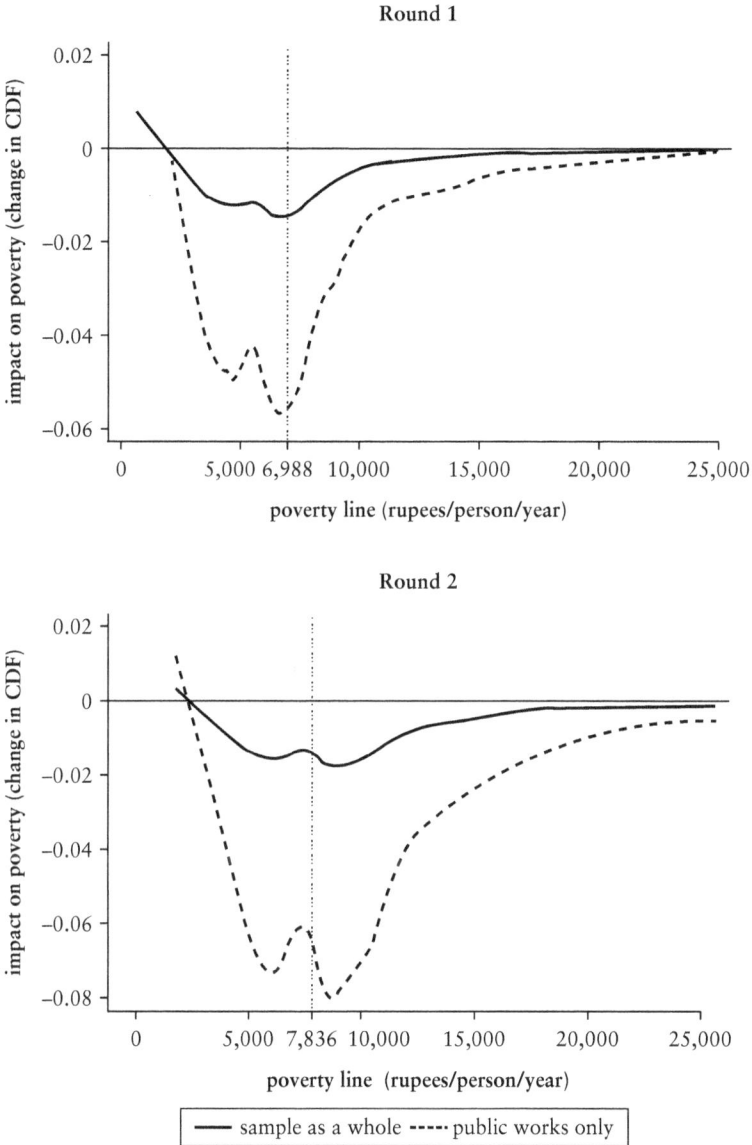

Source: Estimates based on Bihar Rural Employment Guarantee Scheme (BREGS) survey.

Note: CDF = cumulative distribution function.

the employment guarantee will not be realized, and it is difficult to say
just how strong these effects would be even if there were no rationing
up to the 100 day limit. Nonetheless, it would be safe to assume that
without any rationing of work up to the 100 day limit, there would
be spillover effects on other unskilled wage rates, which would favor
the poor. A reduction of 14 percent could well be an underestimate.

Figure 6.5 illustrates the impacts under this stylized scenario
across the full range of potential poverty lines, for R1 and R2, respectively. (Naturally, impacts are even larger among the PW participants, but we focus on the impacts in the population as a whole.)
The 14 percentage point drop turns out to be near the maximum
impact in R1, though slightly below the maximum in R2. Impacts
drop off at lower or higher poverty lines.

Thus, it is evident that there is a large "lost impact" on poverty of
BREGS. Instead of a reduction in the poverty rate of 14 percentage
points or more, we estimate that the impact is roughly 1 percentage
point. As seen from the results of this study so far, none of the
conditions assumed by the idealized version of BREGS holds in
practice. Not all households want the 100 days (see table 2.4). But
more important, there is a large unmet demand for work; even the
"conditional guarantee" (subject to the 100 day limit) is not working. There is also nonnegligible forgone income. And there are gaps
between the wages received and those stipulated by the scheme.

How much of the lost impact is due to the unmet demand for
work? That is, how much greater could the impact on poverty have
been if there was no unmet demand up to the 100 day limit? The
seemingly low impact on poverty reflects, in part, the high proportion of potential workers who wanted work on the scheme but did
not get it, though many of them did not require the full 100 days.

Two key assumptions are made in simulating the potential impact
of BREGS if the expressed demand were satisfied. First, we assume
that the changes in earnings from public works implied by the idealized version of BREGS are passed on fully to current consumption
(that is, the earnings are not saved or invested). Second, we ignore
consumption gains from the extra assets created as well as general
equilibrium effects (noting that the 100 day limit makes it unclear
how great a spillover effect can be expected).

The days of work for households currently participating in the
scheme are scaled up to equal the days they said they would have
liked in the survey, up to a maximum of 100 days. We value the
extra days at the average, household-specific, PW wage rate net of
forgone income. Households that wanted work but did not get it
are given the median of the simulated net earnings on PW for the
actual participants. No changes are made for those not interested in

Figure 6.5 Impacts on Poverty under Idealized Bihar Rural Employment Guarantee Scheme

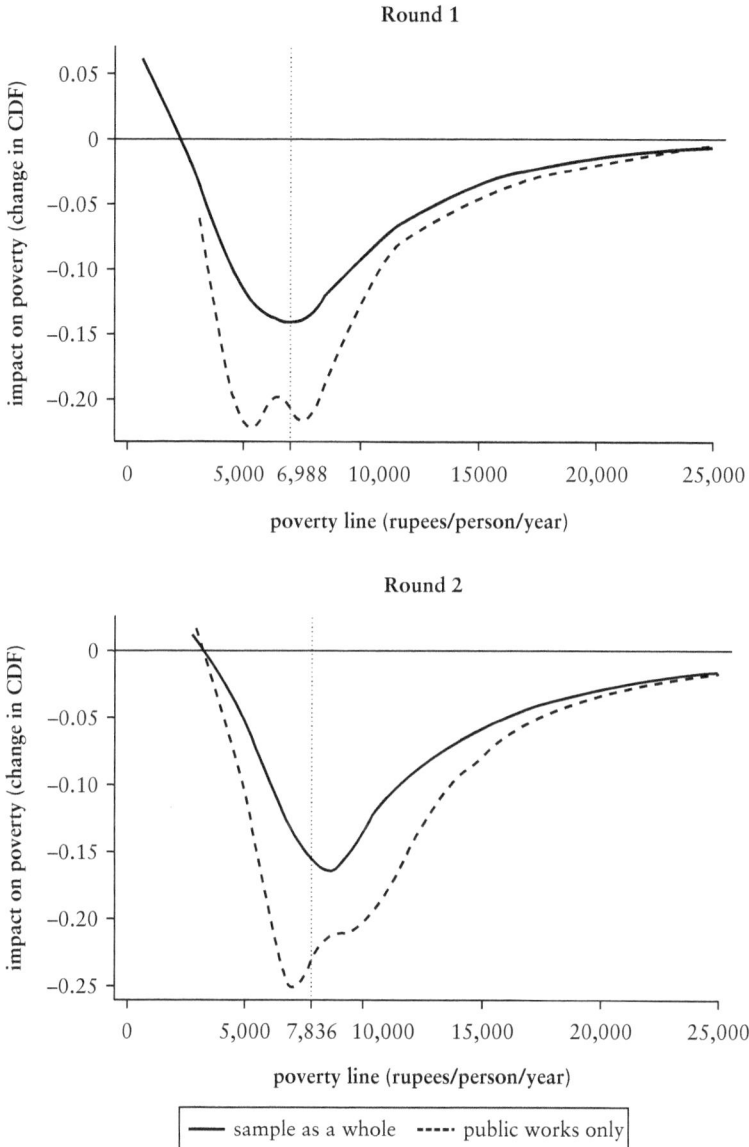

Round 1

Round 2

sample as a whole ----- public works only

Source: Estimates based on the Bihar Rural Employment Guarantee Scheme (BREGS) survey.

Note: See text for a description of simulation assumptions. CDF = cumulative distribution function.

participating. (We can only make this calculation for R2, in which we asked for the number of extra days desired.)

We estimate that satisfying the expressed demand for work on the scheme would have decreased the poverty rate in R2 from 42.3 percent to 33.7 percent. Satisfying the unmet demand for work would have increased the scheme's impact on poverty from about 1 percentage point to more than 8 percentage points.

How much of the lost impact is due to the gap between the actual wages received and the stipulated wages (as discussed in chapter 4)? To address this question, we simply reestimate the impacts by raising the wage rates actually received to the level of the stipulated wage rate for that date up to the 100 day limit, and keep all else constant. Closing this gap would have resulted in a poverty rate of 49.1 percent in R1 and 40.3 percent in R2, as compared with the preintervention rates of 51.4 percent and 42.3 percent, respectively. Thus, the wage gap accounts for about 2 percentage points of the lost impact—much less than that attributable to the unmet demand.

Thus we see that more than two-thirds—about 10 percentage points—of the 15 percentage points of lost impact in R2 is attributable to the ways in which the scheme is not fulfilling the provisions of the Act. The rest is due to forgone income, which is hard to avoid.

A second simulation allocates the same total public resources that were spent on BREGS in a different way. In calculating the cost of the scheme, we include both wage and nonwage costs from the administrative data. The precise budgets we use are Rs 858.42 per rural household in R1 and Rs 1,194.92 per rural household in R2.[3] The simplest alternative is to then give every household (regardless of whether poor) these amounts—a uniform transfer—so that the total across households equals the sum of money actually spent on BREGS. This plan requires no targeting. We estimate that this would reduce the poverty rate from 51.4 percent to 49.5 percent in R1, whereas in R2 it would reduce the poverty rate from 42.3 percent to 39.1 percent. Both resulting poverty rates are lower than those under BREGS.

This simulation assumes that there is no leakage of money from the budget for the transfers, which is unrealistic. If we make a seemingly generous allowance for leakage in these transfers, such that 10 percent is lost, then the poverty rates fall to 49.7 percent and 39.6 percent in R1 and R2, respectively—still an improvement in comparison with the BREGS impact.[4]

A third simulation of interest is to once again take the same budget but distribute it equally to all households holding a Below-Poverty-Line (BPL) card. This approach assumes that the government knows who has a BPL card (which is plausible given that they are issued by the government), but that it does not know who is really poor and how poor they are. Our calculations indicate that this alternative would reduce the poverty rate from 51.4 percent to 49.8 percent in R1, and in R2 it would reduce the poverty rate from 42.3 percent to 40.0 percent. In both cases, the poverty rates are lower than under BREGS. Poverty rates are also lower than for the uniform transfer, indicating that BPL cards are more likely to be given to those who are deemed to be poor in our data set. If we make a 10 percent allowance for leakage in the transfers, the poverty rates fall to 49.9 percent and 40.2 percent in R1 and R2, respectively.[5]

It is notable that the impact on poverty using an allocation of transfers based on BPL cards is only slightly greater than that calculated for a uniform, untargeted allocation of the same total expenditure. This outcome indicates that the assignment of BPL cards is only slightly more pro-poor than if they were handed out with an equal chance of anyone getting the card.

Table 6.1 summarizes the various budget-neutral simulations reported above. The calculations suggest that in 2009 the extra earnings from BREGS had slightly less impact on poverty through the income gains to workers than would have occurred through either a uniform transfer of the same gross expenditure (to everyone, whether poor or not) or a uniform transfer to those holding a BPL card (with only a slightly larger impact in the latter case). When one allows for 10 percent leakage from the transfers, there is hardly any difference in the poverty impacts in 2009—BREGS, uniform transfers of the same budget, or transfers of the same budget to BPL card holders would all have achieved a 50 percent poverty rate, as compared with an estimated preintervention rate of 51.4 percent. However, the picture looks less favorable for BREGS in 2010. For that year, we find that the scheme would not have done as well as either of these alternatives,

Table 6.1 Summary of Estimated Poverty Impacts Holding Total Public Spending Constant

percentage of population below the poverty line

		Round 1	Round 2
Preintervention	(Estimated by deducting net earnings gains from BREGS)	51.4	42.3
Postintervention	BREGS (observed data)	50.0	41.8
	Basic-income scheme	49.5	39.1
	Basic-income scheme with 10 percent leakage	49.7	39.6
	Transfers based on BPL ration cards	49.8	40.0

which would have reduced the poverty rate by an additional 1.5–2.0 percent points, even with a seemingly generous allowance for leakage. The scheme is clearly not justified, relative to feasible options, by its ability to transfer cash to poor people through the self-targeting mechanism. Only with sufficient asset creation benefiting poor people will the balance tilt in favor of this workfare scheme.

Perceptions of BREGS

We can complement this assessment of poverty impacts with perceptions about the scheme and general conditions in the village and their changes during the intervening year. The mean weighted shares of positive answers to perception questions included in the survey are presented by gender in table 6.2.[6]

The answers suggest that households are reasonably positive about their village circumstances, for which they have seen improvements during the survey period. More than half of all men and women in R1 and nearly two-thirds in R2 felt that infrastructure in their village had improved during the past year. A significant share (41 percent and 35 percent, respectively, of men and women in R1 and 46 percent and 42 percent in R2) felt that employment opportunities increased during the past year. More than three-quarters of both men and women reported that wages had gone up. Many fewer (34 percent and 23 percent in R1 and 26 percent and 17 percent in R2) felt that there had been a reduction in short-term, work-related migration from the village.

Optimism on the same issues with respect to BREGS was more muted, and in marked contrast, perceptions were that the impact of BREGS weakened between the two survey rounds.[7] Only 30 percent and 28 percent of men and women, respectively, felt that BREGS had increased access to employment in R1, falling to 23 percent and 16 percent in R2. Fewer still felt that BREGS had led to a decline in work migration: approximately a fifth of men in both rounds and 23 percent and 13 percent of women for R1 and R2, respectively. Respondents perceived that BREGS employment was heavily rationed and not available to them. In R1, only 17 percent of men felt that they could get BREGS work when they asked for it during the previous year and even fewer (12 percent) did so in R2. Women are even more pessimistic: the share who felt that they could get work on a worksite, already a low 18 percent in R1, halved to 9 percent a year later. In both rounds, slightly more than half of male and female respondents trusted that BREGS would still be a source of employment in a year's time.

Table 6.2 Summary Statistics on Perception Variables

| | Round 1 | | | | Round 2 | | | |
| | Women | | Men | | Women | | Men | |
	Mean	Standard deviation	Mean	Standard deviation	Mean	Standard deviation	Mean	Standard deviation
Your household: knowledge of BREGS increased in past year	—	—	—	—	0.39	0.49	0.56	0.50
Your village: infrastructure improved in past year	0.53	0.50	0.57	0.49	0.62	0.48	0.63	0.48
Your village: work increased in past year	0.35	0.48	0.41	0.49	0.42	0.49	0.46	0.50
Your village: wages increased in past year	0.79	0.41	0.83	0.38	0.74	0.44	0.78	0.42
Your village: migration decreased in past year	0.23	0.42	0.34	0.47	0.17	0.38	0.26	0.44
Your village: workers can influence wages	0.56	0.50	0.59	0.49	0.62	0.49	0.67	0.47
Your village: benefits of participating in Gram Sabha	0.15	0.36	0.22	0.42	0.14	0.34	0.22	0.42
Your village: women participate in Gram Sabha	0.24	0.43	0.29	0.45	0.36	0.48	0.42	0.49
Can get work under BREGS when demand it	0.18	0.39	0.17	0.38	0.09	0.28	0.12	0.33
BREGS projects have increased employment	0.28	0.45	0.30	0.46	0.16	0.37	0.23	0.42
BREGS decreased migration of labor	0.23	0.42	0.22	0.42	0.13	0.34	0.20	0.40

(Continued on the following page)

Table 6.2 (Continued)

| | Round 1 | | | | Round 2 | | | |
| | Women | | Men | | Women | | Men | |
	Mean	Standard deviation	Mean	Standard deviation	Mean	Standard deviation	Mean	Standard deviation
BREGS work will be available in village next year	0.52	0.50	0.61	0.49	0.51	0.50	0.59	0.49
Women have right to choose BREGS projects	0.52	0.50	0.56	0.50	0.62	0.49	0.66	0.47
Assets created under BREGS are useful to women	0.46	0.50	0.47	0.50	0.82	0.38	0.80	0.40
Women work in BREGS projects	0.79	0.41	0.75	0.44	0.70	0.46	0.70	0.46
Women treated well at BREGS worksite	0.95	0.22	0.95	0.22	0.98	0.13	0.98	0.14
Women get work if they bring children to BREGS worksite	0.71	0.45	0.67	0.47	0.76	0.42	0.80	0.40
Women paid same wages as men in BREGS	0.89	0.31	0.87	0.34	0.83	0.38	0.80	0.40
Women of household would like to work on BREGS	0.43	0.49	0.42	0.49	0.46	0.50	0.43	0.50
Women of household would be allowed to work on BREGS	0.41	0.49	0.41	0.49	0.47	0.50	0.44	0.50

Source: Estimates based on Bihar Rural Employment Guarantee Scheme (BREGS) survey.
Note: Household-weighted, individual-level data. All perception questions require yes/no answers, where yes is coded 1 and no is coded 0. See annex table 6A.1 for summary statistics for the sample excluding BREGS participants. — = not available.

Annex 6A

Table 6A.1 Perceptions among Nonparticipants

Variable	Male round 1			Female round 1			Male round 2			Female round 2		
	Mean	Standard deviation	Observations	Mean	Standard Deviation	Observations	Mean	Standard deviation	Observations	Mean	Standard deviation	Observations
Your household: Knowledge of BREGS increased in past year	—	—	—	—	—	—	0.54	0.50	1,747	0.37	0.48	2,376
Your village: Infrastructure improved in past year	0.53	0.50	1,751	0.53	0.50	2,401	0.61	0.49	1,765	0.62	0.49	2,410
Your village: Work increased in past year	0.36	0.48	1,682	0.35	0.48	2,108	0.43	0.50	1,700	0.41	0.49	2,149
Your village: Wages increased in past year	0.82	0.39	802	0.79	0.41	955	0.77	0.42	1,709	0.74	0.44	2,212
Your village: Migration decreased in past year	0.29	0.45	794	0.22	0.42	901	0.22	0.41	1,716	0.16	0.37	2,113
Your village: Workers can influence wages	0.58	0.49	1,709	0.55	0.50	2,142	0.68	0.47	1,704	0.62	0.49	2,022
Your village: Benefits of participating in Gram Sabha	0.19	0.39	1,597	0.15	0.36	2,062	0.21	0.41	1,657	0.13	0.34	2,023
Your village: Women participate in Gram Sabha	0.28	0.45	1,641	0.23	0.42	2,180	0.39	0.49	1,673	0.35	0.48	2,149
Can get work under BREGS when demand it	0.13	0.34	1,441	0.18	0.38	1,489	0.08	0.28	1,632	0.07	0.26	1,868
BREGS projects have increased employment	0.23	0.42	1,459	0.27	0.45	1,470	0.18	0.38	1,633	0.13	0.34	1,835

(Continued on the following page)

Table 6A.1 (Continued)

Variable	Male round 1			Female round 1			Male round 2			Female round 2		
	Mean	Standard deviation	Observations	Mean	Standard Deviation	Observations	Mean	Standard deviation	Observations	Mean	Standard deviation	Observations
BREGS decreased migration of labor	0.18	0.38	1,428	0.22	0.41	1,388	0.16	0.36	1,611	0.12	0.33	1,784
BREGS work will be available in village next year	0.54	0.50	734	0.51	0.50	725	0.56	0.50	813	0.48	0.50	707
Women have right to choose BREGS projects	0.54	0.50	1,116	0.52	0.50	999	0.66	0.47	1,304	0.62	0.49	1,332
Assets created under BREGS useful to women	0.43	0.49	1,199	0.46	0.50	1,122	0.80	0.40	1,555	0.81	0.39	1,799
Women work in BREGS projects	0.70	0.46	1,423	0.77	0.42	1,501	0.67	0.47	1,601	0.68	0.47	1,899
Women treated well at BREGS worksite	0.94	0.24	930	0.95	0.22	993	0.98	0.13	973	0.98	0.13	1,016
Women get work if they bring children to BREGS worksite	0.68	0.47	771	0.73	0.45	838	0.82	0.39	878	0.77	0.42	858
Women paid same wages as men in BREGS	0.86	0.35	947	0.90	0.31	995	0.79	0.41	909	0.82	0.38	946
Women of household would like to work on BREGS	0.35	0.48	1,420	0.40	0.49	2,052	0.37	0.48	1,747	0.43	0.49	2,476
Women of household would be allowed to work on BREGS	0.34	0.47	1,416	0.38	0.49	2,031	0.37	0.48	1,747	0.43	0.50	2,462

Source: Estimates based on the Bihar Rural Employment Guarantee Scheme (BREGS) survey.
Note: Household-weighted, individual-level data. All perception questions require yes/no answers, for which yes is coded 1, and no is coded 0.
— = not available.

Perceptions then are consistent with the findings on wages reported in chapter 4, in which we hypothesized that the observed rise in non-PW wages was attributable to the recent growth in casual off-farm employment rather than to BREGS. This seems to accord well with villagers' own perceptions.

When it comes to perceptions about the way in which women are treated on worksites, both men and women are quite positive. Three-quarters of women and just slightly fewer men agreed that women actively participate in BREGS; whereas the same proportions (though reversed by gender) felt that women are not penalized in getting work if they bring children to the worksite. Close to all (95–98 percent) perceived that women are treated well at worksites and close to 90 percent of women and 80 percent of men said that women are paid the same wage.

Notes

1. As a consequence of the smoothing used in creating figure 6.1, the average impact at the median is slightly lower than the precise estimate at that point reported above.

2. We then find that the poverty rate for R1 (again using the R1 median) among PW participants fell from 62.8 percent to 56.8 percent as the result of BREGS—a drop of 6.0 percentage points, as compared with 5.4 percentage points with full forgone income, as indicated by the respondents. For the rural population as a whole, the R1 poverty rate fell from 51.6 percent to 50.0 percent—a 1.6 percentage point decline, as compared with 1.4 percentage points with full forgone income. In R2, the poverty rate for PW participants fell from 54.0 percent to 50.2 percent—a 3.8 percentage point drop, as compared with 2.4 percentage points with the full forgone income from the survey responses—while it fell from 42.6 percent to 41.8 percent in the population as a whole, representing a 0.8 percentage point decline, as compared with 0.7 percentage point with the full forgone income.

3. The administrative data indicate total expenditures of Rs 13,058 million in fiscal year 2008/09 and Rs 18,177 million for fiscal year 2009/10. These amounts were divided by our count of 152 million households in rural Bihar, as implied by the survey weights. Census projections for these years gave slightly higher counts, but it is better to use our survey-based numbers for internal consistency.

4. The results are not very different if we use the estimated leakage in BREGS (assuming the discrepancy between survey responses and administrative data is due to leakage to unintended beneficiaries; see table 4.5). Poverty rates fall to 49.6 percent and 39.2 percent in R1 and R2, respectively, for the uniform transfer.

5. Again, applying estimated leakage in BREGS (see chapter 5) yields very similar results. Poverty rates fall to 50.1 percent and 40.3 percent in R1 and R2, respectively, with a Below Poverty Line–targeted uniform transfer.

6. This uses the entire sample of individuals interviewed in each round. We also calculated the summary statistics for the sample of interviewed individuals from households in which both a man and a woman were interviewed in either round. The results were very similar, so we only report the results for the full sample.

7. It is interesting to note that this optimism holds in the sample of nonparticipants, though less so than in the full sample (that is, including participants). See annex table 6A.1.

Reference

Ministry of Labour and Employment. 2010. *Report on Employment and Unemployment Survey (2009–10)*. Chandigarh: Government of India.

7

Reforming the Bihar Rural Employment Guarantee Scheme: Citizen Awareness

The rights-based, demand-driven nature of the Mahatma Gandhi National Rural Employment Guarantee Scheme (MGNREGS) and its decentralized, participatory approach are two core aspects of the scheme that set it apart from previous public works schemes in India. These aspects of the scheme introduce new challenges in delivery, including developing mechanisms to register demand for work. This chapter uses the quantitative and qualitative work done for this study to assess how the demand-side processes are working, how aware people are of those processes and their rights under the National Rural Employment Guarantee Act (the Act, or NREGA), why some people are more knowledgeable about the scheme than others, and how policy makers can improve knowledge.

Registration and Expressing Demand for Work

To participate, the Act requires that households must first register and get a job card (see the overview). In round 2 (R2) of the Bihar Rural Employment Guarantee Scheme (BREGS) survey, 42 percent of rural households had been issued job cards, up from 34 percent in round 1 (R1) of the survey (see table 7.1).[1] Households without job cards are less likely to get work on the scheme. In both survey rounds, 40 percent of male and about a third of female excess demanders reported the lack of a job card as the reason for not getting work. At the same time, there are a few households (but a

Table 7.1 Not All Households That Want a Job Card
Have One

	Round 1 (percent)	Round 2 (percent)
Households with job cards	34.2	42.2
Among households without job cards:		
Households that are in the process of obtaining a job card	26.0	5.0
Households that want, applied for, but have not gotten the card	33.4	39.6
Reason: no acquaintance with officials	59.2	37.9
Reason: perceive discrimination by officials	29.3	46.7
Reason: without BPL card	3.9	4.0
Reason: with disabled members	2.3	1.6
Reason: cannot afford	2.5	6.0
Households that want but have not applied	11.9	19.3
Reason: unaware of application process	49.0	73.1
Reason: perceive application process too lengthy	10.8	7.2
Reason: perceive unlikely to obtain	20.2	8.1
Reason: deterred by lack of BPL card	11.2	1.2
Reason: deterred by disability	6.4	5.9
Households that do not want	28.7	35.9
Reason: do not need work	30.1	20.5
Reason: deterred by disability	6.2	15.2
Reason: deterred by other program features[a]	63.7	64.3

Source: Estimates based on the Bihar Rural Employment Guarantee Scheme (BREGS) survey.

Note: Households with missing values are excluded from the sample. BPL = Below Poverty Line.

a. These households were not interested in the type of work, or felt the stipulated wage was too low or the number of days available too few.

declining share) that say they do not have a job card but also report getting work on the scheme. We find that 7.8 percent of households without a job card in R1 got work on the scheme, falling to 3.8 percent in R2. However (as noted in box 7.1), we cannot rule out the possibility that some of those interviewed were unaware that they had a job card.

In both years, one in five households reported not receiving a job card even after applying for it. Lack of local contacts and discrimination by functionaries were perceived to be key reasons in both years, with the proportion reporting the latter reason increasing to 47 percent from 29 percent between the two years. Qualitative research indicates that caste and electoral politics may have a role to play in this process (Sunai 2009). Reports for Bihar and other

Box 7.1 Are the Transparency Safeguards Adhered To in Practice?

The job card is an important transparency safeguard; it is supposed to serve as a complete record of adult household members (with photographs) and of all scheme-related activity by the household members. In practice, qualitative research for this report and other field studies suggest that this function is not yet being served. Poor knowledge of processes as well as high levels of illiteracy among Bihar Rural Employment Guarantee Scheme (BREGS) workers exacerbates the problem.

An encouraging finding is that the majority (two-thirds) of job card holders in Bihar have the card in their own possession. This is the first step in ensuring transparency. However, this still leaves nearly a third of job card holders reporting that their card is held by the Mukhiya or other panchayat members and officials (panchayat rozgar sewak, postmaster, and the like). But one-third may be a lower bound; qualitative research suggests that households may be unaware that job cards have been issued in their name and are in the possession of a middleman or functionary. Administrative data indicate that 61 percent (74 percent) of rural households were issued job cards in 2008/09 (2009/10), whereas only 34 percent (42 percent) of households in the BREGS survey reported possession of a job card in approximately the same period. The same research also indicates that passbooks for workers' bank and post office accounts are often held by scheme functionaries or the Mukhiya, leaving room for manipulation and misuse.

We also find that job cards are poorly maintained. The majority of households report that their job cards list at least one adult member, but about 29 percent in round 1 of the survey said their cards do not have the photographs of all listed members. Though job cards and photographs are supposed to be issued free of charge, in both rounds, only about a quarter of job card holders obtained theirs without payment. The rest paid between 40 and 50 rupees, on average. Qualitative research suggests that scheme functionaries often charge for the photographs. In addition, records of work applications, days worked, and wages paid are often not made in the job cards. For instance, when asked about payments received at the last worksite at which they worked, 24 percent of men and 38 percent of women workers did not even know if this information was recorded in the job card. Only 29 percent of men and 25 percent of women workers reported that payments received were recorded in their job cards.

Source: Authors' calculations from the Bihar Rural Employment Guarantee Scheme (BREGS) survey; Indian Grameen Services 2010; Development Alternatives 2009; and Sunai 2009.

northern states have also emphasized the specific barriers faced by women, for example, in getting their names on job cards (Khera and Nayak 2009). Among those who wanted a job card but had not yet applied for one, the main deterrents were a lack of knowledge about the application process, the perception that it was lengthy, and they thought that they would not get a job card even if they were to apply for it (see table 7.1).

We find that the knowledge of rights, and equally important, information about the processes by which to access these rights, remains low, and more so among women (more on this below). In particular, the notion of "demanding" and applying for work is still in its infancy.[2] We find that only a quarter of male (and only 16 percent of female) workers in the sample had actually demanded work at the last worksite at which they worked in R1 (see table 7.2). The rest had simply come to the worksite when it opened, or obtained work through village leaders (including the Mukhiya), scheme functionaries, or even contractors. An encouraging trend is the increase in the proportion demanding work in the second survey round, particularly among female workers.

Women said that they were often turned away from worksites if they came for work without a husband or male relative. It is unclear how widespread this practice is. But the R1 survey indicates that 23 percent of women workers who applied for work at the last BREGS worksite at which they worked did so with their husbands

Table 7.2 Notion of "Demanding" Work Is Weak but Improving

	Round 1		Round 2	
Way in Which Work Was Obtained	*Men*	*Women*	*Men*	*Women*
Asked for work	25.2	16.3	40.5	33.8
Came to worksite	11.8	10.6	11.8	17.1
Called for work by contractor	9.2	14.0	13.2	13.5
Called for work by panchayat rozgar sewak	9.4	14.8	7.0	4.7
Called for work by Mukhiya or Gram Panchayat member	41.1	36.0	26.3	19.6
Other	3.1	7.3	0.2	11.1

Source: Estimates based on the Bihar Rural Employment Guarantee Scheme (BREGS) survey.

Note: Based on responses by workers in the surveyed households to the question of how work was obtained at the BREGS worksite at which they last worked. Observations with missing values (workers that did not respond to the question) are excluded from the sample.

and 52 percent applied as part of a group. It was more common for men (60 percent in R1, but falling to 35 percent in R2) to apply individually for work. Applications as part of a group were even more common in R2 (70 percent for women and 58 percent for men).

Qualitative research also corroborates that many villagers believe that work will be provided when it is available (that is, not necessarily on demand). In some cases, the Mukhiya, the panchayat rozgar sewak (PRS), or other scheme functionaries inform potential workers that work will be available when a worksite is opened. The perception of Mukhiyas and PRSs is that many people do not formally demand work because they are used to a contractor-based system wherein work is allocated rather than demanded (Sunai 2009).

There is little awareness that the right to employment is a universal right for rural households and not limited to specific groups. As a consequence, potential applicants can be excluded based on certain characteristics (for example, widowhood, gender, old age, and disability) or a lack of documentation (for instance, a Below-Poverty-Line [BPL] ration card). We find that although 11 percent of households perceived the lack of a BPL card to be a deterrent to applying for a job card in 2008/09, fewer than 2 percent continued to think so in 2009/10.[3] Another small share of households (6 percent in both rounds) cited disability as the reason for lack of interest in the scheme or for not applying for or getting a job card. Although public works schemes are typically designed for able-bodied individuals, some states have made greater efforts to extend the scheme to persons with disabilities.[4] We find little sign that this has happened in Bihar, however.

There is also some anecdotal evidence that women are discouraged from participating because of a perception that they are less productive. Information campaigns need to stress that all adults are eligible for the scheme and that potential workers need to demand work, individually or collectively, to get it. And it is crucial that such campaigns be designed keeping in mind the high levels of illiteracy in rural Bihar. There is also a need to specifically mobilize weaker groups to encourage their participation in the scheme.

What Do Rural Households Know about BREGS?

The surveyed individuals were asked whether they knew about the existence of BREGS, and if so, they were given 12 questions aimed at testing their knowledge of the scheme's functioning, as well as about their rights under the Act. Table 7.3 provides the mean of correct responses for each of the questions by gender and survey

Table 7.3 Summary Statistics of Knowledge of Bihar Rural Employment Guarantee Scheme Rules

	Round 1				Round 2			
	Women		Men		Women		Men	
	Mean	Standard deviation	Mean	Standard deviation	Mean	Standard deviation	Mean	Standard deviation
A. Full sample								
Heard	Has heard of BREGS							
	0.73	0.44	0.95	0.21	0.88	0.33	0.98	0.15
Score 1	Employment knowledge score							
	1.51	1.52	2.60	1.88	2.10	1.56	3.14	1.83
Days	Knows entitled to 100 or thinks 90 days[a]							
	0.11	0.31	0.37	0.48	0.13	0.34	0.38	0.49
Gender	Knows both men and women can demand work							
	0.51	0.50	0.57	0.50	0.62	0.49	0.68	0.47
BPL	Knows non-BPL families can demand work							
	0.38	0.48	0.53	0.50	0.57	0.49	0.69	0.46
Work lag	Knows work to be provided within 15 days							
	0.02	0.13	0.06	0.25	0.07	0.26	0.14	0.34
Unemployment allowance	Knows about unemployment allowance							
	0.11	0.32	0.29	0.45	0.22	0.42	0.41	0.49
Wage rate	Knows wage rate							
	0.21	0.41	0.44	0.50	0.26	0.44	0.45	0.50
Wage lag	Knows wages to be paid within 2 weeks							
	0.08	0.27	0.12	0.32	0.10	0.30	0.14	0.35
Contractor	Knows contractors not allowed							
	0.11	0.32	0.24	0.43	0.13	0.34	0.27	0.44
Score 2	Facilities knowledge score							
	0.98	1.29	1.39	1.41	1.12	1.20	1.55	1.29
Child care	Knows of child care facilities							
	0.19	0.39	0.19	0.39	0.12	0.32	0.18	0.38

Water	Knows of drinking water facilities	0.42	0.49	0.59	0.49	0.53	0.50	0.67	0.47
Shade	Knows of shade facilities	0.21	0.40	0.36	0.48	0.38	0.48	0.51	0.50
First aid	Knows of first aid facilities	0.18	0.38	0.26	0.44	0.10	0.30	0.20	0.40
Board	Knows of information board	—	—	—	—	0.01	0.11	0.06	0.23
Demand	Knows work has to be demanded	—	—	—	—	0.52	0.50	0.74	0.44

B. Individuals in households in which a man and a woman were interviewed

Heard	Has heard of BREGS	0.72	0.45	0.96	0.20	0.87	0.34	0.98	0.15
Score 1	Employment knowledge score	1.57	1.57	2.60	1.88	2.17	1.58	3.16	1.83
Days	Knows entitled to 100 or thinks 90 days[a]	0.12	0.32	0.37	0.48	0.14	0.35	0.39	0.49
Gender	Knows both men and women can demand work	0.51	0.50	0.56	0.50	0.64	0.48	0.69	0.46
BPL	Knows non-BPL families can demand work	0.39	0.49	0.53	0.50	0.58	0.49	0.68	0.47
Work lag	Knows work is to be provided within 15 days	0.02	0.14	0.06	0.24	0.08	0.27	0.13	0.34
Unemployment allowance	Knows about unemployment allowance	0.13	0.33	0.29	0.45	0.23	0.42	0.41	0.49
Wage rate	Knows wage rate	0.22	0.42	0.44	0.50	0.28	0.45	0.46	0.50
Wage lag	Knows wages to be paid within 2 weeks	0.09	0.29	0.12	0.32	0.10	0.30	0.14	0.35
Contractor	Knows contractors not allowed	0.13	0.33	0.24	0.43	0.13	0.34	0.27	0.44

(Continued on the following page)

Table 7.3 (Continued)

| | Round 1 | | | | Round 2 | | | |
| | Women | | Men | | Women | | Men | |
	Mean	Standard deviation	Mean	Standard deviation	Mean	Standard deviation	Mean	Standard deviation
Score 2	Facilities knowledge score	1.02	1.30	1.40	1.40	1.15	1.21	1.55	1.29
Child care	Knows of child care facilities	0.19	0.39	0.19	0.39	0.13	0.33	0.18	0.39
Water	Knows of drinking water facilities	0.44	0.50	0.59	0.49	0.53	0.50	0.67	0.47
Shade	Knows of shade facilities	0.22	0.41	0.36	0.48	0.39	0.49	0.51	0.50
First aid	Knows of first aid facilities	0.18	0.39	0.25	0.44	0.11	0.31	0.20	0.40
Board	Knows of information board	—	—	—	—	0.02	0.12	0.06	0.23
Demand	Knows work has to be demanded	—	—	—	—	0.50	0.50	0.73	0.44

Source: Estimates based on the Bihar Rural Employment Guarantee Scheme (BREGS) survey.

Note: Household weighted. Approximate sample sizes: Panel A, "Heard of BREGS": $N = 2,800$ for women; $N = 2,300$ for men; Panel B, "Heard of BREGS": $N = 2,000$; Women round 1: $N = 1,500$; $N = 2,000$ for remaining questions.

Questions about the information board and having to demand work were not asked in round 1. Score 1, the "employment knowledge score," is an overall measure of knowledge about the scheme's employment aspects, based on the number of correct answers to the eight employment-related questions. Score 2, the "facilities knowledge score," is an overall measure of knowledge of the facilities and amenities that BREGS mandates must be provided at worksites (child care, drinking water, shade, and first aid kits). BPL = Below Poverty Line; — = not available.

a. A response of "3 months" or "90 days" is treated as a correct response to the question on number of days of worked.

round. We provide the weighted summary statistics for two samples: all interviewed individuals in panel A of table 7.3 and all those from households in which both a man and a woman were interviewed in panel B. (The questionnaire first asked individuals whether they had heard about BREGS. If they answered no, the rest of the awareness questions were skipped for those individuals. Note that the means presented in table 7.3 simply treat these as missing observations rather than including them as zeroes.)

We find knowledge of the details of the scheme to be very low and lower for women than for men.[5] Most men and three-quarters of women had heard about the program by R1, but many were unaware of their precise rights and entitlements under BREGS. The level of understanding of how to go about obtaining work is clearly low. For example, 37 percent of men and 11 percent of women knew that households can work up to 100 days per year; 57 percent and 51 percent (respectively) knew that both men and women can work; 53 percent and 38 percent that a household need not have a BPL ration card to be eligible; 6 percent and 2 percent that work should be provided within 15 days of having demanded it; 44 percent and 21 percent knew what wage should be paid, and 12 percent and 8 percent that it should be paid within two weeks; and only 24 percent and 11 percent that contractors are not allowed on the scheme. The R1 questionnaire did not contain a question about whether the individual knows work must be demanded. However, in R2, 74 percent of men and 52 percent of women answered the question correctly. The only awareness question for which there was no gap between men and women concerned the provision for child care, which 19 percent of all individuals knew about.

As an overall measure of knowledge about the scheme's employment aspects, we use the number of correct answers to the eight employment-related questions. We call this the "employment knowledge score," or "Score 1" for short. This gives averages of 2.6 for men and 1.5 for women out of a maximum of 8. A second measure was created for awareness of the facilities and amenities that BREGS mandates must be provided at worksites (child care, drinking water, shade, and first aid kits). Respondents were asked to identify what facilities were supposed to be provided. The mean number of correct answers was 1.4 and 1.0 out of a maximum of 4 for men and women, respectively. We refer to this as the "facilities knowledge score" ("Score 2").

As can be seen in table 7.3, knowledge of entitlements and BREGS procedures improved with time. The average employment knowledge score increased to 3.1 for men and 2.1 for women between rounds 1 and 2, while the facilities knowledge score rose to 1.6 and 1.1, respectively. But these are clearly not large increases.

Table 7.4, column 1, shows the marginal effects of various individual, household, and village attributes on whether an individual has heard about BREGS. This regression uses all individual observations for R1.

Higher educational attainment at the secondary level and above has a significantly positive effect on awareness of the scheme, as does male gender. We also collected data to calibrate an individual-specific version of the Pearlin Mastery scale, which is a measure of the extent to which individuals perceive themselves in control of factors that affect their lives. We find that the Pearlin scale has a significant positive effect for women but not for men.[6] Being married, or widowed or divorced, as opposed to unmarried, significantly reduces the probability of having heard about BREGS.

Household-level characteristics that are correlated with higher participation in the scheme (see chapter 3) also have a significant positive impact on knowledge. These characteristics include having male and female household members who have engaged in casual work, being from the Mahadalit caste or of the Hindu religion, being related to the ward member or other panchayat member, and having voted in the panchayat election. In contrast, higher wealth as measured by the assets index (as used in chapter 3) and land holdings tend to reduce the likelihood of having heard about BREGS. The scheme is clearly less relevant to wealthier groups. The fact that they know less about the scheme suggests that this type of knowledge is not public knowledge.

Conditional on individual and household characteristics, the attributes of a respondent's village of residence have considerable explanatory power. We find that knowledge is lower in villages that are more unequal (based on distribution of assets). Living in an electrified village that is within five kilometers of the Gram Panchayat or block headquarters also appears to negatively affect knowledge of BREGS. Larger shares of Scheduled Caste households and ones with kutcha houses also have a strong positive effect, as does having a panchayat bhawan, a post office, and access to nonagricultural enterprises within five kilometers of the village. The characteristics of the Mukhiya also emerge as important. A male Mukhiya has a positive effect on knowledge; a Mukhiya employed in agricultural pursuits has a significant negative effect on whether villagers have heard of BREGS.

The regression also tests for whether active associations in the village has an effect. We separately control for the presence of women's self-help groups (SHGs), and civil society organizations

Table 7.4 Regression for Knowledge of Bihar Rural Employment Guarantee Scheme Rules in Round 1

	Heard (1)	Days (2)	Gender (3)	BPL (4)	Unemployment allowance (5)	Wage rate (6)	Contractor (7)
Individual characteristics							
Age	0.005	0.010**	0.005	0.005	0.000	0.003	0.006*
Age squared	-0.000	-0.000***	-0.000	-0.000	-0.000	-0.000	-0.000*
Education							
Literate (< class 5)	0.005	0.061***	0.033	-0.021	0.062***	0.015	0.025
Class 5 pass (primary)	0.014	0.022	-0.046	-0.011	0.048	-0.035	0.015
Class 8 pass (middle)	0.009	0.074**	-0.087**	0.032	0.033	0.006	0.052*
Class 10 pass (secondary)	0.100***	0.115***	-0.017	0.022	0.128***	0.044	0.041
Class 12 pass (higher secondary)	0.151***	0.070	-0.126*	0.065	0.103*	0.012	0.056
More than higher secondary	0.149***	0.174**	-0.030	0.074	0.136*	-0.016	0.055
Household head	0.035	0.038	0.024	0.042	0.037	0.078**	0.008
Spouse of household head	0.008	-0.010	0.001	0.025	0.009	0.060	0.034
Married	-0.077***	-0.048	0.002	-0.095*	0.039	-0.050	0.083**
Widowed or divorced	-0.084**	-0.043	-0.029	-0.118*	0.032	-0.010	0.125***
Male gender	0.240***	0.183***	-0.003	0.198***	0.117***	0.115**	0.145***
Pearlin index interacted with (male)	0.005	0.001	0.018**	-0.000	0.001	0.020***	0.005
Pearlin index interacted with (female)	0.020***	0.004	0.001	0.009	-0.001	0.009	0.014***

(Continued on the following page)

Table 7.4 (Continued)

	Heard (1)	Days (2)	Gender (3)	BPL (4)	Unemployment allowance (5)	Wage rate (6)	Contractor (7)
Household characteristics							
ln (household size)	0.092	-0.128*	-0.043	-0.056	0.043	-0.140	0.099*
ln (household size) squared	-0.032*	0.028	0.014	0.034	-0.018	0.043	-0.023
Share of male adults	-0.043	0.019	0.010	0.115*	0.075	-0.066	0.065
Share of female adults	0.035	-0.057	-0.032	0.046	0.036	0.015	0.017
Share of elderly	-0.066	0.021	0.010	-0.082	0.141	-0.024	0.065
Share of children younger than age 6	0.014	0.089*	0.088	0.056	-0.005	0.001	0.005
Male household head	-0.018	0.049*	-0.013	0.001	0.021	0.061**	-0.012
Age of household head	0.000	-0.008**	0.004	-0.002	-0.003	-0.003	-0.005
Age of household head squared	0.000	0.000**	-0.000	0.000	0.000	0.000	0.000
Maximum education in household							
Literate (< class 5)	0.020	0.029	-0.051**	-0.026	-0.009	0.023	-0.012
Class 5 pass (primary)	-0.005	0.022	-0.048	-0.028	0.007	-0.002	-0.003
Class 8 pass (middle)	-0.001	0.040	0.032	-0.008	0.035	0.046	0.007
Class 10 pass (secondary)	-0.044*	-0.004	-0.104***	-0.045	-0.001	0.005	-0.064**
Class 12 pass (higher secondary)	-0.073**	0.081**	-0.032	-0.101**	-0.018	-0.012	-0.016
More than higher secondary	-0.052	0.167***	0.037	-0.035	0.039	0.045	0.096*

Social group						
Scheduled Caste	0.032	0.044	0.007	-0.022	0.001	-0.050*
Mahadalit	0.068***	-0.009	0.011	0.025	0.087**	-0.024
Other Backward Class	0.019	0.040	-0.004	-0.050**	-0.029	-0.057**
Scheduled Tribe	0.021	0.000	0.039	0.047	-0.036	-0.038
Hindu	0.067***	0.086***	0.046	0.013	0.080***	0.040*
Asset-house index	-0.006*	-0.009	-0.005	0.006	0.004	0.001
Asset-house index squared	0.000	0.001	-0.004*	-0.000	0.001	0.001
Asset-house index cubed	0.000	-0.000	0.001**	-0.000	-0.000	0.000
Land owned	-0.021*	0.035**	0.024	-0.001	0.017	-0.010
Land owned squared	0.002	-0.002	-0.002	-0.001	-0.001	0.000
BPL ration card	0.018	0.004	0.034*	0.009	0.017	-0.005
Know Mukhiya or Sarpanch of panchayat	0.020	0.025	0.122***	0.068***	0.066***	0.051***
Know ward member or other panch leader	0.021*	-0.006	-0.016	0.035**	0.042**	0.034**
Know program officer or block development officer	-0.018	0.023	0.056	0.144*	0.093	0.022
Know any political worker	-0.025	0.103**	-0.041	-0.059	-0.027	-0.031
Household voted in panchayat election	0.040*	0.045	0.027	0.046*	0.091***	-0.014
Household suffered a shock in past year						
Accident	-0.009	-0.040**	-0.008	-0.015	0.022	0.010
Illness	0.030	0.024	0.039	0.059**	0.033	0.035
Job loss	0.018	0.088***	0.043	-0.048*	0.029	0.006

(Continued on the following page)

Table 7.4 (Continued)

	Heard (1)	Days (2)	Gender (3)	BPL (4)	Unemployment allowance (5)	Wage rate (6)	Contractor (7)
Natural disaster	−0.003	0.066***	−0.022	0.014	0.041**	0.066***	0.052***
Other	−0.002	−0.026	−0.059*	0.045	0.024	0.019	0.034
Men in household do casual work	0.066***	0.028	0.010	0.003	−0.015	0.071***	−0.007
Women in household do casual work	0.036***	−0.001	0.002	−0.002	−0.023	0.017	−0.002
No male migration	−0.012	0.038***	−0.012	0.039**	−0.011	0.033**	−0.021*
Regular-salaried worker in household	−0.028	0.061	0.009	−0.000	0.085**	0.035	0.006
Village and GP characteristics							
GP has a panchayat bhawan	0.026**	−0.000	0.008	0.067***	0.051***	−0.016	−0.002
Mukhiya's age	−0.001	−0.000	−0.004***	−0.001	0.002***	0.002**	−0.000
Mukhiya lives in village	0.019	0.061***	0.005	0.046**	0.003	0.002	−0.004
Mukhiya is male	0.031**	0.015	0.089***	0.061***	0.029*	−0.036*	−0.001
Mukhiya completed class 5	−0.035**	0.017	0.111***	−0.012	0.012	−0.003	−0.050***
Mukhiya is a farmer	−0.042***	−0.058***	−0.124***	−0.046**	−0.018	−0.029	0.029*
Mukhiya held a GP post in the past	0.022	−0.018	0.013	−0.029	−0.034*	−0.041*	−0.028
Mukhiya's family held a GP post in the past	0.002	−0.029	0.034	0.002	−0.025	−0.067***	0.013

Mukhiya is a contractor	−0.020	−0.060	−0.107*	−0.163***	−0.001	0.059	0.033
Listing; share of SC households	0.086***	0.113**	−0.045	0.025	0.124***	−0.005	−0.070*
Listing; share of OBC households	−0.014	−0.001	−0.146***	−0.099**	0.044	−0.032	−0.016
Village is predominantly Hindu	0.025	−0.010	0.024	−0.012	0.016	0.020	0.006
Village is electrified	−0.029**	−0.012	0.032*	0.034*	0.024*	−0.003	0.004
Village has a pucca road	−0.020	−0.040**	−0.072***	−0.041**	−0.025	−0.017	−0.009
Within 5 km of bus stop	0.000	0.087***	−0.004	0.014	−0.010	0.023	0.043***
Within 5 km of GP	−0.044***	0.025	0.145***	0.037	0.058***	0.010	−0.023
Within 5 km of town	−0.000	−0.030	0.063**	−0.009	−0.019	0.029	0.033
Within 5 km of block headquarters	−0.057***	−0.015	−0.082***	−0.069***	−0.013	0.027	−0.040**
Post office in village	0.036***	−0.015	−0.061***	0.012	−0.006	0.042**	−0.044***
Nonagricultural enterprises within 5 km of village	0.072***	−0.057**	−0.079***	0.009	0.024	−0.084***	0.016
ln(mean asset index in village)	0.024	0.058	−0.288***	0.124**	0.060	0.045	−0.067*
Asset inequality in village	−0.394***	−0.558***	−0.543***	−0.658***	−0.387***	−0.374***	−0.157
Listing; share households with kutcha house	0.139***	0.067	−0.114**	0.162***	−0.148***	0.091*	0.046
Listing; share BPL households	−0.026	0.130***	0.087	0.065	0.092**	0.184***	−0.021
Flood in village in past year	0.058***	−0.038**	−0.100***	−0.052***	−0.036**	−0.052***	−0.050***
Drought in village in past year	0.039***	0.023	0.069***	0.059***	−0.020	−0.055***	0.050***
Any shock in village in past year	−0.055***	−0.057**	0.001	0.022	−0.015	0.008	−0.005

(Continued on the following page)

Table 7.4 (Continued)

	Heard (1)	Days (2)	Gender (3)	BPL (4)	Unemployment allowance (5)	Wage rate (6)	Contractor (7)
Good relations among village social groups	−0.008	−0.022	0.043	0.073**	0.020	0.059**	0.053***
Self-help group in village	−0.039***	−0.038**	−0.085***	−0.110***	−0.044***	−0.026	0.012
Civil society organization in village	−0.016	0.024	0.036*	0.011	0.019	0.069***	−0.007
BREGS Vigilance Committee in village	0.031**	−0.001	−0.074***	−0.050**	0.016	−0.005	−0.007
Other associations in village	−0.031*	−0.064***	−0.068***	−0.029	−0.020	0.010	−0.009
Observations	4,792	3,977	4,000	3,991	3,994	3,974	3,985
R^2	0.185	0.158	0.105	0.098	0.130	0.128	0.086

Source: Estimates based on the Bihar Rural Employment Guarantee Scheme (BREGS) survey.

Note: Round 1 data. If individual had not heard about BREGS, answers to other questions were coded as missing. Full definitions of each knowledge question are given in table 7.3. The omitted education category is illiterate. BPL = Below Poverty Line; GP = Gram Panchayat; km = kilometers; OBC = Other Backward Class; SC = Scheduled Caste.

*, **, and *** indicate significance at the 10 percent, 5 percent, and 1 percent levels, respectively, based on robust standard errors.

(CSOs) that specifically focus on the Act, an NREGA Village Vigilance Committee (NVVC), and others (comprising farmers, laborers, trade, caste groups, and agricultural or milk cooperative societies). Some 45 percent of villages in the sample have at least one women's SHG, only 22 percent have active BREGS-related CSOs, and 77 percent an NVVC. The other groups are generally individually much less common, although 84 percent of villages have at least one that is active. People in villages with a women's SHG and "other" groups are less likely to have heard about the scheme, perhaps because the presence of these groups reduces their need for BREGS. Those in villages with an NVVC are more likely to have heard of BREGS. Having a BREGS-related CSO appears to have no bearing on whether people have heard about the scheme.

The columns from 2 onward in table 7.4 present the probit estimates for whether individuals answered each of the specific knowledge questions correctly in R1. (We dropped the questions with which respondents were least familiar to save space.) As noted above, if an individual stated that he or she had not heard of BREGS, none of the knowledge questions were asked, and a zero was entered for each of the subsequent knowledge questions. This raises the possibility of selection bias with respect to the sample of individuals who had heard of BREGS and answered the questions. However, the tests did not suggest that this was likely to be a problem.[7] We therefore conclude that the people who said that they did not know about BREGS are not systematically different from those who said they did. We exclude them and run the probits only for those who answered the specific knowledge questions.

Many of the attributes that determined whether individuals had heard of BREGS (male gender, higher levels of education, the gender-specific Pearlin scales, being Hindu, political connections—knowing the Mukhiya, Sarpanch, ward member, or panch, and having voted—as well as attributes of the Mukhiya and of the village) also influenced knowledge of the various aspects of the scheme.

As with the "heard of BREGS" question, the level of asset inequality in the village has a strong negative effect on the level of awareness in almost all cases. Having suffered a household-level shock from a natural disaster tends to raise knowledge. Natural disasters at the village level also result in more people knowing about BREGS. However, the direction of the effect on knowledge about the scheme's details depends on the shock. Floods tend to significantly reduce knowledge whereas droughts have the opposite effect. This outcome may reflect the reality that BREGS worksites tend to be impossible to set up in times of flooding and that the scheme closes down during the rainy season, leading to fewer opportunities to learn about the scheme.

It is interesting that the only cases in which there is no significant male knowledge advantage concerns the questions about whether women are equally welcome to participate and whether child care is provided. The only case in which BPL household status has a statistically significant (and positive) effect is for the question concerning whether eligibility requires that one be a BPL household. These findings suggest that people retain information about issues that specifically concern them and matter to them.

Living in a village that reports good relations between different village groups significantly raises the probability of correct answers on a number of knowledge questions; being from a village with active CSOs positively affects knowledge about the wage rate but negatively affects that concerning the scheme's mandated worksite facilities. However, the presence of a women's SHG consistently significantly reduces awareness. If these groups are dispensing micro-credit to women, they might have a reduced need to know about the scheme. Alternatively, the finding may reflect that women's groups locate where there is the most pressing need for them, that is, where knowledge is lower.

Intrahousehold Gender Differences in Knowledge

It is apparent from the above discussion that men and women have different perceptions about their circumstances, as well as disparate levels of awareness about BREGS, and do not necessarily share information within the household. When we limit the sample to households in which members of both genders were interviewed, we find the gender gap in knowledge declines, but the differences are negligible. Table 7.3, panel B presents the means of correct answers for the different knowledge questions for men and women separately in this sample. A comparison with the means in panel A shows that with some exceptions, awareness is somewhat higher for both genders and the percentage difference between them slightly reduced. The mean knowledge gap calculated over the 12 questions decreases to 0.123 from 0.132. A regression on this reduced sample reveals that the coefficient on male gender remains positive and significant for all knowledge questions and is actually larger conditional on individual, household, and village characteristics.[8] Thus, the conditional mean difference in knowledge favors men even more than does the unconditional mean.

We also estimated separate male and female knowledge regressions for individuals in households in which a member of the opposite sex was also interviewed. The regressions controlled for the male or female individual's own characteristics as well as those of the other surveyed individual's characteristics, and household and village attributes as before.

We found some interesting differences between the male and female estimates. More education and higher Pearlin scores have similar effects on knowledge. More education from secondary schooling on increases the probability that women have heard of the scheme but does not do so for men. When significant, the effects of education are always positive for women; in contrast, more education for men is a mixed blessing from the point of view of getting the BREGS knowledge questions right. For example, progressively more education relative to being illiterate is significantly associated with progressively higher probabilities by men of erroneously believing that women are not allowed to work on BREGS. Yet, education levels higher than middle school for the interviewed woman in the same household helps him answer this same question correctly. More years of schooling of the interviewed woman tends to be associated with greater knowledge on the man's part. The opposite is true with respect to women's knowledge. Their fellow male household member's education tends to negatively affect their knowledge when it matters at all.

Similarly, a higher score on the Pearlin scale significantly influences women's knowledge of their rights but has far less effect on men's awareness. Indeed, men's higher Pearlin score leads them to erroneously think that the household needs to have a BPL card to participate in BREGS. Furthermore, a higher Pearlin score for the interviewed female has a positive effect on the male interviewee's knowledge but not vice versa. A positive effect of the household's share of children under age six on knowledge of the mandated requirement that water be provided at work sites is significant only for women.

Being close to the Mukhiya is equally important for men and women in determining knowledge. For men, there are also significant positive effects of being close to the ward member and from voting in the elections. Neither effect is apparent for women. The household's having faced a shock related to a natural disaster significantly heightens men's knowledge of multiple aspects of BREGS but not women's. On the whole, village characteristics appear to influence knowledge similarly for men and women, conditional on household and individual characteristics.

To summarize the above discussion of the determinants of knowledge, we find certain factors to be consistently important. At the individual and household levels, one can think of these as falling roughly into two categories of attributes—those that enhance a person's knowledge and understanding, and those that render the information more relevant and meaningful to those individuals. In the first category, higher levels of education and higher scores on the Pearlin scale are dependably significant attributes that help individuals process and retain information. Political connections create opportunities to access the work that an individual may not have otherwise and in that sense will also help people take on information that may concern them. Being from the Mahadalit caste (typically the most disadvantaged), or being from a household whose members have engaged in casual work in the past, has a low level of wealth, and has suffered a shock, fall in the second category of attributes that make knowledge about BREGS vital to one's household's well-being. Male gender, given men's responsibility as main breadwinners, can also be seen to fit this category. In addition, a number of village-level characteristics that may largely reflect supply-side issues also emerge as very important. High asset inequality is negatively associated with knowledge; having a panchayat bhawan and certain characteristics of the Mukhiya, such as if he lives in the village, increase knowledge whereas others, such as the Mukhiya being a farmer or landowner, tend to reduce it.

A Pilot Information Campaign

In the present setting, it may be that people are too unaware of their rights or of how to demand their rights for the program to function as intended. However, full information may not be sufficient for the scheme to improve. First, being aware of one's rights is not the same as being empowered to demand those rights. The BREGS target groups tend to be illiterate or barely educated, to come from the castes most discriminated against, and to lack political clout. It may take more than awareness for them to be able to make demands from those to whom they are subordinates in every way. There is also the preliminary issue of whether new contradictory information can even be processed and accepted in the face of evidence to the contrary from one's leaders, patrons, and other figures of authority in one's community. As we have seen, a household's political connections and vote history, and local officials' characteristics, have significant effects, both positive and negative, on knowledge. Second, knowing the rules and how to obtain work may not be sufficient in the presence of very real supply-side issues that may play a substantial role in limiting participation (as further discussed in chapter 8).

A key question is whether demand- or supply-side constraints are the more important handicap to higher participation and a better working scheme, and whether improving one without changing the other can still enhance the scheme's functioning. Knowledge of public program eligibility and take-up procedures is a necessary condition for people to demand their rights, but is it sufficient? Would raising awareness on its own embolden people to demand employment and put sufficient pressure on local governments and officials to overcome supply-side limitations?

To shed light on these key questions, we piloted a demand-side intervention aimed at increasing individual knowledge. Alternative modes of information campaign were initially explored through several open-ended focus group discussions with BREGS participants and nonparticipants, and men and women separately, in Nalanda and Patna districts. In Nalanda, information about the scheme was read out by facilitators; in Patna, the team showed short video clips on the scheme produced by the Ministry of Rural Development and provided additional information through facilitation and discussion. The film format attracted considerable interest in the focus groups. Feedback gathered in the field after the discussions suggested that a facilitator was needed for viewers to retain the information provided through such video clips and to provide the most recent information. The demand-side pilot was thus designed as a film on the program to be shown to households, in the presence of a facilitator.

Based on these preliminary findings from the fieldwork, and with the cooperation of the Rural Development Department of the government of Bihar, we produced a film to convey explicit information about rights and entitlements under BREGS. The film was tailored to Bihar's specific context and program guidelines. Bihari actors acted out an entertaining and emotionally engaging story-based plot whose purpose was to provide repeated information on how the scheme works, who can participate, and how to go about participating. The film was produced by a local nongovernmental organization, Praxis (Institute for Participatory Practices).

The film was disseminated between mid-February and mid-March 2010 in a randomly selected subsample of 40 out of the 150 villages that were surveyed in R1. Compliance at the village level was complete. Because the 150 villages were drawn randomly from all villages in rural Bihar, we can infer mean impacts of a village receiving a screening of the film for rural Bihar. However, it is important to recognize that this evaluation design (in common with other randomized control trials) only identifies mean impact. We cannot conclude that exposure to the film would have that impact in all villages. In practice, there will be heterogeneity in the impacts. We return to this issue.

As a check on the randomization (if something went wrong that we do not know about), we tested for differences in the sample means of the 75 village variables used in the analysis (including village means of household variables). The difference in sample means was only statistically significant at the 5 percent level for three of the 75 variables. (Some significant differences are to be expected by chance even when fully randomized.) The treatment and control samples are clearly well balanced.

In each village, the film was shown in two separate locations at different times. At each location, the film was screened twice, followed by a question and answer session and distribution of handouts. Concerted efforts were made to announce and advertize the upcoming screenings widely in advance. Local officials such as the Mukhiya and Sarpanch, opposition leaders, and local BREGS officials were specifically invited to attend. The film was typically shown in a common area, such as an open ground, school building, or community hall. In 93 percent of the showings, the facilitators noted that the majority of people watched both screenings of the film. On average, about 365 people (38 percent women) attended at least one of the two back-to-back screenings at a given location. In a third of the villages, the Mukhiya attended the show as did the mate; the PRS attended in half the treatment villages, and the local opposition leader did so in close to 60 percent. People in the majority of shows (89 percent) reported that the information was somewhat new, and the movie generated a lot of discussion in 29 percent of the showings.

Impacts of the Information Intervention

The intervention aimed to raise awareness and through that to also favorably affect the scheme's outcomes. We begin with the single-difference estimates of the impact of showing the movie in a household's village on knowledge and other outcomes. Table 7.5 gives the movie's estimated impacts on knowledge about BREGS, for men and women separately, as well as for the full sample. These are regression coefficients of knowledge scores on the village assignment of the movie.[9] The dependent variable is a dummy variable taking the value 1 if a respondent was aware of BREGS or got the right answer to the relevant question, and 0 otherwise. Thus, the regression coefficient

Table 7.5 Estimates of the Effect of the Movie on Knowledge about the Bihar Rural Employment Guarantee Scheme by Gender

	Whole sample			Women			Men		
	Film in village	Constant	Observations	Film in village	Constant	Observations	Film in village	Constant	Observations
Heard	0.028**	0.915***	5,012	0.047***	0.867***	2,782	0.006	0.976***	2,230
Score 1	0.497***	2.465***	4,655	0.368***	2.006***	2,464	0.696***	2.977***	2,191
Days	0.118***	0.221***	4,597	0.117***	0.104***	2,429	0.130***	0.351***	2,168
Gender	-0.022	0.654***	4,635	-0.007	0.622***	2,452	-0.037	0.690***	2,183
BPL	0.042*	0.615***	4,636	0.048	0.559***	2,453	0.039	0.676***	2,183
Work lag	0.062***	0.088***	4,629	0.038*	0.064***	2,450	0.094***	0.114***	2,179
Unemployment allowance	0.094***	0.286***	4,635	0.081**	0.201***	2,451	0.117***	0.381***	2,184
Wage rate	0.116***	0.322***	4,637	0.082***	0.239***	2,452	0.165***	0.413***	2,185
Wage lag	0.048***	0.106***	4,609	0.025	0.093***	2,438	0.078***	0.122***	2,171
Contractor	0.047**	0.184***	4,634	-0.011	0.132***	2,449	0.121***	0.242***	2,185
Score 2	0.020	1.317***	4,655	-0.068	1.140***	2,464	0.144	1.514***	2,191
Child care	0.075***	0.128***	4,644	0.073***	0.100***	2,458	0.081***	0.160***	2,186
Water	-0.041*	0.604***	4,645	-0.063*	0.546***	2,458	-0.009	0.668***	2,187
Shade	-0.026	0.445***	4,644	-0.067**	0.394***	2,457	0.027	0.502***	2,187
First aid	0.016	0.142***	4,642	-0.008	0.102***	2,457	0.049	0.186***	2,185
Board	0.023**	0.028***	4,996	-0.004	0.014***	2,773	0.058***	0.045***	2,223
Demand	0.049**	0.605***	4,989	0.027	0.515***	2,767	0.083***	0.717***	2,222

Source: Estimates based on the Bihar Rural Employment Guarantee Scheme (BREGS) survey.

Note: Regressions using household weights and individual outcomes. Based on round 2 data only. If an individual had not heard about BREGS, answers to other questions were coded as missing. Full definitions of the knowledge questions are given in table 7.3. BPL = Below Poverty Line.

*, **, and *** indicate significance at the 10 percent, 5 percent, and 1 percent levels, respectively, based on robust standard errors.

is the difference in the mean knowledge score between those who lived in a village that was assigned the movie and those who lived in a village that was not. The constant gives the knowledge estimate for the control group. Given that the village assignment was random by design, and there was complete compliance (meaning the movie was shown as planned in all selected treatment villages), the estimated difference in means is unbiased.

The movie had a significant effect on knowledge of the existence of BREGS for the sample as a whole, although the effect was small (a 3 percentage point gain) and only significant at the 5 percent level. However, it should be recalled that knowledge of the existence of BREGS was high to begin with. Also note that a larger and more significant effect on knowledge is found among women, who (as noted above) were less aware initially.

There was a significant impact on knowledge about how many days of work are available, with a 12 percentage point increase in the proportion who got this right being attributed to the movie (significant at the 1 percent level). The impact was slightly higher for men than for women.

For men, but much less or not at all for women, the movie had a large effect on knowledge of the fact that work has to be provided within 15 days, that wages are to be paid within two weeks, and that contractors are not permitted under the legislation; these impacts are all significant at the 1 percent level for men.

Awareness of the provision for an unemployment allowance if work could not be provided also rose substantially as a result of the movie, with a larger effect for men (12 percentage points) than for women (8 percentage points). Similar effects were evident for knowledge of the wage rate, with a large and significant effect of the movie, though again, stronger for men than for women.

The fact that child care is to be provided was little known in the control group, but rose appreciably for those living in villages where the movie was shown, rising from 13 percent to 20 percent. The impact was similar for men and women. Among women, but not men, there was a puzzling negative effect on knowledge that the scheme requires that drinking water and shade be provided at worksites.

There was a sizable and significant effect of the movie, among men, but not women, on knowing that work has to be demanded. Some 72 percent of men knew this in the control villages, rising to 80 percent with the movie. It is striking that there was no impact on women's awareness that work had to be demanded, given that barely half of them knew this in the control villages. It may be that because women typically go to BREGS worksites with male family members or as part of groups, this is information they do not feel they need to retain.

Following the same estimation method as used for table 7.5, table 7.6 presents estimates of the movie's impacts on a number of other outcome indicators. Rows 1 through 22 report on differences in perceptions about a number of factors, while the last four rows give impacts on actual aspects of how the scheme functioned after the movie: demand, participation, days of work, and wages.

The perceptions that BREGS projects have increased employment and led to a decline in migration rose appreciably and significantly as a result of the movie for both genders. For example, the feeling that one can get work if one asks doubled from the 9 percent for the control group. Similarly, the perceptions that one can get work on BREGS when one demands it, and of improvements in BREGS work opportunities for the household, were appreciably and significantly raised by the movie. The first increased from 43 percent for men in the control villages to close to 60 percent for those living in villages where the movie was shown, and from 35 percent to 51 percent for women. There was a doubling in the perception among both men and women that BREGS work opportunities have increased between the two rounds of the survey.

In general, perceptions of improvements in village infrastructure, greater work opportunities, and lower migration in the village (not linking this to BREGS like the previous questions) were significantly raised by the movie, although not always for both genders. When asked whether migration has decreased in their villages, 13 percent more men and 9 percent more women agreed in the villages where the movie was shown than in the control villages. Similarly, perceptions that village infrastructure has improved were significantly higher among women, though not for men, in the villages where the movie was shown.

There is a small effect on men's perceptions that women can choose BREGS projects, but no such effect for women. However, the movie has a strong significant negative effect on the perception of men and women that the assets created have been useful to women, and for men only that women participate in BREGS work. No other perceptions concerning women were affected by the movie.

There are no significant effects on actual or desired participation, wage rates, or days worked (table 7.6). Although we find significant impacts of the movie on both knowledge and perceptions of work opportunities (and infrastructure), we find no impacts on actual work or wages. It may be that perceptions are informed by factors that are not yet evident in the objective data, although the time period and timing of the intervention should have sufficed to

Table 7.6 Estimates of the Effect of the Movie on Perceptions and Bihar Rural Employment Guarantee Scheme Participation by Gender

Dependent variable	Whole round 2 sample			Women			Men		
	Film in village	Constant	Observations	Film in village	Constant	Observations	Film in village	Constant	Observations
1 Can influence wages	0.033	0.637***	4,408	0.016	0.617***	2,259	0.053	0.659***	2,149
2 Benefits of participating in Gram Sabha	0.104***	0.152***	4,356	0.096***	0.112***	2,267	0.115***	0.197***	2,089
3 Women participate in Gram Sabha	0.088***	0.367***	4,507	0.087***	0.340***	2,395	0.090**	0.398***	2,112
4 Get work under BREGS when demanded	0.085***	0.084***	4,201	0.072***	0.069***	2,125	0.100***	0.099***	2,076
5 BREGS projects have increased employment	0.084***	0.176***	4,173	0.067**	0.147***	2,096	0.105***	0.206***	2,077
6 BREGS decreased migration of labor	0.093***	0.140***	4,071	0.087***	0.108***	2,028	0.102***	0.172***	2,043
7 BREGS work will be available next year	-0.032	0.563***	1,906	-0.041	0.520***	831	-0.030	0.599***	1,075
8 Women have the right to choose BREGS projects	0.047*	0.632***	3,188	0.030	0.614***	1,515	0.064*	0.649***	1,673

9	Assets useful to women created under BREGS	−0.088***	0.832***	4,013	−0.090***	0.844***	2,039	−0.088***	0.821***	1,974
10	Women work in BREGS projects	−0.072***	0.721***	4,211	−0.045	0.717***	2,162	−0.104***	0.726***	2,049
11	Women treated well at BREGS worksite	0.003	0.981***	2,602	−0.004	0.983***	1,274	0.010	0.978***	1,328
12	Women get work if they bring children to worksite	0.008	0.779***	2,322	0.010	0.762***	1,104	0.009	0.795***	1,218
13	Distance women would be willing to go to work on BREGS worksite	9.180	61.741***	3,063	36.132	61.053***	1,584	−24.708	62.457***	1,479
14	Women paid equal wages as men	0.021	0.807***	2,454	0.004	0.824***	1,198	0.038	0.790***	1,256
15	Women of household would like to work on BREGS	−0.013	0.454***	4,929	−0.011	0.467***	2,740	−0.015	0.437***	2,189
16	Women of household would be allowed to work on BREGS	−0.017	0.458***	4,913	−0.019	0.473***	2,724	−0.014	0.440***	2,189

(Continued on the following page)

Table 7.6 (Continued)

Dependent variable	Whole round 2 sample			Women			Men		
	Film in village	Constant	Observations	Film in village	Constant	Observations	Film in village	Constant	Observations
17 Knowledge of BREGS increased in past year in your family	0.163***	0.427***	4,834	0.163***	0.348***	2,637	0.166***	0.522***	2,197
18 BREGS work opportunities improved in past year for your family	0.105***	0.119***	4,798	0.110***	0.110***	2,606	0.098***	0.129***	2,192
19 Infrastructure improved in village	0.068***	0.611***	4,888	0.087***	0.602***	2,671	0.044	0.621***	2,217
20 Work increased in village	0.063**	0.424***	4,560	0.048	0.407***	2,410	0.081**	0.444***	2,150

	(1)	(2)	N	(3)	(4)	N	(5)	(6)	N
21 Wage increased in village	0.018	0.755***	4,627	0.017	0.740***	2,472	0.018	0.771***	2,155
22 Migration decreased in village	0.112***	0.184***	4,506	0.094***	0.148***	2,355	0.134***	0.225***	2,151
Scheme outcomes after the movie									
23 BREGS participation	-0.010	0.054***	5,012	-0.009	0.035***	2,782	-0.009	0.078***	2,230
24 BREGS days	-1.232	4.690***	1,047	-0.586	2.842***	430	-1.704	6.011***	617
25 BREGS wages	-72.841	406.176***	1,047	-52.766	261.668***	430	-88.228	509.487***	617
26 Desired participation in round 2	-0.012	0.532***	5,012	-0.021	0.446***	2,782	0.002	0.641***	2,230

Source: Estimates based on the Bihar Rural Employment Guarantee Scheme (BREGS) survey.

Note: Regressions using *weights* and *individual* outcomes. Based on round 2 data. If individual had not heard about BREGS, answers to other questions were coded as missing.

*, **, and *** indicate significance at the 10 percent, 5 percent, and 1 percent levels, respectively, based on robust standard errors.

capture any real effects. It appears more likely that the perceptions were distorted by the movie. Having watched the movie, people came to think that the scheme was working better for the village as a whole than their own objective experiences would suggest.

The results in tables 7.5 and 7.6 use R2 data. We can also exploit the panel data structure to test further for impacts of the movie on the various transitions discussed earlier. First, consider the group of "excess demanders" in R1. Did the movie encourage those exposed to it to take up work on the scheme in R2? The answer is a clear "no." The regression coefficient of the probability of taking up work among the R1 excess demanders on the dummy variable for whether the movie was shown is 0.001 for men and –0.006 for women, and neither are significantly different from zero at the 10 percent level.

Nor was there any impact on those who were neither actual participants nor excess demanders in R1. Among this group, the regression coefficient of the probability of either taking up work or becoming an excess demander on the dummy variable for whether the movie was shown was not significantly different from zero at the 10 percent level.

We also calculated difference-in-difference (DD) impact estimates of the movie on knowledge for all individuals, as well as for men and women separately. As we expect given the randomization, the movie's estimated DD impacts are quite similar to those found for the single difference and reported above. However, small-sample properties mean that there may be some dissimilarities between the randomized in and out villages. Thus, the DD estimator provides extra cleaning for time-invariant selection bias that may be present as the result of any small-sample bias. The DD impacts tended to be larger but less statistically significant. For example, the movie's effect on women having heard of BREGS is nearly double that estimated with the single difference. The major disparity with the previous estimates concerns awareness of the mandated facilities. Using R2 data only, we find significant impacts on knowing about the child care provision as well as negative effects on being aware of the water and shade provisions. There is no sign of movie impacts on any of these variables when we use both survey rounds. We also test whether the movie had any effect on the number or the change in the number of worksites that opened in the GP. There is no effect on either.

Table 7.7 turns to impacts of the movie on transitions from not knowing to knowing about BREGS. There may only be a small overall impact on the proportion of people who get the answer right, as we saw above using R2 data. Yet the small increase in awareness could coincide with a learning process together with a forgetting

Table 7.7 Effects of the Movie on Learning about the Bihar Rural Employment Guarantee Scheme

	Heard	Days	Gender	BPL	Work lag	Unemployment	Wage rate	Wage lag	Contractor
				Panel A: "STILL RIGHT"					
Whole sample									
Film in village	0.028***	0.256***	−0.061	0.032	−0.038	0.132**	0.207***	0.109	0.127
Constant	0.946***	0.384***	0.676***	0.662***	0.313***	0.468***	0.407***	0.130***	0.274***
Observations	3,100	717	1,583	1,346	149	605	937	252	459
Men									
Film in village	−0.002	0.246***	−0.075	0.071	−0.056	0.205***	0.207***	0.020	0.181*
Constant	0.990***	0.449***	0.689***	0.681***	0.389***	0.510***	0.460***	0.198***	0.361***
Observations	1,511	548	838	819	106	449	620	157	307
Women									
Film in village	0.052***	0.285**	−0.046	−0.019	−0.013	−0.072	0.196**	0.192	0.011
Constant	0.907***	0.162***	0.663***	0.636***	0.102*	0.369***	0.309***	0.078**	0.108***
Observations	1,589	169	745	527	43	156	317	95	152
				Panel B: "LEARNING"					
Whole sample									
Film in village	0.022	0.115***	−0.009	0.069*	0.068***	0.106***	0.129***	0.082***	0.058*
Constant	0.789***	0.161***	0.644***	0.594***	0.084***	0.263***	0.302***	0.087***	0.167***
Observations	649	2,167	1,346	1,577	2,770	2,318	1,975	2,650	2,459
Men									
Film in village	−0.155	0.110**	0.030	−0.001	0.090***	0.100*	0.109**	0.098***	0.149***
Constant	0.941***	0.264***	0.662***	0.692***	0.105***	0.349***	0.398***	0.107***	0.198***
Observations	75	915	647	664	1,373	1,035	856	1,315	1,172

(Continued on the following page)

Table 7.7 (Continued)

	Heard	Days	Gender	BPL	Work lag	Unemployment	Wage rate	Wage lag	Contractor
Women									
Film in village	0.049	0.120***	−0.044	0.117**	0.047	0.113**	0.140***	0.066**	−0.025
Constant	0.764***	0.091***	0.628***	0.525***	0.064***	0.195***	0.236***	0.068***	0.141***
Observations	574	1,252	699	913	1,397	1,283	1,119	1,335	1,287

Source: Estimates based on the Bihar Rural Employment Guarantee Scheme (BREGS) survey.

Note: "Still right" is defined as being aware in round 1 and staying aware in round 2. "Learning" is defined as not being aware in round 1 but answering correctly in round 2. If an individual had not heard about BREGS, answers to other questions were coded as missing. Definitions of each knowledge question are given in table 7.3. BPL = Below Poverty Line.

*, **, and *** indicate significance at the 10 percent, 5 percent, and 1 percent levels, respectively, based on robust standard errors.

process that may reduce the net impact. So it is of interest to isolate the learning process. To do so, we need to bring in the baseline and panel. Panel A of table 7.7 shows impacts for the subset of people who answered questions about BREGS correctly in R1 to see whether the movie reduced the incidence of forgetting, and hence influenced the share that are "still right." Panel B then shows impact estimates for the subset of those who answered incorrectly in R1 and are "learning" about the scheme.[10] Did the movie help them learn?

The movie had significant, mostly positive, effects on retaining information about some of the scheme's stipulated rules between the two survey rounds. For example, it significantly helped both men and women remember that BREGS offers 100 days of employment per household and at what wage rate. It enabled men to recall that an unemployment allowance is mandated when work is not provided and that contractors are not allowed. It reinforced awareness of the existence of the scheme for women who had heard about BREGS in R1. Women who knew in R1 that child care facilities should be provided were significantly reminded of this by the movie. However, being from a village that showed the movie appears to have had a negative effect on men's and women's recollection that worksites must provide drinking water.[11]

Panel B of table 7.7 turns to the movie's impacts on learning about aspects of the scheme that people had been ignorant of in R1. The movie significantly helped increase knowledge about a majority of the 12 knowledge questions for both men and women. For example, 12 percent more individuals who are from movie villages than those from control villages learned about the allowed number of work days, 12 percent more women that participation does not require a BPL card, 13 percent more people about the wage rate, 8 percent more people about the prescribed time for wage payments, and 15 percent more men that contractors are not permitted. For mandated facilities, the movie only influenced learning about child care.

The movie could have heterogeneous effects according to people's characteristics—including both those attributes that help one retain and digest information and those attributes that make that information more relevant to some individuals and less so to others. In particular, we postulate that education, self-mastery (as captured by the Pearlin scores), caste identity, and being politically connected matter to how much the movie affects knowledge.

Table 7.8 gives the results. We found some signs of heterogeneous impacts. For instance, compared with those with primary education, illiterate individuals were more likely to feel that their knowledge of BREGS improved and that infrastructure has gotten better.

Table 7.8 Tests for Heterogeneity in the Impacts of the Movie

	Education: primary school vs. illiterate	Standard error	Pearlin 2 - 1	Standard error	Pearlin 3 – 1	Standard error	Caste 2 - 1	Standard error	Political 2 - 1	Standard error	Male - female	Standard error
Heard	-0.037	0.023	0.028	0.033	0.013	0.039	0.019	0.022	-0.052	0.062	-0.040**	0.021
Score 1 (employment)	0.171	0.248	0.406*	0.232	0.367	0.304	0.298	0.296	-0.589	0.768	0.329*	0.182
Score 2 (facilities)	0.225	0.185	0.082	0.178	0.130	0.237	0.038	0.180	-0.819*	0.480	0.212	0.135
Can influence wages	-0.048	0.058	-0.030	0.063	0.013	0.086	-0.095	0.066	-0.172	0.153	0.038	0.047
Benefits of participating in Gram Sabha	-0.004	0.060	0.033	0.066	0.112	0.082	0.020	0.067	-0.305**	0.126	0.019	0.044
Women participate in Gram Sabha	-0.080	0.064	0.104	0.066	0.154*	0.086	-0.104	0.070	-0.089	0.137	0.003	0.049
Get work under BREGS when demanded	-0.048	0.042	0.019	0.039	0.101*	0.060	-0.109**	0.046	0.043	0.071	0.028	0.033
BREGS projects have increased employment	-0.018	0.059	0.048	0.058	0.180**	0.077	-0.101	0.062	0.021	0.097	0.038	0.044

BREGS decreased migration of labor	0.036	0.061	0.024	0.052	−0.032	0.065	−0.093*	0.054	−0.009	0.088	0.015	0.043
BREGS work will be available next year	−0.003	0.096	0.152	0.131	0.096	0.15	0.174*	0.105	0.018	0.212	0.012	0.079
Women have the right to choose BREGS projects	−0.009	0.061	0.149*	0.077	0.105	0.101	0.014	0.073	−0.120	0.180	0.033	0.055
Assets useful to women created under BREGS	0.026	0.057	0.054	0.057	0.131**	0.063	0.024	0.054	−0.171	0.150	0.002	0.042
Women work in BREGS projects	0.138**	0.059	−0.003	0.058	0.008	0.082	0.132**	0.060	−0.149	0.116	−0.059	0.046
Women treated well at BREGS worksite	0.014	0.016	0.021	0.030	0.035	0.031	−0.012	0.011	0.030	0.077	0.013	0.015

(Continued on the following page)

Table 7.8 (Continued)

	Education: primary school vs. illiterate	Standard error	Pearlin 2 - 1	Standard error	Pearlin 3 - 1	Standard error	Caste 2 - 1	Standard error	Political 2 - 1	Standard error	Male - female	Standard error
Women get work if they bring children to worksite	0.049	0.069	−0.031	0.076	−0.034	0.110	−0.185***	0.055	−0.374***	0.101	−0.001	0.056
Distance women would be willing to go to work on BREGS worksite	0.102	0.068	0.014	0.070	0.067	0.087	0.186**	0.075	−0.318***	0.117	0.033	0.050
Women paid equal wages as men	−0.006	0.051	0.041	0.063	−0.014	0.084	0.072	0.057	−0.061	0.140	−0.004	0.048
Women of household would like to work on BREGS	0.001	0.051	0.059	0.063	0.026	0.085	0.019	0.056	−0.064	0.141	0.006	0.048

Women of household would be allowed to work on BREGS	-0.109*	0.060	0.069	0.065	0.051	0.085	-0.072	0.066	-0.220*	0.127	0.003	0.046
Knowledge of BREGS increased in past year in your family	0.042	0.053	-0.003	0.045	0.022	0.065	-0.145***	0.052	-0.327***	0.121	-0.011	0.038
BREGS work opportunities improved in past year for your family	-0.140**	0.060	-0.154***	0.059	-0.170**	0.083	-0.211***	0.063	-0.026	0.139	-0.043	0.046
Infrastructure improved in village	-0.086	0.065	0.129*	0.067	0.163*	0.088	-0.121*	0.068	0.028	0.122	0.033	0.049
Work increased in village	-0.080	0.051	-0.013	0.048	0.054	0.075	-0.132**	0.055	0.024	0.127	0.000	0.041
Wage increased in village	-0.051	0.061	0.088*	0.051	0.057	0.070	-0.183***	0.058	0.003	0.112	0.040	0.044

(Continued on the following page)

Table 7.8 (Continued)

	Education: primary school vs. illiterate	Standard error	Pearlin 2 - 1	Standard error	Pearlin 3 - 1	Standard error	Caste 2 - 1	Standard error	Political 2 - 1	Standard error	Male - female	Standard error
Scheme outcomes after the movie												
BREGS participation	-0.021	0.019	-0.01	0.034	0.023	0.037	-0.025	0.041	0	0.052	0	0.021
BREGS days	-5.098**	2.138	-0.23	2.098	1.293	2.297	-0.546	1.873	-1.529	1.371	-1.118	1.535
BREGS wages	-487.300**	204.172	35.65	207.564	169.881	220.525	-37.958	183.366	-113.54	135.939	-35.462	147.347
BREGS wages received	-106.035	148.744	107.668	192.594	237.912	210.289	168.739	157.837	-106.74	130.428	43.038	133.216
Desired participation in round 2	-0.016	0.061	0.027	0.063	-0.085	0.084	0.026	0.059	0.016	0.139	0.023	0.047

Source: Estimates based on the Bihar Rural Employment Guarantee Scheme (BREGS) survey.

Note: Estimated using a single difference on round 2 data. Estimates give the difference in estimates between the specified groups. The stratifications are as follows:

education: 1= illiterate, 2 = literate and up to class 5 pass, 3 = more than primary;

caste: 1 = Mahadalit, 2 = all others;

Pearlin: 1 = scale < 3; 2 = scale = 3, 4, or 5; 3 = scale > 5;

political: 1 = person voted, close to Mukhiya, or close to ward member, 2 = none of these are true.

The movie resulted in 5.1 more days of employment for them than for the more educated as well as 487 rupees (Rs) more in wages (implying a daily wage rate of Rs 95, which is almost exactly the average BREGS wage in R2). Although this could be considered a nonnegligible gain, it is confined to current BREGS participants; the movie had no impact on participation by illiterate individuals. A relatively higher Pearlin scale results in higher impacts on a number of perceptions. For example, going from Pearlin 1 to 2 increases the employment knowledge score by 41 percent. Impacts on quite a few perceptions also vary by caste. Typically, impacts of the movie are significantly higher for Mahadalits, although in some cases, they are lower for them than for higher-level castes. There are also notable differences between those who do and do not have political connections. The movie's impacts were significantly different with respect to the facilities knowledge score and a number of perceptions. In all cases, the impacts are larger for the unconnected.

In summary, we find that the movie helped both men and women remember and retain information about the scheme's rules and raised knowledge among those unaware of the rules in R1. It also had appreciable and significant impacts on the perceptions of both men and women on the functioning of the scheme. This is particularly the case among individuals who are likely to find this information relevant, such as illiterate individuals and Mahadalits (typically the most disadvantaged groups). In addition, impacts are larger for more empowered and politically connected individuals. However, there are no significant effects on actual employment or wages except among illiterate participating individuals, for whom the movie appears to have helped secure extra work on existing BREGS projects.

Annex 7A

Table 7A.1 Knowledge among Participants, Excess Demanders, and the Rest

Round 1	Participants						Excess demanders						Rest					
	Whole		Male		Female		Whole		Male		Female		Whole		Male		Female	
Variable	Mean	SD	Mean	SD	Mean	SD	Mean	SD	Mean	SD	Mean	SD	Mean	SD	Mean	SD	Mean	SD
Heard	1.00	0.00	1.00	0.00	1.00	0.00	0.98	0.13	0.99	0.09	0.97	0.16	0.67	0.47	0.87	0.34	0.58	0.49
Score 1	2.98	1.61	3.22	1.56	2.15	1.50	1.99	1.86	2.35	1.97	1.54	1.60	1.81	1.70	2.47	1.86	1.38	1.43
Days	0.42	0.49	0.48	0.50	0.20	0.40	0.22	0.41	0.30	0.46	0.12	0.32	0.20	0.40	0.37	0.48	0.09	0.28
Gender	0.63	0.48	0.64	0.48	0.59	0.49	0.52	0.50	0.55	0.50	0.49	0.50	0.53	0.50	0.54	0.50	0.52	0.50
BPL	0.64	0.48	0.67	0.47	0.54	0.50	0.44	0.50	0.50	0.50	0.37	0.48	0.40	0.49	0.46	0.50	0.35	0.48
Work lag	0.05	0.23	0.06	0.24	0.04	0.19	0.04	0.19	0.06	0.24	0.01	0.12	0.04	0.20	0.08	0.27	0.02	0.13
Unemployment allowance	0.24	0.43	0.28	0.45	0.11	0.31	0.20	0.40	0.26	0.44	0.13	0.34	0.20	0.40	0.35	0.48	0.10	0.30
Wage rate	0.60	0.49	0.65	0.48	0.45	0.50	0.32	0.47	0.38	0.48	0.24	0.43	0.23	0.42	0.36	0.48	0.14	0.35
Wage lag	0.16	0.37	0.18	0.39	0.11	0.31	0.09	0.29	0.10	0.30	0.09	0.28	0.08	0.27	0.08	0.28	0.08	0.26
Contractor	0.24	0.43	0.28	0.45	0.12	0.33	0.16	0.37	0.21	0.41	0.10	0.30	0.17	0.38	0.25	0.43	0.13	0.33
Score 2	1.80	1.38	1.88	1.36	1.52	1.42	1.12	1.34	1.26	1.38	0.96	1.28	1.02	1.32	1.18	1.40	0.91	1.25
Child care	0.22	0.42	0.22	0.41	0.24	0.43	0.19	0.39	0.18	0.38	0.19	0.40	0.18	0.38	0.19	0.40	0.17	0.38
Water	0.76	0.43	0.79	0.41	0.67	0.47	0.47	0.50	0.54	0.50	0.40	0.49	0.44	0.50	0.50	0.50	0.40	0.49
Shade	0.48	0.50	0.52	0.50	0.35	0.48	0.26	0.44	0.32	0.47	0.19	0.39	0.23	0.42	0.29	0.45	0.20	0.40
First aid	0.35	0.48	0.37	0.48	0.27	0.45	0.20	0.40	0.23	0.42	0.17	0.38	0.18	0.39	0.21	0.41	0.16	0.37
Board	—	—	—	—	—	—	—	—	—	—	—	—	—	—	—	—	—	—
Demand	—	—	—	—	—	—	—	—	—	—	—	—	—	—	—	—	—	—

Round 2	Participants						Excess demanders						Rest					
	Whole		Male		Female		Whole		Male		Female		Whole		Male		Female	
Variable	Mean	SD	Mean	SD	Mean	SD	Mean	SD	Mean	SD	Mean	SD	Mean	SD	Mean	SD	Mean	SD
Heard	1.00	0.00	1.00	0.00	1.00	0.00	0.99	0.08	1.00	0.05	0.99	0.10	0.84	0.37	0.94	0.24	0.79	0.41
Score 1	3.60	1.56	3.75	1.58	3.30	1.48	2.65	1.77	3.11	1.84	2.18	1.57	2.24	1.70	2.89	1.86	1.85	1.46
Days	0.38	0.48	0.43	0.50	0.26	0.44	0.26	0.44	0.38	0.49	0.15	0.35	0.20	0.40	0.36	0.48	0.11	0.31
Gender	0.68	0.47	0.72	0.45	0.60	0.49	0.67	0.47	0.69	0.46	0.65	0.48	0.61	0.49	0.65	0.48	0.60	0.49
BPL	0.79	0.41	0.77	0.42	0.82	0.39	0.63	0.48	0.69	0.46	0.58	0.49	0.57	0.50	0.63	0.48	0.53	0.50
Work lag	0.18	0.39	0.20	0.40	0.15	0.36	0.12	0.33	0.14	0.35	0.11	0.31	0.06	0.24	0.10	0.30	0.04	0.19
Unemployment allowance	0.46	0.50	0.48	0.50	0.40	0.49	0.34	0.47	0.42	0.49	0.26	0.44	0.24	0.43	0.36	0.48	0.16	0.37
Wage rate	0.67	0.47	0.68	0.47	0.67	0.47	0.32	0.47	0.41	0.49	0.23	0.42	0.29	0.46	0.41	0.49	0.23	0.42
Wage lag	0.18	0.39	0.18	0.38	0.19	0.39	0.12	0.32	0.13	0.34	0.10	0.30	0.10	0.30	0.13	0.34	0.08	0.28
Contractor	0.27	0.44	0.30	0.46	0.22	0.42	0.19	0.39	0.26	0.44	0.12	0.33	0.18	0.39	0.28	0.45	0.12	0.33
Score 2	1.91	1.25	1.96	1.29	1.80	1.15	1.38	1.26	1.54	1.27	1.21	1.23	1.10	1.21	1.36	1.28	0.94	1.13
Child care	0.28	0.45	0.27	0.45	0.28	0.45	0.14	0.35	0.16	0.37	0.12	0.33	0.12	0.32	0.16	0.37	0.09	0.29
Water	0.80	0.40	0.79	0.40	0.80	0.40	0.62	0.49	0.67	0.47	0.56	0.50	0.51	0.50	0.59	0.49	0.46	0.50
Shade	0.59	0.49	0.58	0.49	0.59	0.49	0.46	0.50	0.51	0.50	0.41	0.49	0.37	0.48	0.46	0.50	0.31	0.46
First aid	0.25	0.43	0.31	0.46	0.13	0.33	0.16	0.36	0.19	0.40	0.12	0.32	0.11	0.31	0.15	0.35	0.08	0.27
Board	0.09	0.28	0.11	0.32	0.04	0.19	0.02	0.14	0.03	0.18	0.00	0.07	0.03	0.18	0.06	0.25	0.02	0.13
Demand	0.82	0.38	0.83	0.37	0.80	0.40	0.74	0.44	0.79	0.41	0.68	0.47	0.46	0.50	0.62	0.49	0.38	0.49

Source: Estimates based on the Bihar Rural Employment Guarantee (BREGS) survey.

Note: See text for definition of variables. BPL = Below Poverty Line; SD = standard deviation; — = not available.

Notes

1. Note that the estimates of job card ownership from the 2009/10 National Sample Survey (NSS) reported in chapter 1 are even lower (17 percent of rural households). As noted previously, a specialized survey (the BREGS has an entire module with questions on the job card) is more likely to capture scheme-specific information than a general household survey.

2. Field studies suggest that this is true in most states across India (see, for example, Drèze and Khera 2011). These studies also typically find that the unemployment allowance is rarely paid in lieu of providing work. In most cases, the allowance is paid following a social audit process in which the information is made public and pressure is brought to bear on local officials.

3. Some 4 percent of households in both rounds cited the lack of a BPL card as the reason for not obtaining a job card despite applying for it.

4. For example, Andhra Pradesh revised the scheme's Schedule of Rates to enable disabled workers to earn the scheme wage following a detailed analysis of effort required. In 2008, Madhya Pradesh enabled the elderly and persons with disabilities to undertake lighter work, such as plantation and provision of worksite facilities work (National Consortium of Civil Society Organizations 2009).

5. Unsurprisingly, participants tend to be more aware of the program (see table 7A.1).

6. The original scale consists of a seven-item scale developed by Pearlin and others (1981). Each item is a statement regarding the respondent's perception of self, and respondents are asked how strongly they agree or disagree with each statement with four potential response categories. The original scale ranges from 4 to 16. We transformed the questions into yes/no answers, which proved to be a better approach in this setting based on our field tests. Our scale is then created by adding up the answers, thus ranges from 0 to 7.

7. We tested for selection bias with the standard Heckman method using a probit for each individual awareness question. We found the Mills Ratio to be insignificant in every case.

8. We run this as a linear probability model so that we can compare the coefficient on gender across the two regressions (which cannot be done across probit estimates).

9. The "svy" command in STATA, which takes into account survey design for estimation purposes, was used to ensure that the regression coefficient on the assignment dummy variable was equivalent to the difference in weighted means. This also takes clustering into account.

10. These are selected subsamples, so caution should be taken in drawing inferences for the population. Nonetheless, these tests are of obvious interest with regard to those subsamples.

11. Note that it does not make sense to examine impacts on the composite indices (Score 1 and Score 2) for this subsample or the next, so they are left out of the table.

References

Development Alternatives. 2009. "Report on Scoping Study for Design and Development of Alternative Implementation Model(s) on NREGS." Background note prepared for the Bihar Rural Employment Guarantee Scheme study. Development Alternatives, Inc., Washington, DC.

Drèze, Jean, and Reetika Khera. 2011. "The Battle for Employment Guarantee." In *The Battle for Employment Guarantee*, edited by Reetika Khera. New Delhi: Oxford University Press. 43–80.

Indian Grameen Services. 2010. "Exploring Shelf of Works for Flood Affected Area of North Bihar." Report prepared for the Rural Development Department, government of Bihar and the World Bank. Indian Grameen Services, Kolkata, India.

Khera, Reetika, and Nandini Nayak. 2009. "Women Workers and Perceptions of the National Rural Employment Guarantee Act in India." Paper presented at the FAO-IFAD-ILO "Workshop on Gaps, Trends and Current Research in Gender Dimensions of Agricultural and Rural Employment: Differentiated Pathways out of Poverty," Rome, March 30–April 3.

National Consortium of Civil Society Organizations. 2009. "NREGA Reforms: Building Rural India—First Annual Report of the National Consortium of Civil Society Organizations on NREGA, 2008–09." National Consortium on NREGA, Madhya Pradesh, India.

National Sample Survey Organization (NSSO). 2009/10. "Socio-Economic Survey Sixty-Sixth Round Schedule 10: Employment and Unemployment." Government of India, New Delhi.

Pearlin, Leonard, Elizabeth Menaghan, Morton Lieberman, and Joseph Mullan. 1981. "The Stress Process." *Journal of Health and Social Behavior* 22 (4): 337–56.

Sunai Consultancy Pvt. Ltd. 2009. "Process Qualitative Observation Report, Feb–Mar 2009, Four Blocks of Muzaffarpur and Saharsa Districts of Bihar." Background note prepared for the Bihar Rural Employment Guarantee Scheme study. Sunai Consultancy, Bihar, India.

8

Reforming the Bihar Rural Employment Guarantee Scheme: Administrative Processes

The foregoing analysis tells us that the Bihar Rural Employment Guarantee Scheme (BREGS) is performing far short of its potential. Despite the high demand for work on the scheme, many people who want work do not get it. And many of those who do get work get fewer days than desired and end up with lower wages than stipulated for the scheme. In chapter 7 we also saw that some important demand-side constraints, such as poor awareness and disempowerment on the part of potential beneficiaries, limit the scheme's performance.

This chapter examines the scheme's delivery mechanisms more closely to identify the points at which practice differs significantly from intent and how performance might be improved. The supply-side constraints identified in this chapter are relevant to both the income gains to poor people from the extra employment on BREGS *and* the value to them of the assets created by the scheme. The creation of productive village assets that promote future livelihoods is a secondary objective of BREGS, and it is typically accorded lower priority than employment generation. However, as seen in chapter 6, the cost-effectiveness of BREGS in reducing poverty through the income gains to workers alone is questionable. As shown in that chapter, a simple cash transfer program based on Below-Poverty-Line (BPL) ration cards could do better, even allowing for administrative costs and poor targeting of BPL cards. So the value to poor people of the assets created should be an important concern in efforts to improve the scheme because it may tip the balance for or against this type of scheme.[1]

We find bottlenecks in the planning and work sanctioning processes that contribute to delays in opening worksites and frequent
interruption of work. The resulting unpredictability of work provision is likely to make labor supply decisions more difficult, with
households less likely to consider BREGS as a reliable source of
employment in times of need. For instance, only about half—
59 percent of men and 51 percent of women in 2009/10 (round 2 of
the BREGS survey, R2)—believed BREGS work would be available
in their village in the next year. More important, only 12 percent of
men and 9 percent of women felt that BREGS work was available
when they needed it in the past year.

A Closer Look at the Scheme's Administration

Planning for Work

According to the scheme's guidelines, the elected village council, led
by the Mukhiya, is responsible for preparing annual plans for the
projects to be undertaken under the scheme. This annual planning
process is intended to generate an annual plan—a shelf of works and
a labor budget (that is, an estimate of person days that the shelf of
works can generate). These plans are meant to be validated through
a village meeting (the Gram Sabha) before the necessary administrative and technical approvals are requested.

In practice, the planning process is rarely community driven or
participatory. Confirming qualitative and anecdotal evidence, the
survey reveals that project selection is rarely performed by the Gram
Sabha. In fact, we find that such village meetings are not widely
held.[2] We asked BREGS participant workers in the sample about
the selection of projects at the most recent worksite at which they
worked. Many—36 percent of men and 54 percent of women in
2009/10—did not know how the projects were selected. Among
those who did know, the majority (60 percent of men and 71 percent
of women) felt the projects were largely chosen by the Mukhiya
(figure 8.1). Only a small proportion report selection of projects at
the worksite having been made at a Gram Sabha. Qualitative studies in Bihar (and other states) also typically find that Gram Sabhas
are rarely held for the purpose of finalizing the shelf of works and
that the projects chosen tend to reflect the interests of selected local
groups rather than the Gram Panchayat (GP) as a whole.[3]

The nonparticipatory selection of projects raises the possibility
of elite capture in work selection so that the assets created may be
of use largely to specific groups and local power lobbies rather than

Figure 8.1 Selection of Bihar Rural Employment Guarantee Scheme Works

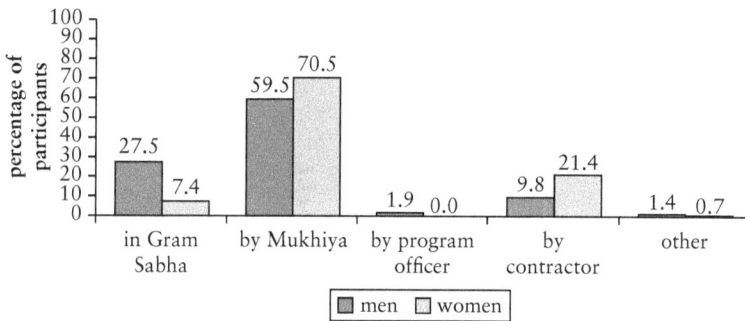

Source: Estimates based on the Bihar Rural Employment Guarantee Scheme (BREGS) survey.

Note: Based on responses of workers who report awareness of the project selection process at the BREGS worksite at which they last worked in round 2 of the BREGS survey. More than a third of men and more than half of women workers were unaware of how the specific project was selected.

beneficial to the village as a whole.[4] In the BREGS survey, we asked people about five assets created under the scheme in their village. We found that knowledge of these assets was poor, particularly among women, with slightly more than half the interviewed women being aware of any of these five assets. Only 13 percent of men and 6 percent of women knew about all five of the assets about which they were asked.[5] However, the majority of those who knew about these assets perceived that they were likely to last at least until the next year and were useful, primarily to those who lived close to them.[6]

In judging the choice of projects, it is necessary to consider local conditions. According to the national scheme guidelines, several types of projects are permissible under the Mahatma Gandhi National Rural Employment Guarantee Scheme (MGNREGS), ranging from rural connectivity to natural resource regeneration.[7] However, as in many states, rural roads are the single most common asset built in Bihar, accounting for nearly half the scheme's total expenditures in the past three years (see table 8.1 for 2008/09). This emphasis on rural connectivity is also reflected in the survey data. Panchayat rozgar sewaks (PRSs) in 98 percent of the surveyed GPs reported kutcha roads in their shelf of works in both rounds of the survey, while the proportion reporting pucca roads and bridges increased from 29 percent to 64 percent between the two years.

However, the variation in the type of project undertaken across Bihar's four agro-climatic zones suggests that the planning process,

Table 8.1 Percentage of Bihar Rural Employment Guarantee Scheme Expenditure by Type of Project, 2008/09

Zone	Water conservation	Drought proofing	Irrigation works	Renovation of traditional water bodies	Land development	Flood control and protection	Rural connectivity
North	12.1	3.5	9.1	7.6	4.7	15.6	47.4
North-East	5.9	2.3	5.1	3.7	2.8	9.4	70.9
South-East	24.1	3.7	15.8	14.2	2.7	4.6	34.9
South-West	23.3	2.6	15.8	15.4	2.3	9.0	31.6
Bihar	14.5	3.0	10.4	9.2	3.4	11.2	48.4

Source: Monthly Progress Reports, Rural Development Department, government of Bihar.

Note: The four agro-climatic zones are defined by the Agriculture Department, government of Bihar. The categories of works are from the list of permissible BREGS projects. The expenditure pattern for 2009/10 is similar, with the exception of an increase in drought-proofing works following the severe drought in 2009.

though not participatory, does take into account local conditions to some extent (see table 8.1). As noted in the overview, nearly three-quarters of Bihar is flood prone while 16 percent of its land area is permanently waterlogged.[8] BREGS planning in many parts of Bihar, particularly in the two northern agro-climatic zones, includes works related to flood control and protection. The share of expenditures on water conservation and microirrigation works is relatively high in many of the southern districts that are prone to drought.

Another consideration has to do with Bihar's population density, which is among the highest in India. This attribute, combined with a shortage of common (public) land, makes it difficult to identify appropriate sites for building community assets. PRSs interviewed in the BREGS survey reported the lack of common land (on which to build village assets) or wasteland (as a source of soil needed for earth filling) as reasons for their inability to undertake certain types of projects in their GPs. As a result, it becomes necessary to promote appropriate projects on individual lands as permissible under the scheme. Administrative data do not indicate the share of expenditure on these projects. However, in the survey, PRSs in 80 percent of the surveyed GPs reported the inclusion of at least some works on the private land of Scheduled Castes and Scheduled Tribes (SC/STs), Indira Awaas Yojana[9] beneficiaries, and of small and medium-size farmers (the last category was included in 2009) in the GP shelf of works.

When BREGS was first introduced, the planning process initially developed in a way that was, for the most part, top down and supply driven with a very limited role for communities, the village council, or the Mukhiya. In fact, the shelves of works left over from the previous public works scheme—Sampoorna Grameen Rozgar Yojana—were used in many districts. Although this approach is understandable in the early days of the scheme, addressing the performance gaps in the planning stage as the scheme matures (see box 8.1) is critical. Participatory planning by the community can promote convergence between schemes at the village level, so as to access all available resources, including those from BREGS, the Backward Regions Grant Fund, and the Village Disaster Management Plan, and develop an integrated village development plan.[10] At present, these are at best fragmented planning exercises lacking a coherent vision and leading to duplication of effort.

Finally, converging with other government schemes optimizes public resources and helps create durable assets. Local area development programs, including watershed management, have the potential to develop village natural resources; they are expected to create, repair, and maintain local resources. Cooperation between

Box 8.1 Informed, Participatory Planning for the Bihar
Rural Employment Guarantee Scheme (BREGS)

As part of the qualitative work for this study, we attempted to understand what is required to undertake informed, participatory planning
in the spirit of the National Rural Employment Guarantee Act. Two
teams carried out assessments of labor demand and a resource mapping exercise in two blocks in each of four districts (Gaya, Khaimur,
Kishanganj, and Purnea) during February and August 2009. In two
Gram Panchayats (GPs), the teams also plotted the relevant data on
a geographic information system (GIS) to facilitate planning.

These teams developed a list of projects based on resource mapping, labor demand assessment, and community participation. They
found that this "unofficial shelf of works" provided a much larger list
of projects than the official shelf of works in the GPs studied. Detailed
resource planning (or land surveys as currently undertaken in Andhra
Pradesh) can provide communities with updated information on
existing village assets and land ownership for siting projects. The
unofficial shelf of works and labor budget developed in conformance
with the work demand assessment also corresponded better to the
availability of workers for BREGS during the course of the year. In
contrast, the corresponding official documents planned for some
work provision every month, without reference to worker preferences
or allowance for seasonality in agriculture.

The team's qualitative work also highlighted two critical requirements for planning. First, the process requires reliable and updated
information on village land use and ownership. The most recent maps
for the two GPs studied dated to the 1960s, resulting in the need for
intensive updating through discussions with village revenue officials,
local leaders, and community groups to obtain an accurate map of the
village.

Second, trained facilitators are needed to help communities plan.
Though Panchayati Raj Institutions (PRIs) and communities have the
advantage of local knowledge, they lack the necessary technical tools
and capacity to translate this knowledge into concrete plans.
Appropriate technical inputs on how to select, sequence, site, and
design works are required. The estimation of costs and labor requirements for each project necessary to develop the overall labor budget
for the GP also requires some engineering skills. Most states, including
Bihar, face shortages in technical staff for the scheme. Andhra Pradesh
and Madhya Pradesh have developed ways to deal with this issue.
Both states have standardized the specific works that could be carried
out under the permissible project types. This standardization has
made the preparation of technical estimates for projects easier at the

(Continued on the following page)

Box 8.1 (Continued)

village level. Madhya Pradesh provides handbooks for its technical staff to generate work estimates, and Andhra Pradesh has integrated the work estimation module in its computerized management information system to allow for automated generation of work estimates.

With the appropriate technical expertise and community participation, the planning process can deliver a shelf of works and labor budget that create assets relevant for the village and have the potential to meet local demand for work. The use of technology, such as GIS for resource mapping, can further provide PRIs and communities with reliable information to plan effectively. GIS can also promote integrated planning by facilitating the exchange of information across government schemes as well as facilitate asset monitoring over time. Gujarat has used GIS to develop composite village maps with information on natural resources and rural assets created by various departments. These maps are being used by Mahatma Gandhi National Rural Employment Guarantee Scheme technical staff as a planning tool to position projects based on technical feasibility and to convince local leaders and communities of the rationale for site selection. GIS has also proved useful in eliminating duplication of projects and in facilitating asset maintenance and monitoring.

Sources: Development Alternatives 2009; Indian Grameen Services 2009; MART 2010.

BREGS and such local area development programs would promote the construction of relevant and durable assets. There are several examples from other Indian states relating to using MGNREGS funds for creating village assets, but with technical expertise (and occasionally material inputs) provided by line departments such as Water Resources (for watershed and irrigation works), Forestry (for plantation-related works), and Agriculture (for works on individual lands). The 2012 MGNREGS guidelines promote this objective by including watershed, agriculture, livestock, fisheries, forestry, and sanitation-related works in the list of permissible MGNREGS projects.

Estimating the Demand for Work

The shelf of works developed through the planning process is supposed to be based on an estimate of labor demand. In practice, the labor budget is typically supply driven and determined by the previous year's performance, with some adjustment based on a rough estimate of likely demand in the current year (Ministry of Rural Development 2011).

Workers are likely to demand BREGS work primarily during the lean agricultural season. The BREGS survey data identify the peak months for BREGS work provision as January through June. Little BREGS work is made available during the rainy season (July–September), when agricultural employment is also low for some of the time.[11] The PRSs in the surveyed GPs reported that most of the projects permissible under BREGS, with the exception of plantations, could not be undertaken for about four months of the year. This gap was usually during the rainy season or after floods (and subsequent waterlogging). In fact, at the time of the survey, BREGS guidelines waived the employment guarantee between mid-June and mid-October, and the state was not obliged to provide work or unemployment allowances during this period.

The central ministry's revisions to operational guidelines in 2012 include undertaking a baseline survey of job card holders in every GP before preparing a labor budget (Ministry of Rural Development 2013). Some states, such as Andhra Pradesh, already undertake detailed labor demand assessments at the start of the fiscal year to prepare a calendar of estimated demand for MGNREGS during the course of the year (see box 8.1). Bihar is attempting something similar through partnerships with nongovernmental organizations (NGOs) and community-based organizations. The Nehru Yuva Kendra Sangathan (an organization of village-level youth clubs) was engaged in 2011 to carry out a survey to increase knowledge of the scheme as well as to explicitly record requests for job cards and demand for work. However, the presence of active youth clubs is patchy across the state, and their capacity to undertake this work is limited. Another promising channel is through the village organizations created under the National Rural Livelihood Mission. These groups have the potential to canvass preferences, at least among their self-help group member households, and to help create a calendar for BREGS work demand. Incorporating this exercise into the planning process and informing workers of the proposed labor budget at an appropriate time (before household labor supply and migration decisions are made) would allow the supply side to be more responsive to demand.

Supplying Work

Matching the expression of demand with the supply of worksites is key to fulfilling the employment guarantee. We find evidence of delays in opening worksites, frequent closures of worksites, and interruption of work in both rounds of the survey. In 33 percent of the surveyed GPs, PRSs reported delays in starting work in round 1 (R1); this figure rose to 43 percent in R2. Several factors could contribute to such delays, such as the absence of approved works that can be quickly initiated in response to demand, insufficient or untimely funding, and inadequate staff for initiating and managing worksites. We examine the first reason here; the latter two factors are examined in the next section, which addresses systemic constraints to BREGS delivery.

In the absence of a ready shelf of works with at least some approved projects, GPs may be constrained in providing work in response to demand. We find that 11 percent of GPs in R2 did not have a shelf of works (an increase from 6 percent in R1). As seen in chapter 3, the presence of a ready shelf of works in GPs was a strong predictor of participation among poor households. Qualitative research for this book reveals significant delays in obtaining the necessary sanctions for the shelf of works proposed by GPs. For instance, in two GPs in Kishanganj district in 2008, it took three to five months to get the necessary approvals from the block and district elected bodies (Development Alternatives 2009; Sunai 2009).

Even when an approved shelf of works exists in the GP, administrative and technical sanctions for a specific project must be obtained before a worksite can be opened. This requirement can introduce further delays in the process. For instance, it took 20–35 days to open road construction projects in the two GPs noted above. In one of them, the entire sanctioning process took so long that the rainy season began and work had to be delayed for another four months (Sunai 2009).[12] In general, insufficient attention is paid to the sequencing and timing of projects. For instance, projects like water harvesting and flood proofing require ample time for the necessary preparatory work, group formation, and consensus building. Breaking ground on such projects just before the monsoons often results in unfinished assets.

In fact, interviews with block officials and PRSs in the surveyed GPs reveal that the problem of intermittent closure of worksites was common and became worse between the two survey rounds. The proportion of GPs reporting work interruptions in at least some of the worksites rose from 44 percent in R1 to 73 percent in R2. This impression is corroborated by the experience of BREGS workers: in both rounds, nearly half of the sample of men and women workers reported interruptions to work at the worksite at which they last worked, often more than once.[13] However, even when household members reported interruption of work at the last worksite,

80 percent of participating households in R1 felt that public works were an available coping mechanism for responding to shocks. By R2, this proportion had fallen to only 57 percent of households, possibly reflecting the increase in the frequency of work interruption. In R1, the main reasons given for work stoppage were rains or flooding. Though these reasons remained important in R2, strikes by workers and work stoppage by officials had become much more widespread. The latter is likely linked to the availability of funds and is examined in the next section. Disputes with farmers were also cited in some of the GPs, perhaps pointing to conflicts over common land.

Worksite Management

We also find departures from the scheme guidelines in the management of worksites and the provision of facilities to workers. For instance, contractors are not allowed under BREGS guidelines; instead, the PRS is expected to function as the agent who mobilizes workers and manages the worksite, with the help of the mate.[14] As seen in table 8.2, we find that the ban on contractors is not being enforced—more than half of male and female workers reported the presence of contractors at the BREGS worksite at which they last worked in R1, and even more in R2. The majority of workers also

Table 8.2 Participant Reports about the Worksite

Participants answering positively that the following are true	Round 1		Round 2	
	Men (percent)	Women (percent)	Men (percent)	Women (percent)
Contractor is on site	52.0	54.1	59.4	62.9
Mate is on site	90.4	79.1	87.8	85.7
Machines are used	39.0	49.0	7.6	7.3
Muster roll is on site	65.8	61.5	70.3	68.9
Attendance is taken on site	94.0	94.4	90.1	90.0
Used own tools	95.7	95.9	92.6	92.6
Site is within own village	67.3	68.1	71.7	74.3
Site is within 5 km	98.6	96.0	99.1	99.5
Money was paid to get work or wages	16.6	19.4	21.5	10.8

Source: Estimates based on the Bihar Rural Employment Guarantee Scheme (BREGS) survey.

Note: Based on responses by workers at the BREGS worksite at which they last worked. km = kilometers.

report a mate being present. It is not entirely clear whether workers fully understand the difference between the two because both
carry out similar functions with only the nature of their contract
with the GP (the implementing agency) being different. There could
thus be some double counting and over- or underestimation of the
presence of mates or contractors based on the responses of workers
in the surveys.

The rationale for banning contractor involvement in BREGS is
to reduce corruption and exploitation. A survey of six North Indian
states finds that worksites where contractors are present are more
likely to have fudged muster rolls,[15] and experienced greater exploitation and harassment of women (Drèze and Khera 2009). However,
contractors also bring project management expertise. PRSs and mates
often lack the capacity to successfully mobilize workers on a fixed
schedule to complete the work and build assets of reasonable quality. Because the mate is responsible for day-to-day management of
the worksite, this is a critical gap and has implications for the quality
of assets being created under the scheme. A concerted effort needs
to be made to build the capacity of the PRS and the mate to enable
them to undertake this task. This strengthening could potentially
include redefining norms for mate selection, providing appropriate
technical training and the necessary tools, and providing incentives
for performance.

The use of machines at worksites is reported by workers,
although the incidence of cases reported declined from 39 percent
and 49 percent of men and women, respectively, at the last BREGS
worksite in R1 to 8 percent of men and 7 percent of women workers
in R2 (table 8.2). It is not clear whether these are labor-displacing
machines (which is the specific category of machines banned). Nearly
everyone reports using their own tools for earthwork rather than
being supplied with tools at the worksite. Fewer than two-thirds of
male and female workers report that a muster roll was maintained
at the last worksite at which they worked, with an increasing trend
over time. But almost all workers in both rounds reported attendance
(in some format) was taken on a daily basis. Worksites were located
in workers' villages in more than two-thirds of all cases and practi-
cally always within 5 kilometers, as prescribed by the guidelines.

Mandated worksite facilities are frequently not provided. The
National Rural Employment Guarantee Act entitles workers to basic
facilities such as drinking water, shade, first aid, and child care at
which women can leave their children when there are more than
five children under age six at the worksite. In practice, these facilities are often not present. The exception is the provision of drinking water—in R2, nearly half of men and women workers reported

Figure 8.2 Worksite Facilities in Round 2

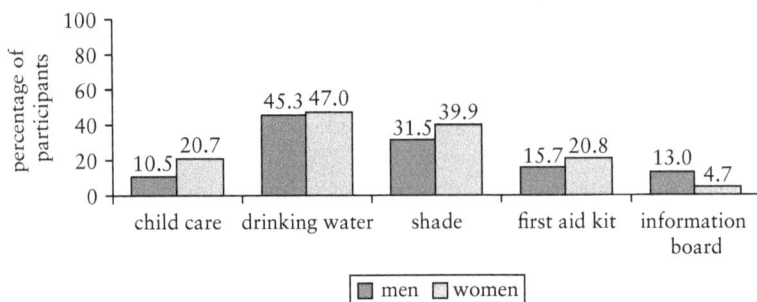

Source: Estimates based on the Bihar Rural Employment Guarantee Scheme (BREGS) survey.
Note: Percentage of participants reporting that the worksite at which they last worked had the facilities. Based on round 2 responses by workers at the BREGS worksite at which they last worked.

its availability at the BREGS worksites at which they last worked (see figure 8.2), which was a somewhat lower share than in R1. Women workers reported an increase in the provision of most facilities, including child care facilities, between the two rounds (from 13 percent to 21 percent). The lack of such facilities can discourage women from participating in the scheme (Sunai 2009).

Wage Payments

The scheme's guidelines require that wages be paid within 15 days of the last day worked. However, the evidence points to delays in wage payments. These delays also discourage participation and reduce the overall impact on poverty.

The survey asked workers how long they had to wait to be paid wages after completing work at the last worksite at which they worked (table 8.3). In R1, 76 percent of men and 79 percent of women workers reported having been paid their expected wages in full at the BREGS worksite. Of course, it should be noted that the amount received may not be equal to the amount owed them had they been paid the stipulated BREGS wage (see chapter 4 for a discussion of wage level shortfalls).[16] In R2, the percentages were 76 percent and 71 percent. Other workers had either received partial payments and were still waiting for the rest, or had not been paid at all by the time of the survey. The latter was true for 13 percent and 14 percent of men, and of 10 percent and 24 percent of women across R1 and R2, respectively. Among those who had

Table 8.3 Time Taken for Payment of Wages after Work Completion

	Round 1		Round 2	
Participants reporting the following	*Men (percent)*	*Women (percent)*	*Men (percent)*	*Women (percent)*
Payment not yet received	13.2	10.2	14.1	24.3
Partial payment received	11.3	11.2	9.7	5.0
Full payment received	75.5	78.6	76.2	70.7
Of which, workers received payments in the following period after completing work				
Daily	15.7	18.3	13.3	6.8
Some amount daily and a lump sum later	20.9	33.9	7.4	4.5
Between 1 and 15 days	52.2	26.5	59.9	70.1
Between 16 and 30 days	7.4	13.2	8.5	6.4
More than one month	3.8	8.2	10.9	12.2

Source: Estimates based on the Bihar Rural Employment Guarantee Scheme (BREGS) survey.

Note: Based on responses by workers at the BREGS worksite at which they last worked. Note that the reference to full payment received reflects merely that workers reported no outstanding payments, even though they may not have received the full stipulated scheme wage (see chapter 4).

received the entire amount expected, about 11 percent of men and 21 percent of women had waited for more than 15 days to be paid in full in R1. By R2, delays beyond 15 days had risen to 19 percent among men and women, with 11 percent of men and 12 percent of women waiting more than one month. Thus, the evidence points to long delays as well as partial payments. At first glance, the high proportion of workers reporting either daily wages or some daily outlay with a lump sum paid subsequently is puzzling. Next we speculate on possible explanations for this occurrence.

There could be several reasons for delayed wage payments. On paper, the payment process is supposed to be as follows: wages due to BREGS workers are estimated on the basis of productivity norms set forth in the rural Schedule of Rates.[17] Scheme functionaries are required to ensure productivity norms are being met by measuring the work done at the worksite. On the basis of the muster roll and work measurement, a payment order is generated that directs banks and post offices to credit worker accounts with the specified wage. Funds are then transferred from the implementing agency's bank account to workers' bank or post office accounts. This cycle is supposed to take no more than 15 days after work completion.

In practice, a number of bottlenecks in these processes in Bihar result in delayed payments. First, holdups often occur in the measurement of work (Development Alternatives 2009; Indian Grameen Services 2009; Sunai 2009). Second, the flow of funds to GPs is erratic and frequently delayed. In both rounds of the BREGS survey, PRSs in the surveyed GPs reported problems of insufficient funds and funds not being available in time. In more than half of the surveyed GPs (52 percent in R1 and 67 percent in R2), these problems were cited as contributing to delays in paying wages to workers. (This issue is explored in more detail in the next section, which focuses on systemic constraints such as weak financial management capacity.) Third, the payment of wages through workers' bank or post office accounts rather than directly in cash adds to the processing time. Since April 2008, the scheme guidelines mandate a move toward financial inclusion with full reliance on payments through personal accounts with financial institutions. But practice is still a long way from that ideal because of the sparse presence and inadequate capacity of financial institutions in rural areas.

In rural Bihar, bank coverage is patchy. In R2, nearly 60 percent of the villages in the sample reported that the nearest bank was more than 5 kilometers distant. Post offices are more accessible: almost all sample villages reported one within 5 kilometers and nearly a quarter of the villages had a post office within the village itself. But most village post offices are small, typically operated by a single postman, and lack the capacity to deal regularly with large volumes of transactions. Nor are they linked to the core banking system that facilitates interbank electronic funds transfers and through which payments can be directly transferred from the implementing agency's BREGS bank account to workers' bank accounts. In the case of post office accounts, funds are transferred first to the district post office before being redirected to the local village-level post offices where worker accounts are held. As a result, payments through post offices introduce further delays.[18]

In fact, we find that more than half of all rural households in Bihar had neither bank nor post office accounts in R2 (see table 8.4). Although the PRS is tasked with helping BREGS workers open bank or post office accounts (at least one per household), about 53 percent of participating households had neither in R1. By R2, this number had fallen to 30 percent. However, the absence of an account does not necessarily constrain households from getting work—fewer than

REFORMING BREGS: ADMINISTRATIVE PROCESSES

1 percent of men and women excess demanders (those who wanted work but did not get it) cited the lack of a bank or post office account as the main reason for not getting work in each round.

The large number of households remaining without bank or post office accounts explains why workers continue to report wage payments made in cash. When asked about the worksite at which they last worked, more than two-thirds of workers, both men and women, reported cash payments in R2 (see table 8.5). For women, however, this represented an improvement from R1, when the majority of women workers (89 percent) reported payment in cash at their last worksite. Naturally, nearly all workers without an account reported cash payments. But even among those belonging to households with

Table 8.4 Percentage of Rural Households with Accounts at Financial Institutions

	Round 1		Round 2	
	All households	*BREGS households*	*All households*	*BREGS households*
Bank account	24.8	23.0	28.2	24.1
Post office account	6.8	19.9	12.3	35.3
Both	2.2	4.0	5.1	10.6
Neither	66.2	53.1	54.4	30.0

Source: Estimates based on the Bihar Rural Employment Guarantee Scheme (BREGS) survey.

Note: Based on responses in the household questionnaire.

Table 8.5 Percentage of Participants Reporting Wage Payments through Various Sources at the Last Worksite

	Round 1		Round 2	
Payment source	*Men*	*Women*	*Men*	*Women*
Post office accounts	12.5	7.5	27.6	25.5
Bank accounts	10.5	3.5	5.8	5.5
Cash				
Mukhiya	27.7	40.0	25.4	29.6
Mate	13.0	14.7	10.9	8.8
Contractor	18.2	20.4	17.5	21.2
Officials (PRS and others)	11.4	11.1	9.5	8.8
Other	6.6	2.9	3.2	0.7

Source: Estimates based on the Bihar Rural Employment Guarantee Scheme (BREGS) survey.

Note: Based on responses by workers at the BREGS worksite at which they last worked.

at least one bank or post office account, more than half the workers, both men and women, reported payments in cash.[19]

By contrast, the PRSs interviewed in the BREGS survey reported that the majority of wage payments are made through worker accounts. In fact, as discussed in chapter 4, qualitative research for this report suggests that delays in fund transfers to worker bank accounts can sometimes lead to the Mukhiya or other functionaries acting as intermediaries and making partial advance payments in cash. These cash advances are paid on a daily basis, in line with usual practice for agricultural casual work, but are typically less than the stipulated scheme wage. Wage payments in the workers' accounts are then transferred to the intermediary when they are received. The difference between the daily wage paid in advance and that stipulated by the scheme and eventually received through the workers' accounts is then pocketed by the intermediary.[20] As seen in chapter 7 (box 7.1), workers' passbooks and job cards are sometimes in the possession of the Mukhiya, the PRS, or some other official or middleman, leaving room for manipulation and leakage. This is a potential explanation for why many workers report receiving daily wages as mentioned earlier and as shown in table 8.3.

Understanding the Supply-Side Constraints on Delivery

Ensuring adherence to the scheme's operational guidelines and transparency safeguards requires appropriate institutional structures with skilled and motivated staff, adequate and timely funds, and robust systems for monitoring and grievance redress. The central government provides 6 percent of MGNREGS expenditures to states to cover the nonwage, nonmaterial costs incurred in implementing the scheme. Yet in 2009/10, Bihar spent about 643 million rupees (Rs), amounting to only about 3.5 percent of total scheme expenditures. This is not because Bihar does not need the extra money. More plausibly, the underspending of the central government's allocation for these other costs reflects the same administrative constraints that have created the rationing documented in previous chapters, as well as other deficiencies in the scheme's performance. This section examines those constraints.

Staffing and Capacity

The BREGS guidelines call for a dedicated cadre of professional administrative and technical staff to implement the scheme. Significant human resources are required at the village level to register households, record every work application, mobilize households to participate in the planning of works, obtain necessary approvals, and initiate work in response to demand, manage and oversee worksites, and ensure timely wage payments. The scheme also places a heavy emphasis on reporting.[21] Whereas the district-level functionaries (the district magistrate, the deputy district coordinator, block development officers, and the assistant engineers) are government officers, the rest of the BREGS staff (including junior engineers and PRSs) consists of contract workers.

When the scheme was first introduced, many states experienced significant delays in appointing contract staff, and Bihar was no exception (Comptroller and Auditor General 2008). In many districts, the existing block development officers were required to perform the program officer (PO) function. The appointment of GP-level PRSs also took time. Extensive recruitment in 2007 and subsequently has led to the filling of these district, block, and panchayat positions. Administrative data indicate that all districts now have a dedicated officer for BREGS, but that vacancies remained significant at the block and GP levels, even in 2011—16 percent of the 534 blocks in the state did not have a PO; 9 percent of GPs in the state did not have a PRS; and 30 percent of GP clusters did not have a panchayat technical assistant (there is supposed to be one for every four GPs).[22]

The issue of technical staff vacancies is reflected in the responses of block officials interviewed in the BREGS survey—although almost all block officials report an average of about 14 PRSs per block (nearly one PRS per GP given that a block has about 15 GPs on average), the majority report only one or two junior engineers and panchayat technical assistants per block. The staffing levels improved between the two survey rounds, but adequate technical staff remains a concern. As many as 73 percent of POs and 80 percent of junior engineers in R1 felt the available BREGS staff in the block was inadequate and contributed to delays in opening worksites, work measurement, and payment of wages. Even in R2, about 66 percent of POs and 56 percent of junior engineers felt more staff was needed. At the GP level, however, only 9 percent of interviewed PRSs viewed staffing as a constraint.

In 2011, the government of Bihar established an autonomous society, the Bihar Rural Development Society, for BREGS implementation. The society seeks to attract experienced government officers and private sector professionals to implement the scheme. Current BREGS staff at the district and lower levels will come under the purview of the Bihar Rural Development Society, opening greater avenues for these contract staff with respect to career development and growth.

Building capacity among BREGS staff and Panchayati Raj Institution (PRI) representatives is a key priority. Field studies highlight low capacity among BREGS staff at the block and village levels, particularly with respect to participatory planning, development of labor budgets, and demand registration. In addition, the scheme guidelines assign a central role to PRIs in BREGS implementation, including planning, execution, and oversight (see box 8.2). BREGS alone required an average GP in Bihar to manage approximately Rs 2.2 million in 2009/10.[23] However, their capacity to perform

Box 8.2 The Role of the Mukhiya

The Mukhiya continues to play an integral role in the implementation of the Bihar Rural Employment Guarantee Scheme (BREGS), acting as the representative of both the workers on one side and the local government on the other.

The panchayat rozgar sewak (PRS) and the Mukhiya bear joint responsibility for scheme implementation. The Mukhiya is responsible for preparing the village plans and can also sanction small works costing up to Rs 5 lakhs.[a] Together, the Mukhiya and PRS are tasked with jointly operating BREGS bank accounts and managing payments. The PRS is responsible for registering demand, facilitating planning and work sanction, supervising worksites, and maintaining records. However, in practice, the Mukhiya frequently carries out these functions; scheme performance often depends on the level of the Mukhiya's commitment. Because the Mukhiya is the local leader and the PRS is an outsider to the Gram Panchayat (GP), possibilities are opened up for conflict or collusion.

Information. Both qualitative studies and the BREGS survey indicate that the Mukhiya and other GP members (such as ward members) remain an important source of information about the availability of BREGS works. In round 2 of the BREGS survey, about 45 percent of men and 29 percent of women workers listed Panchayati Raj Institution (PRI) representatives as the main source of information about the worksite at which they last worked. About 26 percent of male and 20 percent of female workers reported that they had been called to the worksite by the Mukhiya or other PRI representative. Qualitative studies indicate that demand for work is often informally made to the Mukhiya.

Participation. In a third of the GPs surveyed in the BREGS survey, the GP's official work is carried out at the Mukhiya's house. This could potentially constrain the ability of different groups to register for job cards or apply for work, depending on caste and political

(Continued on the following page)

Box 8.2 *(Continued)*

affiliation. In addition, the local political connections and characteristics of the Mukhiya him- or herself can influence participation (see
chapter 3). Thus, households in villages in which the Mukhiya has
held a GP post in the past, is a contractor, and lives in the village are
more likely to get BREGS work.

Work execution. According to the scheme guidelines, the mate in
charge of worksite management is to be chosen by the Gram Sabha.
But more often than not, the mate is selected by the Mukhiya. The
mates perform the project management function of contractors to a
large extent in that they mobilize workers, record attendance, oversee
and manage the worksite, and record preliminary work measure-
ments. Qualitative research indicates that mates are not always held
accountable because of their connections to the Mukhiya.

Source: Authors' observations and estimates from the Bihar Rural Employment Guarantee Scheme (BREGS) survey.
a. One lakh = Rs 100,000.

these functions is weak. Both the scheme staff and PRI representatives also often lack clarity on the modifications to the scheme
guidelines that are periodically issued by the state.

Training and technical support to the scheme staff and PRI representatives, particularly at the village level, is critically important.
This support includes, for example, building capacity for better
financial management, participatory resource planning, and project
management functions. But developing an ongoing system for the
training of about 13,000 contract BREGS workers and PRI representatives in 534 blocks and 8,463 GPs is not an easy task. In fact,
findings from the BREGS survey suggest a lower emphasis on training in R2 compared with R1. Both the POs and PRSs report, on
average, a lower number of training sessions and fewer days spent
in training in R2.

Financial Management

Because MGNREGS is a centrally sponsored scheme, the central
government funds the bulk of the states' MGNREGS expenditures.
As noted previously, the central government also finances up to 6 percent of the state government expenditures on MGNREGS, including
salaries of contract workers, training, and information technology
(IT) monitoring systems. As with other centrally sponsored schemes,

funds are transferred directly from the central ministry to districts. For BREGS, unlike other centrally sponsored schemes, PRIs at the district, block, and GP levels are implementing agencies and play an important role in managing scheme funds. Given the multiple agencies and government levels involved in managing the flow of funds, it is critical for Bihar to have a well-functioning financial management system to keep track of funds' transfer and use.

MGNREGS funds are released by the central Ministry of Rural Development on the basis of state proposals rather than predetermined allocations. These annual state work plans and budget proposals are supposed to be an aggregation of demand for funds from the districts (based on the estimated shelf of works and labor budget). In practice, the initially released central funds are also linked to actual utilization in the previous fiscal year.

Funds are released directly to districts in two (or more) tranches. On paper, the initial tranche in the beginning of the fiscal year is based on the submitted district-level labor budget projections.[24] Once the central funds are released, the state allocation is also released. This initial allocation provides the necessary advance funds to initiate BREGS works. The second (and subsequent) tranches are released once the districts submit utilization certificates indicating that 60 percent of the initial allocation has been exhausted. An audit report is also required if the certificates are submitted after September. Funds are to be transferred to the district within 15 days of submission of the utilization certificate, provided the certificates are found to be accurate. Districts are then required to transfer funds to the implementing agency accounts at the district, block, and GP levels.

In practice, both qualitative research and the BREGS survey find evidence of significant delays in the transfer of funds to GPs. As seen in table 8.6, substantial improvement occurred by R2, but 36 percent of PRSs still reported inadequate funds. Even if sufficient funds

Table 8.6 Flow of Funds

	Round 1 (percent)	Round 2 (percent)
PRSs reporting insufficient funds in past year	61.1	36.3
PRSs reporting funds not available on time in past year[a]	—	64.1

Source: Estimates based on the Bihar Rural Employment Guarantee Scheme (BREGS) survey.

Note: Based on panchayat rozgar sewak (PRS) responses in the Gram Panchayat questionnaires. — = not available.

a. This question was not asked in R1.

were available on average, they were not necessarily available on time, as reported by PRSs in 64 percent of the surveyed GPs in R2. In the majority of GPs in which these instances were reported, this resulted in delays in starting work, in making wage payments to workers, and in paying government functionaries.

Delays can occur at any or all of three stages: the transfer of funds from the central ministry to districts; the release of the state share to districts; and the transfer of funds from the district to the GPs. We analyzed administrative data on the request for and receipt of central and state funds by districts in 2010/11 to identify bottle-necks in the flow of funds.[25] Given the somewhat patchy condition of these data, this analysis can only be indicative of the nature of delays and shortfalls in fund transfers between the central ministry and the districts.

We find that, for all 38 districts, the sanction of the first tranche by the Ministry of Rural Development occurs within two days of the request being made (typically at the start of the fiscal year in April). Very little delay in receipt of the first tranche from the central ministry seems to have occurred for the 25 districts for which we have information. On average, funds were received within 17 days from the sanctioning of the first tranche; the maximum time was 30 days. By mid-May, all 25 districts for which we have this information had received the first tranche.

However, there were delays in the release of subsequent tranches. The second tranche was received by 29 districts by July or August 2010, another three districts received funds by September or October, while the remaining five districts received funds only in January or February 2011. During this period, some districts made repeated requests for funds. In the 19 districts for which we have informa-tion on the dates of both tranches, the average gap between the two tranches was 115 days.

We do not have information at the district level on the additional time it may have taken for these funds to reach GPs. However, a field visit to a block in Bhojpur district indicated further delays in trans-ferring funds to GPs: in October 2010, about 181 GPs (83 percent of GPs in the district) had less than Rs 1 lakh in available funds at the time.[26] The peak BREGS season is the first quarter of the calendar year, so delays in the receipt of funds until this time make it difficult for GPs to open worksites. Furthermore, low funds availability also leads to prioritization of smaller works with estimated costs of less than Rs 1 lakh.

An additional concern is the shortfall between the amount requested by districts and that received in each tranche from the central ministry. In all of Bihar's 38 districts, the amounts received were significantly lower than that requested. For instance, the average labor budget was Rs 1,162 million while the average amount received in the first tranche was Rs 188 million. Combined with the funds already available at the district level from the previous year, these disbursements amounted to only 28 percent of the requested labor budget.

On paper, the first tranche can be up to 50 percent of the labor budget. However, in 2010/11, the actual amount released was based on the expenditures during the first six months of the previous fiscal year. This amount was released only if all documentation for the previous year was complete; otherwise only a partial amount was released. Districts then had to request release of the remaining amount of the first tranche.

Linking the current release to expenditures in the previous year is a problem in a demand-driven scheme such as BREGS, particularly when current circumstances (such as a drought) may result in higher demand than in the previous year. By the end of fiscal year 2010/11, the amount released combined with the amount available from the previous fiscal year came to only about 60 percent on average of the labor budget requested.

The main cause for these delays and shortfalls appears to be the limited financial management capacity at the district and lower levels. For instance, the above data indicate that shortfalls in the amounts released varied substantially across districts, ranging from 18 percent of the labor budget in Madhubani to 91 percent in Muzaffarpur. This variance likely reflects the differences in capacity across districts, blocks, and GPs for managing funds and preparing accurate reports on use. Delays in the submission of accurate documentation by any one GP can delay the entire district's receipt of funds.

In addition to the problems of insufficient and untimely funds availability, Bihar has often been unable to fully absorb available resources (central and state) in the past. This was the case when BREGS was first introduced. In 2006/07, expenditure as a share of total available funds was only 38 percent. Utilization rates have improved significantly since then; in 2010/11, about 82 percent of available resources were spent. This improvement occurred even as the total quantum of resources increased more than 2.5 times. However, expenditures on the scheme can be expected to increase even further as the delivery system becomes more responsive to the currently unmet demand. In the future, addressing the varying capacities of districts to absorb available funds will be critical. As figure 8.3 indicates, not only do utilization rates vary across districts, they also vary from year to year within districts.

Figure 8.3 Utilization of Available Resources across Districts

Annual scheme expenditures as a percentage of total available funds

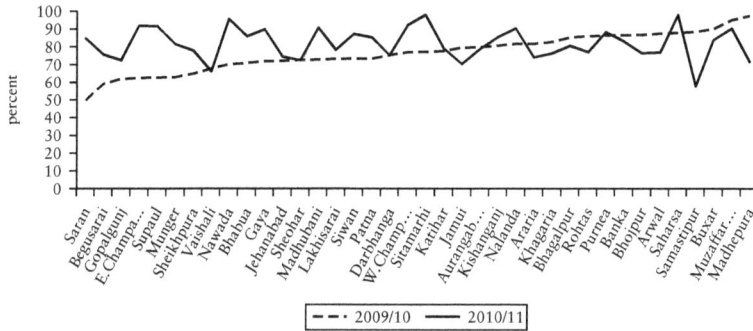

Source: Monthly Progress Reports, Rural Development Department, government of Bihar.

Several initiatives are under way to improve financial management. Because funds are transferred directly from the center to the districts, the state's administrative role to date has been somewhat limited to coordinating between the districts and the central ministry. In recent years, the Rural Development Department, government of Bihar, has increased its oversight of the flow of funds and has introduced systems for better financial management. The government has mandated the appointment of a funds manager in each district to manage releases to GPs and simultaneously introduced a system of fortnightly monitoring of funds available to GPs. The objective is to ensure that no GP has a balance of less than Rs 1 lakh at any time. Transfers are made on the basis of these reports, with utilization certificates being submitted subsequently. The government also recognizes the need to build financial management capacity simultaneously at the district and lower levels.

A State Employment Guarantee Fund has also been established according to the provisions of the national guidelines. Once this state-level corpus fund is fully functional, funds from the central government are expected to be transferred to it and then directly to GPs, thereby reducing the delays that occur in transfers from the district to GPs. In addition, a rolling fund has been provided to minimize delays in wage payments to workers through paying agencies, whether it be post office or bank accounts or other modality of payment.

An IT-enabled system for centralized funds management was also introduced in 2010. This system provides access to information on BREGS account balances in the more than 9,000 district, block, and GP implementing-agency bank accounts on a nearly real-time basis. As a result, the state is able to monitor and respond when cash balances in BREGS accounts in GPs fall too low. This system has introduced transparency in BREGS financial management and enabled the state to monitor and manage its resources across districts. In addition, the modifications planned with respect to accounting applications should also facilitate accurate and timely creation of utilization certificates by districts.

These two initiatives—creating a state level corpus fund and putting in place a centralized funds management system—are expected to smooth funds flows to implementing agencies and simplify accounting requirements at local levels, thereby limiting one potential source of the rationing of work.

Monitoring

There is a strong emphasis on monitoring in BREGS, in contrast with previous such schemes. The National Rural Employment Guarantee Act provides for several mechanisms to increase transparency and accountability. Intensive monitoring and evaluation of program outcomes is therefore critical to learning whether the strengthened provisions have had the intended impact.

In Bihar, BREGS implementation is monitored largely through monthly and fortnightly progress reports submitted by districts and through monthly review meetings. These monthly meetings are held at the block, district, and state levels to review progress and resolve bottlenecks in the delivery of the scheme. The scheme guidelines call for Vigilance Committees to be established in all GPs. However, these committees rarely exist or function. Field-based process and outcome monitoring is limited, partly as a result of the absence of a clearly defined strategy and partly because of the lack of capacity. Social audits are mandated by the scheme guidelines, but, as in most states, progress in undertaking such audits has been slow. The few instances in which NGOs have mobilized communities for social audits in some districts in Bihar have unearthed discrepancies.

The monthly progress reports are district-wide reports on predefined indicators of financial and physical progress in implementing the scheme. The reports are sent by districts to the state and uploaded on the national website (http://nrega.nic.in) in the first week of every month. Although a useful source of information on progress, there are two areas of concern. First, only aggregate data, such as the total number of households provided employment and the number of person days of employment generated, are available at different administrative levels. Detailed data are not available because these district-wide reports are compiled using block-level reports, which, in turn, are aggregated using GP-level reports submitted by PRSs. It is not possible to track beneficiary-level information through this system.

Second, information submitted in the reports is not verified in the field. The PRS is tasked with maintaining the various documents used for this purpose, including registers for recording applications, job card distribution, beneficiary accounts opened, employment provision, receipt of muster rolls (for attendance), works executed, and grievances received. The PRS is also required to maintain the cashbook (for recording funds receipts and expenditures). Technical staff are responsible for maintaining the measurement book for recording work done and wages paid. However, there is no clear mechanism at the block level to verify the authenticity of data in the monthly reports by checking these documents. Field visits to blocks in four districts—Darbhanga, Jehanabad, Madhubani, and Nalanda—indicated that random checks of documents are conducted in some blocks, but that it is not a uniform practice. Fieldwork for the BREGS survey and other field visits also highlighted the difficulty of obtaining a complete record of scheme performance because some documents were available with the PRS, others with the Mukhiya, and some not at all.

In contrast, the national MGNREGS Management Information System (MIS)—NREGAsoft (available online at http://nrega.nic.in)—makes data available on the scheme at the beneficiary level. However, the level of disaggregated information required, the large number and frequency of transactions to be recorded, and the limited IT infrastructure at the block and lower levels present a challenge to making information available in a timely fashion. For instance, because of the lack of adequate IT support and connectivity at the block level, hard copies of documents such as muster rolls and measurement books must be brought to the district headquarters by the PRSs for data entry into the MIS. As a result, there is a significant time lag before the data are available online. The timeliness of this information has improved because the transfer of funds from the central ministry to districts has now been linked to the information available on the MIS.

However, the design of NREGAsoft is such that all transactions (such as the issuance of job cards or recording attendance on the muster roll) remain paper based. Once the paper transaction is complete, data are entered offline and subsequently made publicly available.

In contrast, a transactions-based MIS would make data entry manda-
tory at the same time the transaction itself is processed (for example,
a job card would be printed and issued only when the relevant information is recorded in the MIS). This would make data available in
real time so that they can be used to inform management decisions.
Andhra Pradesh has been using a transactions-based IT system since
the introduction of the scheme in 2006.

Grievance Redress Mechanisms

Bihar has made a commitment to making the BREGS delivery mechanism more accountable to the public and citizens can submit grievances through multiple channels.[27] Citizens can submit grievances
related to BREGS in person, in writing, by telephone, or through
public meetings (janta durbars). The chief minister, as well as most
government functionaries at the state and district levels, holds public
meetings every week at which citizens can voice their grievances and
register petitions (about BREGS as well as other issues). Field visits
to Madhubani district in 2011 indicated that about 80 to 120 complaints, on average, were received at the district meeting and that it
took at least three months to complete the entire grievance redress
process at the district level.

An Information and Public Grievance Cell has been established
to receive and follow up on complaints received at the state-level
meetings. BREGS-related complaints are then forwarded to the relevant authorities for redress. Bihar has also introduced the statewide
Bihar Public Grievance Redress System that works directly under
the supervision of the chief minister's secretariat. This system registers complaints on BREGS and other issues received from different
sources (including public meetings and the online portal) and directs
it to the relevant authority for redress.

BREGS-related grievances can also be received verbally or in
writing. At the block level, the PO maintains a grievance register
to record complaints. Often, verbal complaints go unrecorded and
only the complaints received by the PO in writing are recorded.
To deal with this issue, a call center was piloted to record verbal
grievances and to ensure that grievances are resolved quickly and
efficiently. To be effective, the call center needs to be more closely
integrated with the Rural Development Department's grievance
redress process.

The above channels have enabled proper registration of complaints, but further work is required to promote a coordinated and
effective response to address the reported grievances.

Learning from Experiences Elsewhere

The experiences of similar public works programs in other countries, such as Argentina and Colombia, is instructive. For instance, the Trabajar program in Argentina uses standardized designs for projects and relies on monthly meetings to approve and prioritize project proposals, including for projects proposed by NGOs. Colombia carries out a series of spot checks to assess how the program procedures are being carried out. In both cases, beneficiary-level data (rather than just aggregate information by district) are available for monitoring.

In addition, innovations in implementing MGNREGS are emerging in many states across India, and there are opportunities for learning from these experiences. The main innovations are with respect to streamlining planning processes, improving worksite management, making timely wage payments, and ensuring transparency.

Several states have introduced various innovations to strengthen the planning process in a manner that is best suited to the state-specific context. For instance, Kerala has used its strong PRIs to promote decentralized, comprehensive planning for village assets. Andhra Pradesh has leveraged its relatively decentralized administrative structure and its mature network of self-help groups and village organizations for community mobilization and participatory planning. These groups undertake annual labor demand assessments and land surveys to determine the village assets to be created and the availability of labor for MGNREGS during the course of the year. As noted earlier (box 8.1), Gujarat is piloting the use of geographic information systems for village resource mapping to provide communities with the appropriate technical inputs for planning purposes. Andhra Pradesh and Madhya Pradesh have developed standardized work estimates for a wide range of MGNREGS works to overcome technical staff shortages at the village level. States such as Karnataka and Andhra Pradesh encourage communities to plan MGNREGS works to be undertaken sequentially across identified areas within a village rather than simultaneously in scattered locations across the village. In each of these areas within a village, a comprehensive set of works is undertaken in a logical sequence.

With respect to worksite management practices, states such as Andhra Pradesh and Rajasthan have introduced the concept of fixed labor groups that work together on worksites. Such groups can help mobilize workers and enable them to collectively voice their demands and improve work efficiency. Moving to group measurement of work at the site suggests that wages can vary depending on group effort, thereby providing incentives to monitor individual effort within the group. The number of group members varies; Andhra Pradesh has groups of 10 to 30 members, while Rajasthan promotes 5-member groups. The process of group formation also varies across states. In Andhra Pradesh, group members are typically workers who have worked together on more than one worksite for at least 10 days. To prevent exclusion in the group formation process, work is allocated separately to general groups and to those with disabled individuals. In contrast, Rajasthan allows workers to form their own groups. Field visits to these states suggest that there is greater ownership among workers that work in groups, but further mobilization and awareness generation would be required, in partnership with NGOs and community-based organizations (MART 2010).

In addition, several states have introduced various mechanisms for the selection, training, and performance management of mates who are responsible for managing worksites in lieu of contractors. Some states, such as Madhya Pradesh and Rajasthan, maintain permanent pools of mates per GP, with worksite allocation on a rotating basis. Andhra Pradesh has an incentive-linked payment system for mates to encourage better performance. Rajasthan provides a tool kit to mates to help them in record keeping and measurement at the worksite (MART 2010).

Some states have successfully streamlined the flow of funds to implementing agencies and set up appropriate disbursement mechanisms to ensure timely wage payments. For instance, Andhra Pradesh has a centralized electronic funds management system that allows near-real-time tracking and funds management across implementing agencies. Full integration of this system with the management information system and a tightly monitored delivery process ensures that wage payments are made within a week of work completion. Some states, including Madhya Pradesh, make advance funds available (linked to the volume of estimated MGNREGS work) to GPs, thus making it easier to open worksites in response to demand. Others have placed advance funds, or a "float," with post offices to enable wages to be paid into beneficiary accounts while waiting for funds to be transferred from the implementing agencies.

Several states have put mechanisms in place for strengthened monitoring, transparency, and accountability in implementation. For instance, Rajasthan is well known for implementation of various transparency safeguards. Muster rolls are present at most worksites, daily attendance is taken in front of workers, wages are paid based on group work and measurement, and job cards are updated at the time of payment. An active civil society, the Mazdoor Kisan Shakti Sangathan, has strongly encouraged community monitoring through social audits. Andhra Pradesh has established a strong IT-enabled management information system to restrict the possibilities of corruption and manipulation. This web-based system has a local language interface that handles registration, work planning, worksite management, and wage payments, and allows public access to reliable, timely, and comparable information from the field.[28] Andhra Pradesh was the first state to institutionalize social audits as early as 2006, with a focus on follow-up action by the administration in the aftermath of such audits. Tamil Nadu has used administrative monitoring effectively through daily audits of the muster rolls. Inspection officers visit worksites regularly to check the information reported in the muster rolls, thereby reducing the scope for "ghost workers" (World Bank 2011).

In several states (for example, Andhra Pradesh, Chhattisgarh, Jharkhand, Madhya Pradesh, and West Bengal), the district administration has partnered with civil society organizations to mobilize communities for demand registration, participatory planning of works, and grievance redress and monitoring (National Consortium of Civil Society Organizations 2009, 2010). These innovations across India present an opportunity for poor states to make the MGNREGS delivery mechanism more responsive to demand and thereby reduce the rationing of work on the scheme.

Notes

1. For further discussion of the importance of asset creation to the cost-effectiveness of workfare schemes, see Ravallion (1999).

2. Nearly two-fifths of households reported no Gram Sabha had taken place in the Gram Panchayat (GP) in the year preceding the survey in 2009/10. A further 16 percent of households were unaware of whether a Gram Sabha had been held in their GP. Among households that reported that a Gram Sabha had taken place, about half attended the meeting. In 2009/10, the majority of men (78 percent) and women (86 percent) perceived no benefits to participating in Gram Sabhas as they are currently held.

3. See Sunai (2009) and Indian Grameen Services (2009) for Bihar; PRIA (2007) for other states.

4. For a broader discussion of this issue in light of evidence from other programs, see Mansuri and Rao (2013).

5. Note that this could also be attributed, at least in part, to the poor quality of administrative data on assets created under the scheme. The GP questionnaire (see chapter 2) was used to collect data on five assets created under BREGS in the preceding year in the surveyed village. All individual

respondents were asked questions on these five assets. The study did not survey worksites or investigate the quality of assets.

6. See also Indian Grameen Services (2009).

7. These include projects for water conservation, drought proofing (including plantation and reforestation), minor and micro-irrigation, land development (including on the individual land of Scheduled Tribe and Scheduled Caste households, small and medium-size farmers, and other specified groups), renovation of traditional water bodies, flood control and protection (including drainage in waterlogged areas), rural connectivity, and others. In 2012, the list of permissible projects was expanded to include agriculture, livestock and fisheries, rural sanitation, and watershed-related projects.

8. Flood Management Information System (FMIS), Water Resources Department, government of Bihar, available at http://fmis.bih.nic.in/history .html. There were severe floods in six districts in the two northern zones in 2008/09. In contrast, rainfall was scant during the 2009 monsoons, and drought was declared in 26 districts.

9. Indira Awaas Yojana is a cash transfer to poor rural households to enable them to construct or repair their houses.

10. The Backward Regions Grant Fund is an untied grant to GPs in backward districts that can be used at their discretion for building assets such as roads and school buildings.

11. The survey's village questionnaire indicates the peak months of agricultural activity in Bihar to be March and April (wheat harvest), June–August (paddy planting), and October–December (paddy harvest and wheat sowing).

12. States such as Andhra Pradesh, Madhya Pradesh, and Rajasthan have made concerted efforts to streamline and shorten the process for obtaining approvals for the annual shelf of works and to ensure that at least some of the projects listed in the shelf of works have the necessary administrative and technical sanctions. As a result, worksites can be opened promptly in response to demand (MART 2010).

13. Unsurprisingly, in R2 nearly three-quarters of men and women who reported instances of interruption of work at the last worksite at which they worked also felt that BREGS work was not available when they wanted it.

14. The mate is a BREGS worker who is assigned the responsibility of managing the worksite, including taking attendance and overseeing daily operations.

15. The muster roll is a record maintained at the worksite of the daily attendance of workers and payments made for the period of a week or fortnight.

16. Chapter 4 also reports information on wage payment delays, but based on responses averaged across all worksites that the household members worked on in the year preceding the survey.

17. The rates are intended to be such that an able-bodied worker can produce the output that could earn him or her the stipulated scheme wage.

18. See Drèze and Khera (2009) for a discussion of the downsides of reliance on post office and bank accounts.

19. Studies from other states note that women may not have access to their earnings if the bank account is opened in the name of the male household head. In Andhra Pradesh, household accounts are opened in the name of the woman.

20. A study of six northern states speculated that contractors are likely to step in and run worksites when funds are delayed because they can ensure timely payments and keep the work going (Drèze and Khera 2009).

21. See, for example, Ambasta, Shankar, and Shah (2008) for suggestions on the appropriate technical and administrative staff strength required to adequately implement the scheme.

22. Information from the Rural Development Department, government of Bihar, as of December 2011.

23. Total scheme expenditures in 2009/10 were Rs 26,320 million (Rural Development Department, Government of Bihar); there are 8,463 GPs in Bihar.

24. In theory, these, in turn, are derived from the labor budgets put forward by GPs as developed during the bottom-up planning exercise.

25. These data were made available by the Rural Development Department, government of Bihar, and compiled from letters from districts to the Ministry of Rural Development for fund releases and data on receipt of funds from the Central Plan Scheme Monitoring System. The data are somewhat patchy. For the first tranche, we have information on the dates of the requests and the amounts requested and received for all 38 districts, but we have information on the dates of the receipt of funds for only 25 districts. Comparable information across tranches restricts us to 19 districts.

26. One lakh equals Rs 100,000. Analysis of road construction worksites in two GPs in Kishanganj district indicated that it took about a month for the block to receive funds from the district and a further four or five months to release these funds to the GPs. However, it is possible that this delayed transfer to the GP was not due to bottlenecks in the funds flow but deliberate because the worksites could be opened only after the rainy season was over (Development Alternatives 2009; Sunai 2009).

27. Bihar is one of the forerunners in the implementation of the Right to Information Act in India and in enacting the Right to Public Services Act in 2011. Under the Right to Public Services Act, citizens are entitled to standards in public service delivery, and civil servants are held personally accountable in the event of failure to comply with these standards. This provides another channel for ensuring improved service delivery, although BREGS does not yet come under the ambit of this act.

28. See National Consortium of Civil Society Organizations (2009) for an assessment of how such integrated end-to-end IT systems can contribute to improved MGNREGS outcomes.

References

Ambasta, Prathamesh, P. S. Vijay Shankar, and Mihir Shah. 2008. "Two Years of NREGA: The Road Ahead." *Economic and Political Weekly* 43 (8): 41–50.

Comptroller and Auditor General. 2008. "Performance Audit of Implementation of National Rural Employment Guarantee Act (NREGA)." Report by the Comptroller and Auditor General of India.

Development Alternatives. 2009. "Report on Scoping Study for Design and Development of Alternative Implementation Model(s) on NREGS." Background note prepared for the Bihar Rural Employment Guarantee Scheme study. Development Alternatives, Inc., Washington, DC.

Drèze, Jean, and Reetika Khera. 2009. "The Battle for Employment Guarantee." *Frontline* 26 (1).

Indian Grameen Services. 2009. "Exploring Shelf of Works for Flood Affected Area of North Bihar." Report prepared for the Rural Development Department, government of Bihar and the World Bank. Indian Grameen Services, Kolkata, India.

Mansuri, Ghazala, and Vijayendra Rao. 2013. *Localizing Development: Does Participation Work?* Washington, DC: World Bank.

MART. 2010. "The Synthesis Report: Institutional Review of MGNREGS in Andhra Pradesh and Madhya Pradesh." Background note prepared for the BREGS study. NOIDA, India.

Ministry of Rural Development. 2011. "Reforms in MGNREGA Implementation." Government of India, New Delhi. Available online at http://nrega.nic.in/circular/Reforms_in_MGNREGA01092011.pdf.

———. 2013. "Report of the Committee for Revision of MGNREGA Operational Guidelines." Government of India, New Delhi. Available online at http://nrega.nic.in/circular/Report_Committee_Revision _guidelines.pdf.

National Consortium of Civil Society Organizations. 2009. "NREGA Reforms: Building Rural India—First Annual Report of the National Consortium of Civil Society Organizations on NREGA, 2008–09." National Consortium on NREGA, Madyha Pradesh, India.

———. 2010. "NREGA Reforms: Building Rural India—Second Annual Report of the National Consortium of Civil Society Organizations on NREGA." National Consortium on NREGA, Madhya Pradesh, India.

PRIA (Society for Participatory Research in Asia). 2007. "Role of Panchayati Raj Institutions in Implementation of NREGA, National Study Phase II." Society for Participatory Research in Asia (PRIA), New Delhi.

Ravallion, Martin. 1999. "Appraising Workfare." *World Bank Research Observer* 14: 31–48.

Sunai Consultancy Pvt. Ltd. 2009. "Process Qualitative Observation Report, Feb–Mar 2009, Four Blocks of Muzaffarpur and Saharsa Districts of Bihar." Background note prepared for the Bihar Rural Employment Guarantee Scheme study. Sunai Consultancy, Bihar, India.

World Bank. 2011. *Social Protection for a Changing India*. Human Development Unit, South Asia. Washington, DC: World Bank.

Glossary

Block	The administrative level above the Gram Panchayat and below the district.
Block development officer (BDO)	A civil servant responsible for the administration of a block.
Block program officer (PO)	Hired on contract by the state government for overseeing and monitoring the Bihar Rural Employment Guarantee Scheme (BREGS) implementation in the block.
BPL ration card	The "Below Poverty Line" card that defines the poverty status of rural households and determines entitlements to various government programs.
District	The administrative level above the block and below the state.
Gram Panchayat (GP)	A cluster of villages; the lowest unit of administration. Also used to refer to the elected body at the panchayat level.
Gram Sabha	A meeting that includes all the adult citizen residents of the village. The Gram Sabha elects representatives to the GP.
Kutcha	Crude or temporary structure (usually used to describe housing or road quality).
Mahadalit	In Bihar, Mahadalits, comprising the poorest and most disadvantaged among Scheduled Castes, have been notified as a separate sub-category by the state government.
Mate	A BREGS worker who is assigned the responsibility of managing the worksite, including taking attendance and overseeing daily operations.

Mukhiya	The elected leader of the Gram Panchayat, responsible for the implementation of development programs at the panchayat level.
Muster roll	A record maintained at the BREGS worksites of the daily attendance of workers and payments made for the period of a week or fortnight.
Panchayat bhawan	A building where the GP conducts its official work.
Panchayati Raj Institutions (PRIs)	The group of locally elected bodies in the three-tier (GP, block, and district) system of local government.
Panchayat rozgar sewak	Hired on contract by the state government for implementing the scheme at the GP level.
Pucca	A solid, permanent, or proper structure (usually in the context of the roof or walls of a house, or a road).
Sarpanch	The elected leader of the panchayat judiciary body.
Schedule of Rates	The payment rates for various tasks, intended to be such that an able-bodied worker can produce the output that could earn him or her the stipulated daily MGNREGS wage.
Shelf of works	Annual list of MGNREGS projects for each GP.
Ward	A division of a GP, which has representation in the GP elective body.
Ward member	The representative of the ward in the Gram Panchayat.

Index

This is a subject index only. Boxes, figures, notes, and tables are indicated by b, f, n, and t following the page numbers.

ECO-AUDIT
Environmental Benefits Statement

The World Bank is committed to preserving endangered forests and natural resources. The Publishing and Knowledge Division has chosen to print *Right to Work?* on recycled paper with 50 percent postconsumer fiber in accordance with the recommended standards for paper usage set by the Green Press Initiative, a non-profit program supporting publishers in using fiber that is not sourced from endangered forests. For more information, visit www.greenpressinitiative.org.

Saved:
- 11 trees
- 5 million Btu of total energy
- 931 lb. of net greenhouse gases
- 5,048 gal. of waste-water
- 338 lb. of solid waste

green
press
INITIATIVE

www.ingramcontent.com/pod-product-compliance
Lightning Source LLC
Chambersburg PA
CBHW061004280326
41935CB00009B/822